PSI AND CLINICAL PRACTICE

PROCEEDINGS OF AN INTERNATIONAL CONFERENCE

HELD IN LONDON, ENGLAND

OCTOBER 28–29, 1989

PSI AND CLINICAL PRACTICE

PROCEEDINGS OF AN INTERNATIONAL CONFERENCE

HELD IN LONDON, ENGLAND

OCTOBER 28–29, 1989

Edited By
Lisette Coly and Joanne D. S. McMahon

PARAPSYCHOLOGY FOUNDATION, INC.
NEW YORK, N.Y.

ISBN 0-912328-44-4
Library of Congress Catalog Number: 93-85463

Manufactured in the United States of America

The opinions expressed herein are those of the individual participants and do not necessarily represent the viewpoints of the editors nor of the Parapsychology Foundation, Inc.

PARTICIPANTS

Moderator—Robert L. Morris
University of Edinburgh
Edinburgh, Scotland, U.K.

Jean C. Dierkens   State University of Mons
Mons, Belgium

Peter Fenwick   The Maudsley Hospital
London, England, U.K.

Keith Harary   Institute for Advanced Psychology
San Francisco, California, U.S.A.

Wim H. Kramer   Parapsychology Laboratory
State University of Utrecht
Utrecht, The Netherlands

Vernon M. Neppe University of Washington
Neuropsychiatry Department
Seattle, Washington, U.S.A.

Adrian Parker   University of Gothenburg
Gothenburg, Sweden

Ian Tierney   Keil Centre
Edinburgh, Scotland, U.K.

Robert L. Van de Castle University of Virginia
Health Sciences Center
Charlottesville, Virginia, U.S.A.

Donald J. West   Cambridge University
Cambridge, England, U.K.

Ian Wickramasekera Eastern Virginia Medical School
Norfolk, Virginia, U.S.A.

OBSERVERS

Mary Rose Barrington

Eberhard Bauer

John Beloff

Daniel Benor

Bernard Carr

Manfred Cassirer

Deborah Delanoy

P. Sarah Dodd

Reverend Paul Eardley

Arthur Ellison

F. Gregory

Jane Henry

Brian Inglis

Denise Iredell

Barbara Ivanova

Kate Lang

James McHarg

Martin Meyer

Sue Miles

Cynthia Milligan

Darlene Moore

Eleanor O'Keeffe

Arthur Oram

Guy Lyon Playfair

Tony Prichett

Serena Roney-Dougal

Margaret A. Savoy

Sybo A. Schouten

Helen Sims

John R. Smythies

Julie Uran

Susanna Van de Castle

Walter Von Lucadou

Ruth West

CONTENTS

INTRODUCTION

LISETTE COLY: My name is Lisette Coly and as Vice President of the Foundation and on behalf of the Board of Trustees I welcome you to this, the Parapsychology Foundation's 38th Annual International Conference.

Our theme this year is *Psi and Clinical Practice*. The observations of psi processes in clinical experiences and related research by our esteemed panelists and observers are sure to provoke lively discussions coupled with meaningful insights of our topic.

Our founder, Eileen J. Garrett, as most of you are aware, started her formal education in psychical research in London in the 1920s. A well-known psychic, as well as writer, publisher, researcher, and foundation executive, Eileen Garrett was and still continues to be a fascinating and rich subject for clinical study as she offered herself and her alleged psychic gifts for research in an effort to find the answers to the many questions raised by the purported paranormal phenomena she encountered. It is, indeed, unfortunate that she is not with us today as both subject and researcher.

The late Jan Ehrenwald, eminent psychiatrist, described by his colleague, Montague Ullman as perhaps the first of the modern era to undertake a serious assessment of the significance of the telepathy hypothesis for an understanding of paranoia and schizophrenic psychoses, conducted several studies with Garrett. Ehrenwald's comments, taken from his book, *Anatomy of Genius* (1984), are of value not only in describing her, but perhaps other persons observed in clinical practice displaying similar psychic manifestations:

> What then, are the conclusions from our re-examination of Mrs. Garrett as a "psychic," "trance medium," or just subject of psychiatric case history? Evidently, the standard clinical approach scratches the surface only. It is true that her mental dissociation, her "spirit controls"—and their underlying psychodynamics—would suggest the presence of a conversion hysteria. Her colorful reports of hallucinations, interspersed with delusional material, may have brought her to the verge of a psychotic break. But invariably, she bounced back from such episodes, with the core of her personality unimpaired. Similarly, she attained a remarkable control over her trance states

and would snap back into her "ordinary" identity at the drop of the conjurer's hat, as it were. Her apparent split into dual or multiple personalities would again be replaced by a seamless whole. If a clinical label was needed, she could be described as a *holophrenic* like Joan of Arc, Saint Teresa of Avila, or C. G. Jung: the only aberration left would be her striking capacity for existential shifts along these lines.

In one of our last conversations she turned to me and remarked half in jest, half in earnest "I know, Jan, you think I'm crazy, but I love you anyway." Eileen was wrong about the first part of her remark. But I am sure she sensed my boundless admiration for what she stood for. She was an explorer of uncharted territories, where others had merely studied the maps. She walked a tightrope between the extremes of madness and genius—and she did it with grace and an Irish smile. (pp. 172–173).

At this time I would like to introduce you to another of Eileen Garrett's accomplishments and contributions to the field—her daughter, the Parapsychology Foundation's most able second President, Mrs. Eileen Coly.

GREETINGS

EILEEN COLY: Well—I would say madness, genius, grace, and an Irish smile is a formidable act to follow, but varying shades of Eileen Garrett and her gifts I have had to deal with for many years!

Too much time has gone by since our last London conference in 1982, which was devoted to Parapsychology's Second Century. However, it is a pleasure to be here once again and to welcome all of you present today—so many old friends and many others we have been eager to meet in person.

Clinical practice and psi is a most valuable topic and definitely belongs in our ongoing conference series. We are very lucky to have been able to prevail upon today's participants to share with us their observations and work experiences in clinical practice as it pertains to psychic phenomena.

Eileen Garrett once wrote ". . . a great physician, whether of the body, the mind, or both, is no mere mechanic tinkering with a machine-like human body and personality. He is and must be a creative and sometimes daring scientist, who understands full well that in treating the bodies and personalities of human beings he is dealing with something in essence far from machine-like, even though man can build true machines by simulating the human physical or nervous system."

It is now time for me to turn these proceedings over to the capable hands of our conference moderator, Dr. Robert L. Morris, who of course, is well known to all of you as holding the Koestler Chair of Parapsychology at the University of Edinburgh, Scotland. We at the Foundation have followed his career for 20 years or more as a Foundation grantee, conference participant, educator, respected researcher as well as valued friend. Let us now proceed with the work of the conference.

REFLECTIONS ON THE INVESTIGATION
OF SPONTANEOUS CASES

DONALD J. WEST

Looking Beyond "Evidentiality"

The writer has recently conducted a small scale postal questionnaire survey repeating substantially the same question as was used a century ago in the Society for Psychical Research (SPR) "Census of Hallucinations." In effect, respondents were asked whether, when fully awake, they had ever had a vision or heard a voice when there was nothing there and no normal explanation for it. A full report has been submitted to the SPR Editor, but briefly the finding was that at least as high a proportion of persons, questioned as before (over 10%) had experienced a definite "apparition" at some time in their lives. Only a minority, however, had any meaningful significance for the percipient, and the present collection included none of the visions coinciding with the death of the person "seen" which were so prominent in the original Census. My primary intention had been to inquire into hallucinatory experiences with some paranormal content, but, in a somewhat reluctant response to advice, questions about other types of presumptively psychic experience were added, namely fulfilled premonitions, near-death experiences and unexplained movements (spontaneous macro PK). This proved fortunate since the responses raised issues that would not otherwise have been considered.

Many years ago, writing on the topic of "The Investigation of Spontaneous Cases" (West, 1948), it seemed that the only reason for taking an interest in psychic anecdotes was to document beyond reasonable doubt that some people do on occasion have visionary experiences or strong premonitions conveying information that could only have been acquired paranormally. The value of this kind of enterprise is open to doubt. The perfect case—perfect that is from the standpoint of evidential value, proof against explanation as coincidence and availability of corroboration—has proved elusive. Some would argue that the search is fruitless, that anecdotes can never be scientifically convincing since the experiences reported are unrepeatable, unavailable to direct observation, and the details dependent upon fallible human testimony. This attitude seems unduly dismissive. Conclusive proof may be unattainable and accounts that appear convincing may be rare and increasingly hard to come by, but at least there are sufficient data to present a prima facie case deserving of study.

There are other ways of looking at the material besides searching for the exceptionally evidential example. Louisa Rhine pioneered the analysis of psychic anecdotes, identifying basic characteristics and meaningful relationships between them; for instance between strength of conviction and accuracy of information conveyed, or between mode of presentation (e.g., apparition, dream or presentiment) and content of the impression (e.g., death or disaster or emotionally neutral events). She took the accounts sent into the Duke Laboratory more or less at face value without attempting validation, assuming that spurious cases would be too small a minority to invalidate the conclusions. She was possibly wrong about that and might have done better to limit her analysis to cases followed up by interview, but the idea behind her project was sound.

People who send in accounts of their strange experiences to the SPR and similar bodies often do so to obtain confirmation of their own beliefs. Whereas some would dismiss an apparition as mere hallucination or illusion and try to forget it quickly, others might immediately think they had seen a ghost and want to match the vision against the appearance of deceased people living in the place where it was seen. Others might assume the experience to be a warning sign and start searching for premonitory significance. The stories that emerge are inevitably colored, if not distorted, by the subject's preferred interpretation.

One of the advantages of sampling an ordinary population, who have never bothered to produce an account of their experiences on their own initiative, is that they may be expected to have no particular axe to grind and their reports may be more matter of fact and free from unwanted elaborations. Another advantage is that if questions are worded so as to include a wide range of phenomena one may obtain an impression of the relative frequencies of different types of experience. Near death experiences, for example, were less common than apparitions, but reports of unexplained movements of objects were more frequent then either near death experiences or out-of-the-body experiences. Apparitions of unrecognized figures that convey no special message were more common than "veridical" cases. In my recent survey, at least, sightings of unidentified flying objects were infrequent in comparison with other kinds of experience, probably because they were not considered "psychic" by their viewers.

A narrow focus on the search for "evidential" stories diverts attention from the total range of the phenomena, neglects the large mass of material from which "publishable" cases are selected and perhaps overlooks features of importance to explanatory theory. The rarity of well-evidenced cases might lead to the conclusion that spontaneous psi is either an exceptional occurrence or perhaps non-existent. An alternative view would be that evidential cases are exceptional only because real life circumstances rarely permit full corroboration or validation. Many presumptive psychic experiences, although they may be unverifiable, may be in fact paranormal, but even if they are not they may contribute to an understanding of psi related phenomena. The examples which follow are all drawn from the recent survey in which 840 completed questionnaires were collected.

Deja Vu

The phenomenon of deja vu, the feeling that events have been experienced already, provides a good example of the difficulty of sorting out the real from the illusory, the probably paranormal from what need not be paranormal at all. The stock explanation of this common phenomenon is that it is an illusion of mistaken familiarity; the mechanisms responsible for matching past memories with present perceptions are manifesting a temporary hiccup. Deja vu is known to occur with undue frequency in states of fatigue or in association with certain neurological disorders. That is as may be, but sometimes the experience includes a conviction of knowing what is about to happen next. Is this too a complete illusion? Hardly ever does it occur in circumstances in which the person involved can give voice to a verifiable prediction. Various deja vu experiences were reported in the survey, some being dismissed by the respondents as "just" deja vu, others being felt to have been truly premonitory.

Case 429: A 60 year old respondent reported an experience 38 years earlier. "Expectancy that I would 'know' a street in Barcelona *before* turning into it (architecture, shops, etc.) and extremely strong feeling of deja vu *after* doing so. This was a first visit to the city and the street was unlikely to be one that would feature in tourist literature or in a book. I mentioned this to friends with me at the time and have talked about it afterwards. It left a vivid impression and has been my only experience of this kind. I have no theory or explanation to offer."

Case 030: A woman graduate student gave a short but classic account of some typical deja vu episodes: "I have experienced 'deja vu' twice, in the sense of knowing and experiencing an event for the second time. I didn't know whether I had actually experienced the reality the first time, or had 'dreamt' it, but the feelings were a definite set of actions in an outside venue. The most vivid experience was while a schoolgirl and having an identical conversation and actions near a park and feeling definitely that I had done it before."

This story illustrates the near impossibility of establishing whether the feeling of familiarity was an illusion of the moment or a real memory of a premonitory dream from the past revived as its fulfillment began. Such stories are usually dismissed as of no psychic interest, but, on the theory that psi is common place rather than rare, a psi hypothesis remains tenable.

The next example shows how easily premonitions and deja vu experiences can be mixed up in the mind of the person experiencing them.

Case 447: "Back in the 1950–60 era at a time when I was completely unaware of ESP phenomena, I did have several experiences which I could not explain. Meeting people, feeling, knowing, that they would appear round the corner of the street and this did happen. Feeling that an old friend was about to knock on the door and rising to answer the door before the knock came. Driving the car in areas where I had never been before and knowing what was there on the other side of the hill in exact detail, including movement of people, cars, etc."

Impressions that one knows what is going to be said or done immediately before it happens might be explained as deja vu illusion. If the mistaken impression of familiarity occurs while someone is speaking, the person listening could think he had predicted what was being said. On the other hand, if psi is common place the impression could conceivably derive from real premonition.

Case 779: "I have many occasions when I have anticipated the actual words or the meaning of what various people have said to me, without there having been any indication in previous conversation to pre-suggest this to me." This respondent, a middle aged architect, also recalled one presentiment that was dramatically fulfilled. He had felt an extraordinarily strong impression of something wrong while on a beach with his family. He left them and raced back to the parked car where his parents were to find that his father had had a stroke.

The feeling of deja vu is sometimes accompanied by a conviction that having been through something before one knows what is going to come next. Unless circumstances permit the experient to give voice to a prediction there is no telling whether this is an illusion. A self-critical psychology lecturer gave the following account.

Case 1041: "In September 1973 I visited Bristol for the first time to give my first conference paper. In a break in the proceedings one afternoon, I walked from the university with another graduate student friend to find and explore the Clifton suspension bridge. On the way there I suddenly had the feeling (which I reported to him) that I knew the scene we would encounter around the next corner. It was an unremarkable suburban 'village green' sloping down and away to our left, and when we arrived it was as I expected (although I do not remember if I had told my friend in advance just *what* I was expecting to find).

"The experience had a distinctive and 'spooky' quality, unlike errors of memory or everyday misattributions. I have no knowledge of a previous visit to Bristol, and my attempts at a 'normal explanation'—that I had perhaps seen the area in a TV series—seem implausible. . . ." He continued, nevertheless, to speculate about what TV program he could possibly have seen to account for it.

That a new but familiar-looking scene might have been previewed on television is an interesting idea, but neither the hypothesis of a true premonition nor the hypothesis of false recognition is capable of disproof.

Unexplained movements

Sporadic physical effects which lack any obvious cause are among the most puzzling of the spontaneous occurrences attributed to the paranormal. Being as a rule seemingly impersonal events they do not so readily attract explanation in terms of haunting or extrasensory perception. As with other kinds of experience some people will attribute paranormality to incidents others would pass over with little notice. The following example illustrates this.

Case 260: This anonymous respondent, a 27 year old computer software programmer, wrote: "Once, when I was extremely angry, and concentrating very bad, a pile of coins on my table top collapsed sideways (while I was out of the room). I realize that this could be easily faked or deluded, but I don't think so. (I am well out of adolescence now—this event occurred about 4 years ago.)"

One can but wonder whether, had he not been in an angry mood, he would have looked for any out of the way explanation for the fall of the coins. The next example poses a slightly more difficult puzzle.

Case 353: A woman of 22 wrote: "When I was 17, at school, I was struggling to wake up, and just as I did so was hit just below my left eye by a mirror which had been previously hanging on the wall several feet to the right of the bed. The effect was a small cut, a black eye and some troubled surprise as to how the mirror travelled across the room. I tried to discover what might have caused this and, there being no logical explanation, have since hovered between romantic superstition (the house was built on a monk's graveyard, and a suicide had occurred there etc., etc.) and a vague belief that adolescent anxieties have been known to cause otherwise inexplicable events. I cannot say which—or whether either—provides an answer which satisfies me." No further particulars were available as the respondent did not answer follow up inquiries.

The following two examples were still more puzzling.

Case 109: A graduate student age 22 gave a careful and precise description when interviewed following the completion of his questionnaire. The event had happened some 6 months previous when he was staying alone in his parents' house working on night shifts at a vacation job. On getting up one afternoon in preparation for going to work he found that a cupboard in the living room, which was about 2 feet high, with a speaker and a wooden elephant on top of it and telephone directories and papers inside, was no longer in its place in the corner. It was displaced some 10 feet across the center of the room, turned round, with doors open and the things from on top on the floor. The house was securely locked, with only a cat and a small dog with him. The usual occupants were far away and he knew of no one with a key. It seemed hardly rational "for someone to come into a house, disguising the fact that he came into the house, and moved the furniture, solely to get me to believe that it had moved of its own accord." For the dog to have done it, "it would have had to have edged the cupboard away from the wall and then pushed it . . . It's done nothing like it before or since and I wouldn't have believed it." He committed himself to no particular theory, insisting that the incident was "unexplained" rather than "inexplicable."

Case 873: While staying on her own in an old inn a middle-aged woman lecturer awoke during the night and had the feeling, which she had never had before, of a presence in the room. The next morning she found her rings, a wedding ring and a thickish silver one, lying on a table by the window. Both had been squashed into an oval shape, to the extent of being uncomfortable to wear. She immediately associated this with her experience in the night. It was all the more curious because, normally, she never removes her wedding ring at night.

The only obvious "normal" explanations for these last two cases that come to mind are lying by the respondents or actions performed while asleep, neither of which seem likely. There were other cases involving more than one person which could not be explained by the unconscious action of a single individual.

Case 282: The respondent recalled an incident in 1946 when he had been sent, following an operation, to a servicemens' rehabilitation center and he was sleeping in a room with six others. Suddenly, in the night, chaos broke out in the room next door but one, where there were about nine men. He remembered seeing the gas lights changing to an eerie glow and he saw men running scared from the room where, apparently, heavy palliasses were thrown about and belongings moved of their own accord. Men who had been through battles and were not easily frightened were very scared by what happened. The next night all was quiet as usual and there were no more disturbances. The incident was much talked about and memorable. No one ever admitted to a practical joke.

If one is to take seriously anecdotes relating to visions and premonitions one must also take seriously stories of unexplained physical effects. Laboratory evidence for psi includes both extrasensory and psychokinetic effects, so one should not be surprised that stories of spontaneous macro effects also take both forms.

Veridical and Non-Veridical Apparitions

It is conventional in psychical research to distinguish between veridical apparitions that provide unexpected information—for instance, portending the death of the person "seen"—and those that either mean nothing to the percipient or convey nothing new—as in the silent appearances of persons already known to be dead. Community surveys have regularly demonstrated that the incidence of non-veridical apparitions exceeds that of the veridical. Here is a fairly typical example.

Case 443: "I woke up one night in 1953 or 1954, looked around the open door and saw the figure of a young girl about 7 years of age wearing what appeared to be a long nightdress. I was very afraid, although she was very pleasant and friendly looking. It happened in the bedroom of the house I was living in that year." Questioned about it later, the respondent was sure she had been fully awake when she saw through the open door the girl standing there. She knew it was not her own daughter, who was sleeping elsewhere in the house. She could tell it was not real because, though she could not see through it, it was not properly solid. She buried her head in the pillows and did not see it go. The experience was unique for her.

This woman made no attempt to relate the apparition to anyone who had lived in the house before and did not call the figure a ghost, although there are many others who would have done so. It is often possible to find a resemblance between an unrecognized apparition and some person from the past, but coincidence and secondary elaboration are difficult to rule out.

It is commonly assumed that spontaneous visions such as this are self-generated hallucinations, entirely analogous to the visions experienced in dreams, but that still leaves unanswered the question of what triggers these (for most people) rare and unexpected occurrences. Once one is prepared to entertain the possibility, in the death wraith apparitions for example, that the experience has its origin in some external event, the same possibility cannot be ruled out in other instances.

Case 814: This was an example of a vision seen in a reputedly haunted place. It happened in September 1967 when the percipient was about 20 and working temporarily as a guide at Iona Abbey in Scotland, a place reputedly haunted. He gave particulars of what happened in an interview with Dr. Gauld who had collected the sample of questionnaires in which this case appeared. It was dusk and he was walking along one side of the cloister towards his room when he glimpsed between the pillars of the cloister a figure around the corner on the other side of the cloister. When he reached the corner himself he saw a figure dressed in a long black garment, like a Benedictine monk, disappear from the cloister through a blocked up door at the far end. He was very scared and went at once to the warden to relate what happened. He was told he was not the first to have an odd experience there. The next year, again at Iona, he spoke to a girl working there as a cook who told him that she too had glimpsed a dark figure in that part of the cloister. In response to a follow-up inquiry an official of the Abbey reported having heard of many strange experiences there but no sightings of the dark figure.

Like so many sightings of unrecognized figures the correspondence with what others may have "seen" in the same place at different times is hard to establish. In this instance the percipient could not recall the name of the girl who may have seen the same figure. Cases in which two or more persons witness the same figure simultaneously provide a stronger reason for questioning whether all apparitions are completely self-generated by the individual percipient. Several examples were obtained in the present survey, but in no case were the precise details of each person's experience properly analyzed.

In one example (Case 694) two young teenagers, alone in the house, heard mumbling from the next room, like a nun reciting a rosary. (It was a Catholic family.) They both ran out of the house, went to a nearby telephone and called the home number, thinking someone might reply, but "of course" no one did. In another case (622) a man and wife, out strolling one night, both saw a figure holding what seemed like a lantern light coming through the bushes towards them. Simultaneously convinced it was something unreal they turned tail. The experience left a profound impression remembered by both over many years. In yet another case (1148) a woman was awaken one night by something tugging at the bedclothes. On looking up she saw an illuminated figure of an old man. She screamed, waking her husband. The figure withdrew, apparently passing through the wall, leaving only some light still glowing. The husband also saw the figure, but as a more blurred image with none of the details she was able to recall. The account she wrote referred to a happening a quarter of a century ago, but she had a vivid picture of it still. She was one of a minority of respondents who reported having had numerous psychic experiences at different times in her life.

Coincidences

These were not asked about specifically, but a few accounts of strange coincidences were received.

Case 423: This respondent wrote that she had "no ESP experiences to report but you might be interested in the following coincidences." Her first example was as follows: "Two years ago I was returning from an acupuncture session. I was feeling quite emotional and had been regretting the fact that I knew so little about my mother's family and her life in Poland before the war. I wanted to get home as quickly as possible, so I took the first bus that came along and because I would have to change sat downstairs instead of in my usual place upstairs. I suddenly noticed a passport photograph stuck into the seat in front of me and I thought 'That's my mother!' She died in 1972. Of course it wasn't her, but it was a young woman with a Polish photographer's stamp on the back. I took it home and found the resemblance to my mother quite striking. The whole incident gave me a feeling of comfort at the time."

Case 871: A man of 30, a university lecturer, wrote: "Shortly after my father's death my mother and I were sorting through his possessions deciding what to keep . . . I looked through articles which my mother had sorted out and vice versa. During the course of this I discovered my father's glasses and was unsure whether they should be disposed of . . . The glasses and the brown case they were stored in were put to one side. . . . [Later] my mother wanted to wire a three pin mains plug to some appliance . . . She was unsure how to match up the wires with the pins and this matter had been concerning her while we were sorting out my father's artifacts.

"At this time my mother came across the glasses case that I had found earlier, opened it and found the reading glasses were inside along with a wiring diagram for three pin plugs. As sure as I can be I feel that this diagram was not in the glasses case when I had found them earlier. (I am not sure but I think it is likely that my mother had also discovered the case earlier, also finding no diagram. Either way, neither of us have any recollection of the diagram being in the case at the earlier time.)

"My mother told me that it was common for my father to put objects or messages on scraps of paper inside the glasses case as a means of reminding himself to do things. It tempts one to read these events in terms of a benevolent intervention . . . I think both my mother, who—like me—is willing, to take this as a form of psychic experience, and I realize the memory dependent nature of this attribution . . ."

Cases of this sort raise the possibility that there could be some paranormal human input in the patterning of physical events. Again, this has some parallel with laboratory effects where there are extra-chance correspondences between a subject's thoughts and the output of a random number generator.

Conclusion

Experience in laboratory experimentation has led to the identification of a wider range of possible psi effects than was covered by the early theories of "thought transference." Examination of the full range of spontaneous case reports suggests that the phenomena may be more complex than was envisaged in the theory of extrasensory impressions presented as dreams, premonitions and occasionally as hallucinations. Reports of physical effects, strange coincidences and collectively perceived apparitions do not fit readily into traditional theories. The collectively witnessed physical effects at poltergeist scenes and at some seances cannot be denied, even if thought by some to be invariably fraudulent. In regard to the sporadic experiences of individuals, however, there is an intellectual prejudice in favor of the theory that they are all subjective impressions, exteriorized as dreams, as alien thoughts or sometimes as hallucinated apparitions. The raw data from an unselected sample of reported experiences do not altogether support this conclusion. Certainly, a high proportion of visions occur when the percipients are quiet and alone, often when lying in bed; but this is not invariable and we are not really in a position to be dogmatic about what does or does no occur. Popular notions about ghosts, materialized forms, hauntings and supernatural intervention in material events may, after all, reflect aspects that have been neglected. It is important, therefore, to continue to collect examples of all kinds, however a priori implausible.

Many happenings that are believed by those experiencing them to be paranormal occur in circumstances in which the paranormal element is unlikely to be susceptible to confirmation. This is obviously so, for example, in experiences on the borderline between deja vu and premonition. Once the reality of paranormal effects is accepted in some cases, it becomes easier to suppose that they may also be at work in many of the much larger number of cases where the evidence is no more than suggestive and alternative explanations remain possible. We may be discounting much more than we should on the grounds of the (largely unmeasured) effects of coincidence, self-deception and faulty reporting.

These are pure speculations. Data from surveys can also be used to argue an opposite viewpoint. Since so few anecdotes provide compelling evidence for the paranormal, the exceptions may be written off as odd instances in which the testimony is not to be trusted or in which information that might provide clues to a "natural" explanation has been omitted. Skepticism of this sort is supported by the common experience of investigators—borne out by the present survey—that the most exciting and clear cut stories are often the ones that prove most elusive when attempts are made to obtain independent corroboration.

A minority of the respondents who report seemingly paranormal experiences claim that they occur to them with considerable frequency. This poses a challenge to the theorist. If psi is common place, there is no cause to be unduly skeptical about these claims, yet once again experience suggests caution. Few of those who report having frequent psychic experiences are able to produce well-substantiated examples. They often say they have experienced a wide variety of psychic happenings and are firm believers in the paranormal, points confirmed in the present survey. The suspicion arises that they are persons of overactive imagination who perceive and elaborate upon trivial happenings until they convince themselves that they are gifted with special powers and that something otherwise inexplicable has occurred.

These conflicting interpretations can be resolved only by further research. Survey work is helpful in establishing the variety and distribution of purportedly paranormal effects, but it is hardly an economic method of gathering cases that can be considered "evidential." That task demands far more detailed information than the average questionnaire respondent is likely to be able or willing to supply. If the public were made better aware of the importance of recording paranormal experiences, and reporting them promptly to research organizations so that investigators could analyze the events while they were still fresh in the witnesses' minds, then more good quality cases might emerge.

One way forward might be to concentrate on individuals who have frequent experiences, some of them premonitory and hence in principle open to validation if reported in advance of fulfillment. If their claims in this regard could be substantiated it would indirectly support their evidence concerning other types of experience. Keith Hearne (1989) has given personality questionnaires to persons claiming special psychic ability, finding them to be a more "normal" group then might have been anticipated. Since a half of their experiences were said to involve foreknowledge he proposed that such individuals might be prevailed upon, especially if some reward were offered, to lodge their information in advance with a view to subsequent verification. He did not suggest a higher reward for premonitions fulfilled within a reasonable length of time, but that would be an interesting ploy.

REFERENCES

Hearne, K. (1989). A questionnaire and personality study of self-styled psychics. *Journal of the Society for Psychical Research, 55*, 404–411.
West, D. J. (1948). The investigation of spontaneous cases. *Proceedings of the Society for Psychical Research, 48*, 264–300.
West, D. J. (1990). A pilot census of hallucinations. *Proceedings of the Society for Psychical Research, 57*, 163–207.

DISCUSSION

HARARY: I have two quick questions about your very enjoyable paper. First, in characterizing deja vu or other kinds of spontaneous experiences, it seems that we sometimes try to boil that down to one explanation. Is it a neurophysiological phenomenon? Is it a premonition? But isn't it possible that these general headings actually represent an entire class of phenomena that may in fact involve all kinds of different causes? Maybe in some cases it is a precognitive dream; maybe in another case there is a neurophysiological explanation. But it is all subjectively experienced along similar lines even though very different things are going on. The second question pertains to something you said toward the end of your talk, the idea that people who describe a lot of seemingly spontaneous psychic experiences might be exaggerating, might be suffering from delusion, because they can not necessarily prove that they are having those experiences. The point is, that if you ask a person what they have experienced and then they tell you, "I have experienced this and this and this," they are really just answering your question. There is perhaps a hidden assumption there that people want to be considered as people who have lots of psi experiences therefore, they are exaggerating them. But maybe they are just reporting what is actually happening to them. We could expect a certain number of people, a certain percentage of the population, if these are widespread kinds of experiences, to have perhaps a slightly larger share of them than other people. Or perhaps they start attending to them and then they notice them more. But why is that necessarily an exaggeration or did I misunderstand what you were getting at?

WEST: I think I would answer these two questions very simply by saying yes. The first question about deja vu, is it not possible that a lot of different factors are at work and not necessarily the same factor in every case? That is what I am trying to suggest may be so and why I think that one really ought to look at people's experiences in much greater detail and without prejudice, realizing that some may be readily explicable in neurophysiological terms and others may in fact have to have more than that. Now, as to the problem of people who report numerous experiences, it does seem from this survey, and from other surveys that I have read, that the population does seem to be rather dichotomized into those who have, on the one hand, either no experiences or only very occasional ones which they remember for the rest of their lives, and a minority for whom these experiences are claimed to be more or less common place or at least frequent. Now as you say, that mere statistical fact does not tell you anything about whether those frequent experiences are likely to be more or less genuine than the real ones. All I would say is that from long experience of trying to track down the corroboration in the case of those who claim very many experiences, one tends to become a little jaundiced in one's views because it is very difficult to pin some of these people down. That is the only reason why I am inclined to suggest that some of them are, to put a nasty name to it, fantasy mongers, but that is not to say that they all are. I certainly think that these people deserve very careful investigation and that is why I suggested a very simple method of doing it, if they are claiming frequent premonitory experiences, get them to record them in advance.

DIERKENS: Most of the time when people experience altered states of consciousness, peak experiences, or lucid dreams, they have the impression that their lives are somewhat changed, that their paradigm is changed, that they are not after that experience the same as they were just before having experienced that experience. Did you find in your survey that the people felt that change was in their own lives? Did you also find that the new spontaneous events would be of a different kind than the first?

WEST: I cannot really answer that question because the questionnaire only asked about their immediate reactions—what they did at the time following the experience. It did not ask them whether it had a long term effect on their lives. All I can say is that I know that it did not have a long term effect on many of them. Let me give you an example of what I mean. There was one case that I was particularly struck by because it so happened that it was somebody who was known to me as a student, who was a very sensible young woman. She said that she had gone home with the friend who subsequently became her fiance, having been to a cinema. Afterwards they went to his parents' house and as she was walking through the corridor to get to the sitting room, where the door was open (the sitting room was brightly lit), she saw sitting in the arm chair an elderly gentleman. She thought nothing about it and hung up her coat. But when she went into the room the elderly gentleman was not there. She assumed that he had gone into the bathroom which led off the room. She wanted to use the bathroom herself, so she waited in some discomfort for this gentleman to come out. But, of course, he never did. She finally asked her friend, "Has the gentleman finished?" And he said, "What gentleman?" She was able to describe this figure in some detail and he suggested half jokingly that it looked like his grandfather because it was wearing a seaman type sweater, which was a favorite of his grandfather, who had in fact died in that house. She said she did not really know what to think about this now. She had no explanation, and it was just something very curious. If she had been of a different turn of mind, she might have said, "I have seen a spirit, and I now know that there is a spirit world." But she did not.

NEPPE: I thought I would make a few comments particularly in regard to deja vu in that I think my book, *The Psychology of Deja Vu: Have I Been Here Before?* may cover many of the areas that Dr. West has spoken about. In fact, my PhD thesis was in the area of deja vu. One of the major attempts that I made was to try to qualitatively differentiate between different kinds of deja vu experience because it was clear to me, as it has been to several of the speakers, that one was apparently not necessarily dealing with a single, unitary phenomenon. Using this kind of an approach, there are two aspects that bear mentioning. First one does requires enormous attention to detail. You can screen out specific phenomena; having done that initial screen, you may be able to narrow your very broad population; but, thereafter, there is no substitute for developing a rigid, rather detailed, qualitative questionnaire (if you can quantitate it, all the better) which will also allow open-ended amplification. The accumulated data must initially be based on operational definitions. In the instance of deja vu, the operational definition must differentiate between the deja vu experience and the precognitive experience. Using this kind of framework, I demonstrated that there were four nosologically quite distinct kinds of deja vu experience occurring, in the four quite distinct populations which populations I examined, namely: normals, who have what I call "associative deja vu"; subjective paranormal experients, (a group of people operationally defined by the large number of subjectively veridical psi experiences of a variety of different kinds) who have "subjective paranormal experience deja vu"; "temporal lobe epileptic deja vu," which incidentally is different from other forms of deja vu in other epileptics and in non-epileptic temporal lobe disfunction; and, "schizophrenic deja vu," which may be a broader group and may occur in other psychotic groups. One can qualitatively differentiate these using such techniques as multi-dimensional scaling. These groups are discriminated in a completely different qualitative kind of way.

WEST: I would only respond in a slightly humorous way by saying that there is yet another category of deja vu which I experienced myself in youth when I had a very talkative lady relative who used to go on and on. Sometimes I had the impression that I had heard what she had to say before. I was never clear whether she had in fact repeated herself or whether I was having a deja vu experience.

WICKRAM: I am not a parapsychologist so my question is a request for information. I was intrigued by Dr. West's paper and I was wondering if he or anyone else had in any systematic way quantified the frequency of specific types of paranormal events that occur spontaneously as opposed to similar types of events elicited under controlled laboratory conditions? In the pain literature we have systematic, parametric differences between the parameters of experimental pain and the parameters of clinical pain. For example, the placebo rating of experimental pain is about 10%, and the mean placebo rating for clinical pain is 33%. So, I am wondering, are there any systematic differences in terms of the types of people who are high scorers in spontaneous situations in the natural habitat as opposed to people functioning in the laboratory?

WEST: I think it is a very complex question. First of all, you have to know what are the relative frequencies of different types of experiences occurring spontaneously, and, of course, there have been a variety of surveys in different countries. The problem here is that they have not all asked about the same thing. There is a tendency to ask about a limited range of psychic experiences in any particular survey, as I did myself. And, of course, the original SPR "Census of Hallucinations" in effect asked only about apparitions. So there is that problem. Then you say, "Are these types of phenomena, like physical effects, premonitory effects, and telepathic effects, similar in relative frequency to what you would get in the laboratory?" Then you have the complication that what you get in the laboratory depends on what you actually do. People in recent years have been interested in PK effects, so they do far more PK experiments than years ago when PK was thought to be something that could not occur in the laboratory. So there is no simple answer to that question.

TIERNEY: Dr. West, you mentioned the term fixity or firmness of belief. One might expect that there would be a correlation between the frequency of paranormal experience and the fixity of belief. Do you have any evidence that that is the case?

WEST: Yes, I do, because we had a rating scale for belief in ESP. The final point on the scale being definitely a fact and, of course, those with frequent experiences tended to say definitely a fact.

BENOR: My question is from my experience as a psychotherapist being very aware that patients of psychoanalytic therapists dream psychoanalytic dreams and patients of Jungian therapists dream Jungian dreams. I wonder if you would feel comfortable about sharing with us your personal beliefs about these phenomena since in doing the questioning of these people presumably your beliefs may have influenced some of the results and some of the responses you got. Also, have you had any paranormal experiences yourself which would lead you to believe or disbelieve in these phenomena?

WEST: These are, of course, very personal questions but I will answer them as frankly as possible. The fact is that in adult life I cannot recall having any paranormal experiences. But I do recall as a boy having what appeared to be premonitory experiences which at the time I did not look upon as something other than very interesting and curious. But, of course, it is many, many years ago and looking back on one's childhood as an old man, one cannot help but doubt one's own recollections. I would not say that I am terribly inclined to believe in these things just because I have a distant memory of having something similar myself. Now as to influencing people's responses, the initial approach was via a written questionnaire which was distributed by a variety of different people so that you could not say that I was personally involved. Of the subsequent follow-up interviews, some were done by me and some were done by Dr. Alan Gauld so that again it was not all dependent on me.

VON LUCADOU: I just want to make a remark concerning your question. While there is little information about the personality characteristics of those people who experience spontaneous PK and those in PK experiments, I could compare a study which has been performed by Hans Bender concerning physical events with my own PK experiments. I found something rather interesting. It seems, to some extent, that apparently with the characteristic of externality and internality, the locus of control, seems to have quite a different outcome with the spontaneous cases. People who report spontaneous cases seem to be more external—they have higher scoring externality; whereas, in the experiment it was the reverse—non-external people tend to be better in PK experiments. To some extent, from a psychological point of view, this seems to be plausible. Another point is extroversion. It seems that in experiments, extroverted people are better than introverts, and in spontaneous cases, it seems that introverts report more physical events. This is also plausible from a psychological point of view, if you assume that people in RSPK cases, focus persons, have a problem which they cannot express by other means and then something happens. But in experiments you have a quite different situation, you have a very artificial situation and you want to get a person to do something very specific and the way to do this is quite different from the sponta-eous case.

CASSIRER: I did not quite understand why Prof. West should be surprised when someone who is "obviously" gullible like myself, claiming to have had psychic experiences, should end up being a firm believer in ESP and other psychic phenomena. What I find extraordinary is that after 400 years of investigation we should still be questioning these things. I am going a little further back than the foundation of the SPR to the witchcraft manifestations of the 16th and 17th centuries when intelligent people were already studying these phenomena, though not with the knowledge and depth of modern sophistication. Now, I may be thought naive in saying that these matters have been established beyond a doubt, but when I investigate a poltergeist case at first hand and see a heavy man violently pushed and nearly forced over, I want to find out why this happened. What is the problem? Not *does* it happen, but *why* and *how* does it happen. This is what really puzzles me.

WEST: About the question of belief, I mentioned that this scale went both ways. There were those saying definitely a fact and those saying impossible or highly unlikely. It was curious to me that those who were on the skeptical end reported virtually nothing. I wondered whether persons with a very skeptical frame of mind actually inhibited these things or repressed them once they had happened.

IVANOVA: In my experience with working with Russian audiences, I think in some cases belief or disbelief has no meaning. I refer to deja vu cases. In general, our audiences do not know anything about it. There is nothing negative written in our press because nobody knows about it and nobody speaks about it. So when I speak about it in my audiences they do not know anything, so belief and disbelief does not exist. But the majority of the people present say that they have such experiences. Half of them will be disbelievers, more or less, and in spite of being disbelievers in parapsychological happenings, they talk in small circles about their experiences. So I think that belief or disbelief does not always play an important role. I am not very sure of it but it seems so to me.

WEST: I only want rather obsessionally to repeat the observation we found which was that of those who said that ESP was impossible, none of them reported any hallucinatory or apparitional experiences. I find that most curious.

ELLISON: This is a question of rather a different kind and I think related to what Donald West was just saying. It is also related to what Manfred Cassirer has said about witches a few hundred years ago. We have not heard anything from the psychologists about defense reactions. We all have, or most of us have here in the West, a paradigm, a philosophy, which is realism. That philosophy of realism is behind almost all of our Western science and is defended very stoutly by defense reactions which psychologists understand much better than I do. Could it not be that what you are finding is a measure of the strength of people's defense reactions? Is this not an important point which should be mentioned? And is it perhaps also related to the fact that no one these days seems to do experiments on themselves? No one has mentioned the sort of experiment I did in which I produced in myself two out-of-body experiences—an experiment like Beard's (in Barrett's time) who produced his apparition to the appearance of people some miles out of London. Why does no one do this? Surely, defense reactions are an important point in relation both to us and to the population in general.

WEST: As a simple answer I do not know. But I think this observation runs through the whole history of the subject. In the 19th century there were descriptions of hypnotists who were able to produce effects on their subjects at a great distance, but one does not have reports of this kind of thing today. There are many things that were reported in the past that are no longer reported, either because they are not attempted or because they no longer happen. I do not know which it is.

CLINICAL APPROACHES TO
REPORTED PSI EXPERIENCES:
THE RESEARCH IMPLICATIONS

KEITH HARARY

When my wife, Darlene Moore, and I first arrived in London, we checked into the hotel and immediately rushed to the Poets' Corner in Westminster Abbey, where some of the most revered figures in literature are memorialized and enshrined. We are both writers, and to be standing in the company of names like Charles Dickens, Geoffrey Chaucer, and Charlotte, Anne and Emily Bronte was, for us, a profoundly moving experience. It struck us both, as we shared remembered lines from the works of these intensely creative people, walking carefully to avoid stepping directly on the graves beneath our feet, how very different they were from one another, and yet, they shared the creative process, the ability to take their deepest feelings and perceptions and express them in a manner that allowed others to experience powerfully their innermost vision.

That creative process is, I suggest, not unlike the process that we call psi. In psi, as in other forms of artistic self-expression, the key to the process is the ability to translate an intangible inner experience into a tangible form. Whatever the nature of the original perception, be it a purely internal phenomenon or one that entails a quasi-sensory interaction with the physical world, it only can consciously be recognized by the perceiver, and clearly reported to others, through a subtle and complex process of creative intrapersonal and interpersonal communication. The perceiver, who simultaneously is like a writer crafting a novel and an artist painting a portrait, must develop the proper verbal and visual language to express himself or herself effectively without distortion. This does not necessarily mean that the successful fulfillment of the process requires the resulting image or description to be photographic. It rather implies that the perceiver's *unique* perspective must clearly and accurately be expressed.

Imagine what life would be like for writers if widespread segments of the literary community and society-at-large mistakenly believed that such creative people all were necessarily psychologically disturbed. We know from numerous research studies, and from our everyday experiences, that such attitudes easily can pervert the perceptions of those who hold them. What if there were such a stigma attached to original forms of self-expression that the ability to write poetry, paint portraits or compose music was looked upon as a mixed blessing in which the gifted also were considered the cursed? How would you react to those reputed to have strong literary, artistic or musical talents, and even to your own creative urges, in such an unhealthy cultural environment? Chances are that you would feel ambivalent, simultaneously drawn to the creative experience as a primal and essential element underlying human nature, yet also reluctant to submit yourself completely to those urges and thereby risk suffering the social consequences of that surrender. Your response to those who openly espoused the creative experience might similarly be ambivalent, bound up in at least equal measures of attraction and avoidance. If you were adventurous by nature, or so impassioned by the creative process that you could not renounce it, or simply rebellious, however, you might feel less ambivalent and more willing to violate the boundaries of social expectation in order to fulfill your need for self-expression. Even if you were not a particularly capable writer, artist or musician, you might affect the role of artisan in an effort to achieve some level of recognition as an avant-garde individual worthy of special attention. Many insecure people, in fact, would eagerly embrace the role of eccentric artist in order to feel more important, adding to the prevailing myth that truly creative people really are psychologically imbalanced.

In the real world, of course, we do not generally approach creative people in such a dysfunctional fashion, although there always have been individuals and subcultures on the cutting edge whose deliberate rejection of the status quo is a fundamental element of the creative process, and who therefore are treated as undesirables by those who embrace it. Our response to psi is, however, dramatically different from our response to any other creative, perceptual and communicative process.

In the field of psi research, we typically respond to those who report psi experiences in just such an ambivalent fashion, often treating them simultaneously as though they are both mad and enlightened, or as if they are worthwhile objects for study who actively are trying to deceive us. This ambivalence is particularly pronounced in our response to those who appear to have demonstrated that their experiences are more than purely subjective, and those who report having spontaneous psi experiences on too frequent a basis.

Rather than reflecting any personal antagonism toward those who appear to demonstrate psi ability or who report frequent psi experiences, however, this reaction most likely reflects a broader discomfort on the part of many of those within the field, including some discomfort with the concept of psi itself. This discomfort may arise from many different sources. It may, for example, reflect the fear on the part of some researchers that those who personally are intimate with psi might better understand its nature than those who are attempting to investigate it from a purely "objective" perspective, and the neurotic need of these researchers to maintain a nominally superior posture relative to such individuals.

It may also reflect the understandable fear on the part of some researchers that they will lose their scientific objectivity and credibility, and potentially be duped, if they approach those who claim to have unusually developed psi ability, or who report psi experiences, in a manner that is too open-minded or egalitarian. Among those researchers who believe that psi is an intrinsically capricious and anomalous process, this ambivalent response may also reflect the belief that those who reportedly experience psi in a consistent fashion must, by definition, either be gifted or deluded if not consciously inventing their reports.

This ambivalence may even reflect the fear of losing control of psi by allowing it to be expressed outside of the controlled environment of the laboratory. In particular, it may represent the fear of allowing psi to express itself freely in a manner that is inconsistent with a favored theory of how it operates, thereby invalidating the researcher's own beliefs (Harary, 1985). But since psi did not originate within the laboratory, and never has restricted its real-life expression merely to fulfilling the theoretical, philosophical or religious expectations of any given group of investigators, such an approach can only limit the scope of the investigation rather than limiting psi itself.

Beyond the idiosyncratic psychodynamics of the psi laboratory, in any event, lies the broader cultural environment and its impact not only on psi researchers but also on the greater population. Just as it does within the field of psi research, this population includes those who are responding to their own experiences, as well as those who are reacting to the reported psi experiences[1] of other people. It is likely that the ambivalent response of psi researchers to such reported experiences has its origins in the similarly ambivalent response of Western culture, which also approaches psi in a highly charged and contradictory fashion that is overly-burdened with negative stereotypes and mass mythology (Harary, 1992b).

In short, we do not approach reported psi experiences, either as researchers or as agents of Western culture, in a manner that is at all objective. The same may be said of the manner in which reported psi experiences are approached in the clinical setting, and the way in which those who have such experiences typically respond to their own situation.

When an individual reports a spontaneous psi experience to a researcher, a clinician, or a friend, he or she usually is seeking some explanation. The response rarely is that the individual in question plainly underwent a still poorly understood, but nevertheless common, creative experience. Instead, we tend to focus on the apparent strangeness of psi, on the specific ways in which the reported experience seems to violate our present understanding of the nature of reality, and on the awesome questions that are raised in our minds in encountering that violation.

Exploring these questions can potentially lead to our expanding our understanding of psi, as well as our knowledge of the universe, or at least may inspire us to expand our vision of our own potential. These are compelling and laudable objectives. But focusing too heavily on the apparent strangeness of psi and its far-reaching conceptual implications without first focusing on more basic issues can also lead us to draw premature conclusions and to turn our attention in the wrong direction. We also may be expected, given this focus, to carry out research that reflects a similar bias.

As psi researchers, this focus can cause us to ask misleading questions about those who appear to show consistent psi ability, or who report frequent psi experiences, which arise from our imbuing these individuals with the same degree of strangeness that we attribute to psi. Sim-

---

[1] In using the term, "reported psi experience," I am intentionally leaving open the question of whether or not any given experience actually may be psi-related. Any human experience is, by definition, subjective. For this reason, terms such as "apparent psi experience" (Harary, 1986a) or "subjective paranormal experience" (Neppe, 1992) may be seen as internally redundant. I therefore have abandoned such terms in favor of the journalistic convention of describing such experiences as "reported" by those who describe them to researchers, clinicians and others.

ilarly, as clinicians, this focus can lead us to treat those who report psi experiences as though they are fundamentally abnormal, and to emphasize attempts to validate or invalidate their experiences, rather than to develop more appropriate ways to respond to their specific needs.

The result, in the laboratory, often is an approach in which psi is treated as an abnormal process, and in which the spotlight is on proving that this abnormal process actually exists. Such approaches typically have a primarily statistical basis, and often downplay psi's creative nature, thereby potentially distorting our vision of the very process that is under investigation by restricting its available range of expression. We see this approach reflected, for example, in Rhine's forced-choice card guessing research, in which the perceiver is told to guess redundantly from among the same five, simple, black and white line drawings (Rhine, 1937).

This experimental method is designed more to meet the needs of the experimenter than to accommodate psi, which expresses itself in everyday life in a far richer and more spontaneous fashion. The focus of this research is linear, with ambiguous distinctions made between telepathy, clairvoyance, precognition and psychokinesis and other conjectural varieties of psi phenomena. It is not process-oriented, because the effort converges more on attempting to distinguish among these blurred theoretical categories, and getting psi to express itself repeatedly in a specific fashion, than it does upon illuminating psi's relationship to the physical universe and its role and meaning in the life of the perceiver.

Moreover, by restricting psi's available range of expression, and overwhelming the perceiver with mental noise[2] such experiments almost invariably lead to a decline in perceiver performance. Rather than establishing that psi performance is innately erratic and unreliable, however, this "decline effect" more likely indicates that the experimental approach itself is flawed because it extinguishes the perceiver's effective ability to process psi impressions. This unimaginative approach

---

[2] I originated the term "mental noise" more than a decade ago to serve as a broad category under which the various cognitive and perceptual processes that tend to interfere with the perceiver's accurate interpretation of psi impressions, and which have been discussed by many researchers over the years, are listed. These include the process of "secondary elaboration" (or free association) discussed by René Warcollier (Warcollier, 1963), "analytic overlay" as discussed in the SRI remote viewing program founded and directed by physicist Harold Puthoff (e.g., Puthoff & Targ, 1976), the interference emerging from short and long-term memories triggered by psi impressions, the interference emerging from perceptual imagery of the perceiver's local environment, and various other cognitive and perceptual processes.

to psi also is so far removed from the more evocative manner in which psi manifests and expresses itself in the real world that it offers little insight to individuals grappling to understand their spontaneous psi experiences, or to clinicians attempting to assist these individuals. In fact, if we take the tacit message of this research to heart, we will likely conclude that anyone experiencing more than a fleeting acquaintance with psi must be abnormal.

If we accept the notion that psi is expressed only under abnormal circumstances, or by abnormal people, then we must logically conclude that something abnormal has occurred when anyone has a spontaneous psi experience. If we carry this perspective into the laboratory, we may also conclude that the appropriate way to encourage psi to manifest in a controlled environment is by making the laboratory experience itself as surreal as possible.

We see this approach most clearly reflected in the ganzfeld experiments currently in vogue among psi researchers. These free-response experiments typically make use of a more imaginative target pool than the Rhine card-guessing experiments, and therefore allow psi a somewhat more expansive range of creative expression than is available in forced-choice studies involving a limited number of symbols. The perceiver in a ganzfeld experiment, however, is placed in a highly structured environment, which involves a combination of sensory deprivation and controlled sensory input, intended to induce a psi-conducive altered state of consciousness by controlling his or her exposure to environmental noise (Honorton & Harper, 1974).

Briefly, ganzfeld perceivers are isolated in a sound-attenuated room with halved ping-pong balls placed over their eyes, and are told to listen to white noise over headphones while a red light shines in their face. They are told to keep their eyes open and to observe *passively* the spontaneous, hypnagogic imagery that is expected to manifest under these conditions while verbally describing this imagery, in a stream-of-consciousness fashion. The target material generally consists of collages, brief film clips or other pictorial information, the contents of which are expected to influence the hypnagogic imagery described by the perceiver.

Many ganzfeld experiments have led to striking correspondences between the perceiver's verbal mentation and the target material, or at least to correspondences that are sufficient to permit a statistically significant number of matches between this mentation and the correct target from among a pool of possibilities for a given trial (Honorton, Berger, Varvoglis, Quant, Derr, Schechter, & Ferrari, 1990). This has led quite a number of researchers to conclude that the ganzfeld does, indeed, induce a special, psi-conducive altered state of consciousness.

This interpretation, however, is not necessarily correct. We cannot assume, for example, that all ganzfeld perceivers are in an identical state of consciousness, or that they are even necessarily in an altered state. Nor should we assume that the perceiver's state of mind is specific to the ganzfeld, or in any way dependant on its paraphernalia. Many ganzfeld perceivers, for example, have reported keeping their eyes closed during this procedure, although the exact number who have done so is not known.[3] Furthermore, even if all ganzfeld perceivers were known to be in a similar state of mind, it still is possible that this mental state might not be the key factor influencing their psi performance. Instead, the social dynamics of the researcher/ perceiver interaction, the psychological atmosphere of the laboratory, the use of the ganzfeld as ritual and, perhaps most importantly, *the nature of the target materials used in these experiments and the creative outlet these materials may make available for psi,* all may play a more powerful role in influencing the success of ganzfeld experiments than any given perceiver's exact state of consciousness.

The weakness of the ganzfeld approach, therefore, is not any failure to elicit some level of psi performance in the laboratory. It may, rather, be that the procedure itself is unnecessary and may lead us to misinterpret the meaning of a successful experimental outcome. Like Rhine's card-guessing experiments, it may also lead us mistakenly to attribute to psi the artificially-imposed limitations of the experimental procedure. This procedure encourages the perceiver to become deeply introspective and demands that he or she describe a free-associated stream of imagery, with all the internal mental noise that may be inherent in such a strategy. By forcefully shielding the perceiver from the immediate environment, and encouraging free association, the ganzfeld therefore may result in exchanging one kind of mental noise for another. It would be illogical to assume that psi is incapable of extending itself into a more expressive range, in a greater variety of conditions, just because it previously has limited its expression in the laboratory to the boundaries we set for it.

From a clinical perspective, the tacit message of the ganzfeld is that

---

[3] One ganzfeld experimenter actually attempted to overcome this problem by taping the perceivers' eyelids to their eyebrows! The perceivers reportedly experienced excruciating discomfort during this series of experiments, and were not especially successful in describing the targets. They may, however, all have been in an altered state of consciousness.

psi is not a process that can easily and consciously be managed by the perceiver under ordinary circumstances. The immediate effect of this message in the laboratory is that the perceiver relinquishes control of the process to the experimenter and to the procedure itself, and may be made to feel less powerful as a result. It is almost as though the ganzfeld perceiver becomes personally less relevant than the experimental method. If we carry the implicit message of the ganzfeld approach into the clinical setting, therefore, we may conclude that anyone claiming to have conscious control over his or her psi impressions in an ordinary waking state would either have to be extraordinarily powerful or extraordinarily deluded, if not unabashedly attempting to deceive us. A more appropriate message might be, however, that the ganzfeld (like many other approaches) shows that psi can manifest even in the most peculiar situations, not because these circumstances are essential, or even particularly helpful, for psi's manifestation, but because psi is an adaptive and creative process that permeates our entire life experience (Harary, 1982b).

If we approach psi as a neutral and normal process that follows the pattern of other creative processes, this more balanced viewpoint also will be reflected in our laboratory methods. It also will have important implications for our treatment of psi experiences in the clinical setting. Perhaps the best historical example of this approach may be found in the dream research conducted at Maimonides Medical Center under the direction of psychiatrist Montague Ullman (Ullman, Krippner, & Vaughan, 1973).

Instead of inhibiting psi by restricting its expression to repetitive symbols, or attempting to regulate psi by overly confining and controlling the perceiver, Ullman and his associates, including psychologist Stanley Krippner and others, developed an original method for observing psi's expression in the naturally creative context of the dream. Most significantly, the inspiration for this research emerged directly from the psychotherapeutic context in which Ullman and a number of professional colleagues noticed that their clients were describing what appeared to be psi-related imagery occurring in their nightly dream experiences. Related reports of psi experiences manifesting in the course of psychoanalysis may be traced all the way back to Sigmund Freud (1953/1934).

By deliberately stimulating psi-related dream imagery in the controlled laboratory environment, Ullman and associates were able to establish that psi can, indeed, play a powerful role in influencing our dream content. This research still leaves open a number of intriguing questions for future study, such as the question of whether the dream state *itself* is especially psi conducive, or whether the natural *meaning-fulness* of the dream experience provides an especially fertile medium for psi's creative expression. Nevertheless, if we carry the message of this research back into the clinical context, then we must consider carefully the potential relevance of psi-related content in assisting our clients in interpreting their dreams. We must also consider the possibility that, since dreams are a ubiquitous human experience, psi experiences also may be ubiquitous.

If psi is a normal creative process that is a common facet of the human experience, and if its manifestation does not require a special state of consciousness, then ordinary people should also be able to express their psi ability under relatively prosaic conditions. Perhaps the best available research evidence in support of this conclusion is beginning to emerge from extended perception[4] studies involving unselected perceivers.

A defining characteristic of this approach is that the perceivers are not in any apparent altered state of consciousness. Nor are they shielded from the immediate environment, or subjected to controlled sensory input as they are in the ganzfeld. They are, instead, wide awake and consciously managing the interpretation of their own psi impressions while *actively* distinguishing these impressions from various forms of mental noise. They also are making sketches to accompany the description they provide of these impressions, providing another important outlet for psi's creative expression. These studies also have successfully been carried out under an extensive variety of environmental conditions, from the noisy confines of the office to the silent depths of the ocean, with no apparent degradation in the results. The perceivers in these experiments have been asked to describe a large assortment of possible targets, from pictorial materials, to objects, to locations, to human beings, making accessible a potentially more expansive range of creative expression than is generally available even in ganzfeld trials. Many extended perception experiments have led to striking correspondences between perceiver descriptions and drawings and the tar-

---

[4] In our ongoing research at the Institute for Advanced Psychology, we have supplanted the older term, "remote viewing," with the more accurate and, we believe, more appropriate term, "extended perception" because: (1) The psi process does not appear to limit its scope to accessing and describing only visual information, and (2) This neutral term is intended to communicate our view that psi functioning exists along a natural continuum that includes all other forms of perception and communication. For this reason, we also find the additional term, "extended communication," and the broader term, "extended abilities," to be useful.

gets themselves, sufficient to permit a statistically significant number of matches with the correct targets (Targ & Harary, 1984).

The emerging evidence from extended perception research suggests that psi ability may be improved with practice, but that it also may involve certain instinctive skills and related capabilities that are widely, but variably, distributed in the general population. In this sense, psi appears to be much like every other creative ability. If we carry the message of this research into the clinical setting, we will treat those who report psi experiences as individuals, rather than as cultural stereotypes. We also will focus on the healthy or unhealthy ways in which these individuals *respond* to their experiences, rather than on the apparent strangeness of the experiences themselves, in determining the nature of this treatment.

It is, unfortunately, a defining characteristic of our response to those who report such experiences that we frequently allow our perspective to be clouded by stereotypical attitudes and misconceptions. We often are so preoccupied with our own response to reported psi experiences, in fact, that we fail to recognize the significant ways in which the impact and meaning of these experiences can vary for each individual. In the laboratory, the clinical setting, and everyday life, we commonly select our reactions from a Pandora's Box of preconceptions, inviting those who share the intimate details of their psi experiences to resolve any lingering questions by losing their perspective along with the rest of us.

Perhaps the most familiar example of this destructive tendency is our eagerness to label selected individuals as "psychic," and the ardent manner in which many people covet, embrace, and even actively compete for the dubious honor of becoming identified with this questionable label. Our use of the psychic label encompasses, succinctly and persistently, the overall lack of vision that characterizes our entire approach to reported psi experiences. It expresses the prevailing attitude that psi involves less of what a given individual *does* than who he or she *is*. This crucial distinction makes the psychic label quite unlike other less loaded terms used to describe a person's pursuit of a creative calling. We may think of artists, writers and musicians as sensitive, passionate, or even eccentric, but we rarely think of them as fundamentally different from the rest of the human race. We do, on the other hand, tend to categorize those we label as psychic in precisely this fashion.

In psi research, this tendency manifests in many different ways, but may be most recognizable in our eternal search for the secret psychological ingredients that comprise the mythical psychic personality

(Schmeidler, 1974). Our search for this formula is the psi research equivalent to the quest for the Holy Grail. It reflects the conviction that our scientific salvation lies not in looking within ourselves to solve the mystery of psi, but in seeking out those who somehow have been chosen to embody this mystery. Just as those who would glimpse the Holy Grail can only achieve their objective by being free of sin, the mythical psychic also is popularly considered to be a creature more spiritually evolved than ordinary mortals.

The narcissistic appeal of this metaphysical attribution no doubt accounts, at least in part, for the eagerness with which many people embrace the psychic label. It also may lie at the root of our ambivalent response to those who are described, or who describe themselves, as psychic. We are simultaneously as attracted to those who are spiritually empowered to provide us with the answers to our deepest and most private questions, as we are viscerally repelled by anyone who would be so conceited as to make any claim to being so enlightened. This response is prevalent not only within the community of psi research, but also at every level of Western culture. It no doubt contributes to such disparate phenomena as the allure of religious cult leaders who claim to have unusually developed psychic abilities (Harary, 1980), and the belligerent renunciation of psi research by many religious atheists (Hansen, 1992).

Our longterm failure to identify a distinct, psychic personality type should provide us with some indication that our effort to do so may be misguided and futile. The problem we may finally be confronting may not simply be a matter of overcoming our prejudicial treatment of those alleged to be psychic. Even if we were to codify a policy of civil rights for psychics, or magnanimously were to concede that those we identify as psychics are essentially as human as the rest of us, the flaw in this approach would be our insistence upon identifying any human being as a psychic in the first place. The category itself is so endowed with conceptual drawbacks and so fraught with historical complications that it cannot help but be destructive both to those who are included within it and to those who are not so included.

A more mature and psychologically sound approach would not be predicated on drawing such absolute and spurious distinctions between those who do and do not have psi ability. It might, instead, be predicated on recognizing that the psi process, like every other creative ability, may comprise a synthesis of associated skills and talents that are common to the human experience and that have little or nothing to do with spiritual enlightenment. A successful writer, for example, must be competent in the rules of language and grammar, must have an adequate vocabulary, and must have a native talent and desire for original self-expression. A successful fine art painter must be proficient in the application of paint to canvas, must have a grasp of art history, and must have a personal aesthetic. Both the artist and the writer must be skilled observers, and must also be fortunate enough to develop their native talents through encouragement and perseverance. All of these specific qualities and capabilities may be recognized and assessed using a variety of approaches, none of which would be so irrelevant and undiscerning as to be oriented toward simply defining a specific artistic personality type.

Similarly, the successful expression of psi ability may require a combination of specific observational and expressive capabilities, all of which may be assessed using a variety of appropriate measures. Once again, it is doubtful that any measure that is so ham-handed as to be oriented toward merely defining a single, psychic personality type could ever be considered appropriate. Perhaps a more appropriate approach would be one that takes account of the specific skills and talents that are directly relevant to the psi process, and that is sensitive to the individualistic manner in which these may manifest and interact with other personality factors on a case by case basis.

The implications of approaching psi functioning as a normal and neutral creative process, both for the psi laboratory and for clinical practice, are significant. In the laboratory, any debate over whether psi ability may be developed through practice or only is inherited would have to be considered pointless. Instead of orienting our research toward the apparent strangeness of psi, we would focus on elucidating the ways in which the psi process integrates itself into the greater spectrum of perception and communication. Instead of developing data dossiers on suspected psychics, we would focus on recognizing the latent potential within each of us for incorporating an awareness of psi into our own creative repertoire. Instead of poisoning the atmosphere with obsolete concepts and battling with one another over meaningless labels, we would focus on redefining and expanding our concept of human potential. Instead of disavowing the personal power of the perceiver, we would focus on developing more effective ways of empowering the perceiver while still fulfilling the highest standards of scientific method.

In the clinical setting, when we encounter a person who reports a psi experience, this suggested approach would orient us toward responding to the specific needs of that individual. Instead of assuming that something unusual has happened to anyone who has had a psi experience, and preoccupying ourselves with attempts to develop normal vs. abnormal explanations for the experience in question, we would honor the integrity of the creative process. Our primary focus would not be on determining whether a given experience involves "real" psi. It would be on assisting the individual who reports the experience in dealing with it effectively and interpreting its personal meaning within the appropriate context of his or her own life.

Despite our research interest in ascertaining the scientific basis for reported psi experiences, as clinicians we must also recognize that the ultimate psychological relevance of any given episode does not depend entirely on whether or not it involves a genuine psi-related interaction. It also depends on the way the individual interprets and relates to his or her encounter with a more expansive sense of self. In fact, any powerful psychological experience can profoundly affect the life course of the individual who has it, without necessarily involving veridical psi, or even having any tangible basis.

Few people would argue, for example, that our nightly dreams represent an actual descent into a separate, Alice In Wonderland reality on the other side of the looking glass of sleep. Yet, countless people have gained transformative insights from exploring the meaning of their dreams precisely because dreams represent the spontaneous, creative expressions of the innermost self. Viewed from this perspective, our dreams can provide us with the ground-level truth of our inner response to our real-world experiences. In this sense, they may provide access to a level of reality that may be "more real than real" because they represent daily life as it subjectively is perceived and symbolically interpreted by the dreamer.

Reported psi experiences may provide us with a similar path to the creative self, but only if we recognize that these experiences are not arbitrarily induced by external forces that overpower the individual. Instead, they emerge from within the individual, with his or her conscious and unconscious consent and active participation. They cannot, therefore, properly be understood without considering the specific life context within which they emerge in each specific case.

If a person reports an experience in which he or she appears to be in extended communication with an alleged unfaithful spouse, for example, it would be irresponsible for any clinician to focus on the question of whether or not such a psi-related communication literally has taken place without addressing the more immediate marital issues that clearly are at stake. Even if it could incontrovertibly be proven that psi is at work in such an experience, we would have to acknowledge—as did Freud (1953/1941)—that its specific focus has hardly been selected at random. We stand to gain greater insights, therefore, by considering the creative manner in which the individual who has such an experience chooses to express his or her specific problems and concerns than we do by limiting ourselves to determining if psi specifically is implicated in that process. Is the alleged unfaithful spouse envisioned in a casual liaison with a total stranger, for example, or is he or she perceived as entering the welcoming embrace of a serious, new romantic interest?

In assisting those who approach us as clinicians and researchers in the hope of receiving an explanation, if not our scientific validation, for their reported psi experiences, we also must openly acknowledge our limitations. More often than not, we do not have the answers such individuals are seeking. We would be doing them a disservice to pretend that we do have those answers. Nor are we frequently in a position scientifically to validate or invalidate any reported psi experience, not only because it is unwise to make lofty pronouncements about an encounter that we have not personally witnessed, but also because our understanding of psi is severely limited. Even in the case of research methodologies that lead to statistically significant results, the effects we observe in the laboratory may not directly be comparable to the spontaneous psi effects that are experienced by ordinary people in everyday life.

The primary law of any clinical interaction is to *do no harm.* The potential for doing harm by pretending to have answers that do not yet exist is enormous. Consider the clinical ramifications, for example, of off-handedly informing a troubled and confused individual who is seeking an explanation of a reported psi experience, or a cluster of such experiences, that he or she must be a psychic. If the individual in question takes this suggestion seriously—which is likely given our posture as "experts" on the subject—the longterm impact of that strange revelation is bound to be destructive. Compounding matters further is the fact that the psychic label literally explains nothing, since the research basis for defining any human being as a psychic is nonexistent.

By the same token, if we nonchalantly inform such a person that a reported psi experience should be classified as telepathy, clairvoyance, precognition, or psychokinesis, or that it represents an encounter with the "paranormal," or falls under some other fuzzy and disputable categorization, we only are proclaiming our inability to provide a more legitimate explanation of what is happening. In every case, the label represents a specific way in which the reported experience appears to be inexplicable, but does not refer to an established psychological and/ or physical process. It is, therefore, irrational to pretend that by using such a label we have made any progress in solving the mystery that the label itself represents. We would be much better off admitting at the beginning of our interaction with anyone concerned about a reported psi experience that, despite more than a century of research, we still know relatively little about the specific psychological and physical mechanisms that eventually may account for psi ability. Even in approaching psi as a creative process, we have not solved the mystery of its perceptual and physical origin. We may, that is, know something about how we process psi information once we have it, but we do not yet know how we get this information. While this limitation does not prevent us from exploring psi's capabilities, and assessing its apparent impact on human behavior, it does restrict our ability to rule out certain experiences as beyond the scope of psi's potential.

We are not currently in a scientific position, for example, to reach any rational conclusion about questions concerning the possibility of survival after death, communication with the dead, or reincarnation. The conservative explanation, that "ordinary" psi functioning may account for information that appears to be channelled from beyond the grave, will always be more scientifically acceptable than raising the specter of an afterlife, unless we establish that psi has definable limits. And even this conservative, psi-oriented explanation of apparent survival-related experiences should be held in abeyance pending more conventional psychological, social and cultural explanations of the observed phenomena reported in such cases.

This does not mean, however, that we should approach those who believe they are in contact with the dead, or who report other similarly outrageous experiences, as potential candidates for psychiatric incarceration. It only means that we should be honest with such people about the inability of our present science to answer many of their questions. For all we know, they may be in touch with a level of reality that is beyond the scope of our present science. As long as we bear in mind that we should be treating the individual and not the reported experience, however, admitting the limitations of our present knowledge will not necessarily limit our ability to intervene clinically when people have problems in coping with such episodes.

In a practical sense, any effort at clinical intervention should be focused on helping those who are dealing with reported psi experiences to maintain a balanced sense of self. It should not be focused on encouraging them to share our philosophical vision. Unless the individual in question is undergoing a psychotic episode, or otherwise is dangerously out of touch with the everyday world, the ultimate arbiter of the meaning of any particular reported psi experience must always be the individual who has it. He or she is, after all, the one who ultimately must live with that experience. As researchers, we can only work toward expanding the scientific knowledge base available to these individuals.

As clinicians, we can only encourage them to maintain a balanced and rational perspective as they move toward integrating their experiences into their lives.

Even if we suspect that a given individual may be so unbalanced, and so out of touch with the everyday world, as to require hospitalization, we must base that assessment primarily on the individual's broad symptoms and behavior. The way in which he or she responds to any reported psi experience often is more relevant than the specific details of the experience itself. It is possible for a person to be mentally ill, and yet to be correct in interpreting a particular experience or cluster of experiences as psi related. It also is possible for him or her to be psychologically fit, and yet to be mistaken in reaching this same conclusion.

In attempting to develop appropriate clinical strategies for assisting individuals to deal effectively with their reported psi experiences, we may find the following six categories to be useful:

1. *Those who report a lifelong, or otherwise longterm, history of psi experiences that appear primarily to have a veridical basis*: Such individuals may find themselves struggling with resolving personal identity issues raised by the unhealthy messages they receive about their experiences from other people, and more generally from Western Culture. They often attempt to deny their experiences in an effort to avoid being judged as abnormal by others or, conversely, may overemphasize their experiences in an effort to acknowledge and encourage others to recognize an aspect of their existence that they perceive as valuable. This overemphasis, which is common among those who identify themselves as "psychic," may lead to social and other problems, or may complicate existing longterm problems (such as child abuse) that may have precipitated the reported psi experiences. The common desire of these individuals to find a community that is more sympathetic to their experiences than the prevailing culture may make them vulnerable to cults that appear to promise, but may not actually provide, such a refuge. All of these issues may be mitigated by their absorption in an ethnic, religious or other established subculture that is openly sympathetic toward reported psi experiences.

2. *Those who report a short-term history of psi experiences, or only a single such experience, whose experiences appear primarily to have a veridical basis*: Such individuals typically find themselves coping with resolving the questions that these experiences can raise about their worldview, but also may find themselves struggling with personal identity issues raised by their experiences. They may attempt to resolve their questions by denying their experiences or by altering their view of reality and sense

of self, including by identifying themselves as "psychic". Their shifting worldview and changing sense of self may lead to social and other problems, or may complicate existing longterm problems, and may make them vulnerable to cults. Once again, however, these issues may be mitigated by their absorption in an established subculture that provides a positive and supportive context for reported psi experiences.

An example from my own clinical experience occurred in the case of a client who reported having correctly identified all 25 cards in a shuffled Zener deck, in a single, controlled experimental run modeled after the studies conducted by J.B. Rhine. The client reportedly was so stunned by her own performance, and found her self-image and view of reality so shaken by that experience, that she abandoned her life as she had known it and spent more than seven years in a religious cult. Although she believed that the cult would provide a supportive context within which she could explore her own potential, she found herself being personally and financially exploited by the cult's leaders while her actual needs never were addressed. The client was able to leave the cult, and returned to a happier and more productive life, when she realized that psi experiences are widespread in the human population and that her own reported experience did not imply that she was fundamentally different from other people. Rather than returning to her original worldview, however, she allowed her experience (in combination with other expansive experiences) to instill her with a greater sense of wonder and curiosity in her everyday life.

3. *Those who report either a long or short-term history of psi experiences, or only a single such experience, and whose experiences appear to represent a mixture of veridical and imaginative elements*: Such individuals may be like many of us in their uncertainty about where the boundaries of actual psi begin and end. In some instances, however, they may have found the veridical aspects of their reported experiences to be so unsettling that their sense of reality has become unstable. They also may be turning to psi-related beliefs to compensate for problems and disappointments that remain to be resolved in other aspects of their life, or may be trying to distract others from these difficulties by claiming to be psychic and/or reporting embellished versions of their actual experiences. They often confront many of the same sorts of problems that are encountered by those who have long or short-term reported psi experiences that primarily are of a veridical nature.

4. *Those whose reported psi experiences primarily are of a fanciful or hallucinatory nature, but who do not appear to be suffering from any disabling psychological disturbance*: The experiences such individuals report may be drug-induced or otherwise psychophysiologically driven, may have

a social or environmental basis, or may simply be the result of an over-active imagination. These experiences also may be indicative of an underlying effort to communicate directly with the inner self by casting the unconscious mind in the role of "objective" observer. Conversely, they may represent an effort to avoid directly confronting certain thoughts and feelings by projecting them onto an "independent" source of wisdom, or blaming them on an "outside" hostile or otherwise dis-ruptive agent.

An example from my own clinical experience occurred in the case of a group of night shift workers in the medical records department of a major California medical center, a number of whom independently reported witnessing the recurrent appearance of an apparition. The reports provided strikingly similar descriptions of this alleged appari-tion, which greatly distressed many staff members and interfered with the normal routines of the department. Instead of attempting to de-termine if the alleged apparition had any veridical basis, I approached it in a group counseling session as a vehicle for discussing the complex interpersonal dynamics and stressful working conditions within the de-partment. The session centered on assisting the staff members in un-derstanding and expressing both their responses to the reported ap-parition and their responses to their colleagues and work environment, and on communicating to them that their efforts were appreciated by department management. The session helped to alleviate much of the stress of the overall situation, and created an atmosphere in which complex psychodynamics were less likely to contribute to what could have become increasingly bizarre reports of alleged apparitional phe-nomena. No subsequent apparitional sightings were reported in the department (Harary, 1982a).

In another example, I recently was contacted by a woman who re-ported hearing voices in her mind that she believed were spirits pro-viding her with psi-related information. Although the voices did not appear to interfere with her ability to function in her daily life, they were becoming a source of concern. They did not, however, appear to be providing her with any objectively verifiable information. In fact, the information they appeared to provide very often turned out to be wrong. Although it was tempting to bluntly invalidate the woman's experience, I focused instead on what her reported experiences meant to her. I also pointed out that an experience did not have to have an objectively verifiable psi component in order to be personally mean-ingful, but that it was important not to let the voices in her mind in-terfere with her life. She concluded, with that encouragement, that the voices reflected her own innermost thoughts and concerns and vowed to deal more directly with these in the future. I then advised her to seek additional counseling that might help her to deal more directly with these underlying concerns.

I also have observed related examples during various field investigations of alleged poltergeist and haunting phenomena. Sometimes the reported phenomena appear to be the result of alcoholic delirium, or the effect of other drugs on human perception and cognition. They also may be the result of other psychophysiological and social phenomena. In one case, for example, a woman who suffered from epileptic blackouts reported finding furniture inexplicably tossed about her home on numerous occasions. Other household observers were able to confirm, however, that the woman was personally throwing the furniture around in the course of her seizures, although she apparently did not remember having done so when the seizures ended. In another case, an adolescent girl who apparently felt unable to express her repressed feelings of rage and frustration directly to her parents, deliberately manufactured a "poltergeist" by physically moving large pieces of furniture and throwing smaller objects around when her parents were not watching.

A final example from this fascinating category occurred in the case of a man who reported hearing indistinguishable voices coming out of his air conditioner, and yet who appeared to be psychologically fit in every other respect. It turned out that his air conditioner was malfunctioning, and that he was perceptually interpreting the low, voice-like sounds it was making as unrecognizable speech. Such environmental curiosities often can complicate reported psi experiences, particularly those involving alleged haunting or poltergeist phenomena, because they often are interpreted as an integral aspect of these experiences. The epileptic woman described earlier, for example, interpreted the sounds of a leaky waterpipe echoing in her closet from two stories below as additional "proof" that a poltergeist was loose in her home.

5. *Those who are suffering from a disabling psychological disorder, and whose reported psi experiences primarily are of a pathological nature*: The experiences such individuals report emerge directly out of an intense psychological disturbance, and often contain pronounced elements of paranoia and delusions of grandeur. They severely interfere with the individual's ability to cope with the everyday world, but emerge from within a broad constellation of clinical difficulties rather than acting as the source of these problems. They frequently respond to a variety of medications, including mega-vitamins, anti-depressants and other drug therapies. They may be of short or long-term duration, and occasionally appear to contain some veridical elements that may be the result of

selective reporting or the inclusion of actual psi episodes in an otherwise delusional worldview.

In one such case from my own clinical experience, a woman reported hearing voices in her mind that she claimed were providing her with verifiable psi information about every aspect of her daily existence. She found that these voices grew silent whenever she took the mega-vitamins prescribed by her psychiatrist. She was reluctant to take her medication, however, because she believed that doing so was the equiv-alent of murdering the "spirits" in her head, whom she claimed had established the reality of their existence by providing her with veridical information. The voices, however, were making it impossible for the woman to function because they entirely preoccupied her waking thoughts. Rather than focusing on the alleged veridical nature of these voices, and attempting to prove them wrong or to offer a logical ex-planation for the information they provided, I focused instead on the woman's desire to lead a more productive and enjoyable existence. As a result of this discussion, the woman decided to continue seeing her psychiatrist and to continue taking her prescribed medication on a regular basis. She wrote to me one year later, reporting that the voices in her head had finally fallen completely silent and that she was happy to be leading a normal life.

In a related example, a former member of a well-known religious cult reported feeling the constant presence of the group's leader in his waking thoughts, and interpreted this experience as his being under "psychic attack" for having abandoned the group. This terrifying ex-perience continued through the course of intensive "exit" counseling with other former group members, but later all but evaporated under the anti-depressant Anafranil which is used to treat obsessive compulsive disorder. These same symptoms reportedly were experienced by other former members of this particular group, and reportedly also responded to similar medication in those instances. Because a number of cult groups have been known to drug their members surreptitiously, this situation is suspicious. There are, however, also a number of other possible social, psychological and/or neurophysiological explanations for this reported clinical phenomenon.

6. *Those who are responding to the reported psi experiences of others*: These may be researchers involved professionally in studying psi ability, cli-nicians whose clients report such experiences in the course of treatment, or lay persons who hear about such experiences from an acquaintance, friend or loved one. In every relationship, a certain level of intimacy and trust is intrinsic in the sharing of a reported psi experience, as is the possibility of helping or harming the individual who takes that risk.

For this reason, especially as clinicians and researchers, we owe it to these individuals to come to terms with our own deep feelings and ambivalence toward reported psi experiences before taking it upon ourselves to advise other people on this subject.

It also is frequently the case that those who are exposed to the reported psi experiences of others are deeply affected in the process. This is particularly the case among those who are exposed to apparent firsthand demonstrations of psi ability, who may experience the same sorts of problems encountered by those who have their own, firsthand, short-term psi experiences. This particular vulnerability often is exploited by the leaders of religious cults, who may arrange fraudulent demonstrations of their professed psi abilities in an effort to attract followers to their group.

In counseling former members of the Peoples Temple following the Guyana tragedy, for example, I learned that its leader, the Reverend Jim Jones, frequently conducted fraudulent demonstrations of his professed ability to heal the sick, to perform extraordinary feats of extended perception, and even to raise the dead. These bogus demonstrations were so convincing to his followers that a great many became convinced that he literally was God incarnate (Harary, 1992a).

The best defense against this kind of exploitation is public education. If we approach psi as a normal and neutral creative ability that is widely distributed in the general population, rather than as an exceptional gift that is bestowed on only a handful of spiritually advanced psychics, we make it much more difficult for demigods like Jim Jones to attract followers and harm the public. In addition, if we educate the public about the subtle nature of psi experiences, about all that we have gleaned from spontaneous case reports regarding the ways in which these experiences do and do not tend to manifest in everyday life, and about the need for scientific rigor and consumer savvy in evaluating special claims pertaining to psi abilities, we will go a long way toward preventing another Jonestown holocaust.

While the above categories should not be considered absolute or all-inclusive, they do provide a useful framework for developing effective and responsible clinical approaches to reported psi experiences. In developing these clinical strategies, however, it also is imperative to keep in mind that reported psi experiences often have a positive impact on the lives of those who have them.

In spite of the obstacles that people often face in coping with these experiences, therefore, it would be a mistake to conclude that they are better off left unexplored. Often, such experiences are an indication of a continuing process of personal growth, an active reaching out from within toward a greater sense of connectedness with the world, with other people, and with one's higher potential. Reported psi experiences also may represent a healthy response to a hostile and alienating external environment, in which an intense inward focus provides an emotional Underground Railroad to a unique domain of freedom.

Viewed in the context of this self-actualization process (Maslow, 1964), reported psi experiences may be recognized as one facet of a much larger creative process involving the continuing redefinition and expansion of our concept of self and our place in the universe. It would be wholly inappropriate for any clinician to suggest to someone whose reported psi experiences are indicative of such a positive process that he or she is abnormal, delusional, or otherwise psychologically disturbed.

Even if the individual in question is having difficulties in integrating a reported psi experience, or a cluster of such experiences, into his or her existing self-image and worldview, this does not mean that the individual should be counseled to abandon the process. Rather, the individual should be supported and encouraged to proceed with the process at a comfortable pace, in a psychologically sound and socially appropriate fashion.

Achieving this clinical objective requires the development of an advanced psychological approach that considers the meaning of human behavior not only according to traditional standards and guidelines, but which also takes into account our expanding understanding of the broader range of human potential and experience. It not only requires insights into human behavior, but also an awareness of human capability, including our need to extend beyond the limits of our individual boundaries, and our search for meaning (Harary, 1986b).

By addressing the individual's response to his or her reported psi experiences, and not over emphasizing the apparent experiences themselves (strangeness of the experiences themselves), we may encourage and facilitate this process. We will also, no doubt, find this strategy having a positive impact on our own approach to psi, and we may find ourselves transformed by that creative experience.

REFERENCES

Freud, S. (1953). Dreams and the occult. In G. Devereux (Ed.), *Psychoanalysis and the occult* (pp. 91–109). New York: International Universities Press. (Reprinted from *New introductory lectures on psychoanalysis*, 1934, London: Hogarth Press)

Freud, S. (1953). Psychoanalysis and telepathy. In G. Devereux (Ed. and Trans.), *Psychoanalysis and the occult* (pp. 56–68). New York: International Universities Press. (Reprinted from *Gesammelte Werke*, 1941, *17*, 25–40)

Hansen, G. (1992). CSICOP and the skeptics: An overview. *Journal of the American Society for Psychical Research, 86*, 19–63.

Harary, K. (1992a, March/April). The truth about Jonestown: 13 years later—why we should still be afraid. *Psychology Today*, pp. 63–67, 72, 88.

Harary, K. (1992b). Spontaneous psi in mass mythology, media and western culture. In B. Shapin & L. Coly (Eds.), *Spontaneous psi, depth psychology and parapsychology* (pp. 200–219). New York: Parapsychology Foundation.

Harary, K. (1986a). A critical analysis of experimental and clinical approaches to apparent psychic experiences. (Doctoral dissertation, The Union Institute). *University Microfilms, International*, No. 8720617.

Harary, K. (1986b). Toward an advanced psychology. Paper presented at the American Society for Psychical Research Symposium on Psi and Psychotherapy, November 8, 1986.

Harary, K. (1985). The fear of success in psi research. In R.A. White & J. Solfvin (Eds.), *Research in parapsychology 1984* (pp. 101–103). Metuchen, NJ: Scarecrow Press.

Harary, K. (1982a). The marshmallow ghost: A group counseling approach to a case of reported apparitions. In W.G. Roll, R.L. Morris, & R.A. White (Eds.), *Research In parapsychology 1981* (pp. 187–189). Metuchen, NJ: Scarecrow Press.

Harary, K. (1982b). Psi as nature. *European Journal of Parapsychology, 4*, 377–392.

Harary, K. (1980). Practical approaches to coping with unusual experiences. In W.G. Roll, (Ed.), *Research in parapsychology 1979* (pp. 41–42). Metuchen, NJ: Scarecrow Press.

Honorton, C., Berger, R.E., Varvoglis, M.P., Quant, M., Derr, P., Schechter, E., & Ferrari, D.C. (1990). Psi communication in the ganzfeld. *Journal of Parapsychology, 54*, 99–139.

Honorton, C., & Harper, S. (1974). Psi-mediated imagery and ideation in an experimental procedure for regulating perceptual input. *Journal of the American Society for Psychical Research, 68*, 156–168.

Maslow, A. (1964). *Religions, values, and peak-experiences*. Columbus: Ohio State University Press.

Neppe, V. (1992). Anomalous experience and psychopathology. In B. Shapin & L. Coly (Eds.), *Spontaneous psi, depth psychology and parapsychology* (pp. 163–180). New York: Parapsychology Foundation.

Puthoff, H.E., & Targ, R. (1976). A perceptual channel for information transfer over kilometer distances: Historical perspective and recent research. *Proceedings of the IEEE, 64*, 329–354.

Rhine, J.B. (1937). *New frontiers of the mind*. New York: Farrar & Rinehart.

Targ, R., & Harary, K. (1984). *The mind race*. New York: Villard.

Schmeidler, G. (1974). The psychic personality. In Mitchell (Ed.), *Psychic exploration* (pp. 94–110). New York: Putnam's.

Ullman, M., Krippner, S., & Vaughan, A. (1973). *Dream telepathy*. New York: Macmillan.

Warcollier, R. (1963). *Mind to mind*. New York: Collier.

DISCUSSION

PARKER: I would like to add more comments than actually ask a question. I would like to make a conclusion from your indication that we may be getting nowhere looking at the personality, searching for a personality trait that relates to psi. I think I entirely agree. Psychic experiences may be something that is not related to personality in itself;

but perhaps, as Arthur Ellison was saying, it is something to do with the defensiveness of personality, an openness to unusual experiences. It is perhaps unfortunate that the term is defense mechanism. This implies sort of a somewhat mechanistic view of the functioning of personality. But maybe that is an area that we have to look at more intensively. I am actually one of the psychologists interested in this field. We also have to look at how people react to these experiences. I think psi and personality come to interact very closely. Some people are very threatened by psi and give it all sorts of weird interpretations in terms of UFOs or it becomes some sort of psychotic experience. Other people can integrate psi into their personal way of functioning and it can, in some cases, become a growth aspect.

HARARY: Obviously I agree with you. If psi becomes normalized in Western culture we may see a lot of the personality variables that researchers and clinicians tend to associate with psi ability evaporating, or at least becoming less important. A lot of the Ways in which people respond to their reported psi experiences are quite bound up in the messages conveyed by the culture, including the media. The researchers, the clinicians, and those dealing with their own experiences are all responding to those messages as well as feeding into them on various levels. When we get beyond that cultural malaise we may find that psi in its natural state has quite a different impact on the individual, one that is ultimately connected to positive change and personal growth.

KRAMER: I like your attitude on the measuring very much—let's stop seeing psychic phenomena as special and accept that they are just normal human experiences like any other experience. That is true. I think as a clinical psychologist you have to accept that; otherwise, you cannot help your clients. I think it is the same in psychology where the clinical psychologist and the experimental psychologist are always dealing with two different kinds of people, actually different ways human beings function. One is looking at them as people functioning in everyday life and the other one is looking at human beings functioning under special conditions. The problem is, and you made it clear at the beginning of your speech about writers, that the same way you can call a psychic weird you can call a writer weird. So, don't let us talk about crazy things but let us talk about being special. The problem, of course, with writers is the same as with psychics. You have normal writers and, of course, you also have writers who, and excuse the clinical term, are nuts. My personal problem is, how can you discriminate between them? I mean by simply reviewing the experience and saying the psychic phenomena are normal human phenomena, is, in a clinical sense, acceptable but it also can be a problem because some things which really are nuts are going to be labelled special. That can create a lot of problems in everyday life, as I have encountered. How do you deal with that?

HARARY: When you ask which psychics are really psychics and which psychics are nuts, you are still dealing with the difficulties inherent in labeling anyone as a psychic in the first place. We desperately need to move beyond the question of who is or is not psychic because then we get caught up in asking the even more loaded and peculiar question of who is more psychic than whom. I have witnessed a lot of competition for that dubious achievement deliberately being encouraged in the field of psi research, and the human impact, not to mention the impact on our view of psi, is really terrible. People climb all over each other to try to say, "No, I am more psychic than you are." "No, I am. I got this one right." You would think they were fighting over the last soda cracker on a lifeboat. The desire to be proven psychic, which is really a desire for special recognition, is often used to manipulate people. As the researcher you can say, "I'll give you a cookie and tell you that you are psychic if you do what I say and even go along with some of this questionable data and the unwarranted claims that are being made about it." It seems incredible that anyone would be willing to go along with that suggestion, but being thought to be a psychic is so important to some people that it does seem to happen. But, if we eliminate the idea that there are psychics and then there is everyone else, we also eliminate the question of who is an authentic psychic and who is lying or deluded, not to mention the question of who is more psychic than whom. If we approach the psi process as a normal, creative experience we can say, "Well, there are some people who are genuinely experiencing psi functioning at a particular moment and maybe even are practiced or talented at it and then there are some people who are on the other end of the continuum completely imagining things." But you do not put any special charge on the process itself by placing those who experience it, or who are familiar with it, in a separate category of human being. By the way, people who are completely imagining things often experience real psi as well at other points in their life. It is just that the particular thing they are telling you about at the moment is not necessarily psi. So we should begin by eliminating the idea that if you have psi experiences then you are this thing, this type, this person, this entity, and whatever that means to you. Often it means all kinds of terrible things within Western culture. You look at the movies and television and people who are described as being psychic are described as everything from extraterrestrials to witches to crazy people. Let us finally take that burden away from people who have psi experiences. Then we will not even have to ask who is psychic. Then, if you want to focus on it clinically, you may find yourself asking, "Is the experience real?" Well, how can you not have a real experience? The experience is subjectively real. At that point, what you are really left with is the question of how people deal with their experience. Now as an experimental researcher you can ask, "Well, is this really psi or is it something else or am I being fooled here?" There are a lot of questions you can ask. In fact, you will find that people are, in a way, more willing to freely express themselves in the laboratory, as far as psi goes, if they do not feel that they are suddenly going to be viewed as a certain personality type as a result. So if you just eliminate that whole category, those dead-end shortcuts are gone. Now you have to focus upon individual human beings, with how they are relating to their experiences, and with the scientific question of what is really happening and what it means. Then, even in the laboratory, you take the charge off the process and make it neutral. You say, "Getting a positive result in a psi experiment does not mean that you are a great guy or spiritual or a swami or anything like that. There aren't any cookies here. If you want to work together, great. We appreciate it. We will study psi together but that is as far as it goes." Then things become easier and healthier for everyone involved in that adventure.

KRAMER: That means you bring it back to a more general problem, that some people claim they are psychic like some people claim they are writers. The problem is how to distinguish between the real writers and the false ones.

HARARY: Well, I suppose that in the case of people claiming to be writers you can always read their work.

KRAMER: Well, that is a problem too because sometimes I read a book and I do not like it but everyone else says he is a fantastic writer.

HARARY: One of the really horrific things that has taken place in Western culture is that being psychic has become a popular aspiration. The title is not only handed out often for political and other manipulative reasons within the field of psi research but it is also handed out and taken on as a stereotype in the culture, in ways that are just appalling. I mean it is the last thing that I would ever want to be associated with. Often what people mean when they want to be called psychic is, "I have a certain worldview." Now there are people who use that term and really are trying to say to you, "Look, I have a lot of experiences that I cannot quite explain but, you know, the best way I can say it is to use this shorthand term and then hope that you will know what I mean, which is a really deep, personal, meaningful, powerful, and beautiful thing." But that is not how it is going to be taken by the person who is listening and thinking about a fortune teller sitting in a tent with a crystal ball or some other offensive image. You are better off eliminating the shortcuts so you can just talk about the experience. The people who say to you, "I am a psychic," let us face it you do cringe a little, don't you? Don't you worry? Aren't you skeptical? The next thing you say is, "Prove it," or "What do you mean?" or "Who do you think you are?" So it is not good for them either.

KRAMER: From a counseling point of view, the problem is that when someone says, "I am a writer" and he cannot write at all, no one is bothered by it. When someone says, "I am psychic," and he claims that in society, then suddenly people start to react differently to him or her. So that means that the claim to be a psychic has a much broader impact than the claim to be a writer.

HARARY: It has a powerful impact both on the people you say that to and on you, yourself saying it. Particularly the people listening to you are going to think of everybody else who ever said that and everything they have ever seen associated with the psychic concept in the media. What I would say as a clinician to a person who approached me in that way would be, "Look, you are not fooling me. I know that certain things exist that we do not have an explanation for yet. I think they do; they seem to. Either that or I will be really fascinated to know how I have been fooling myself all these years and that will be clinically fascinating. But why do you want to call yourself a psychic? What are you getting out of this? Why are you taking on that identity? What are you trying to explain? What are you trying to say about who you are? What are you trying to say about who you are in relation to other people? And what do you mean by that term because other people who use it mean a lot of different things?" I would really work seriously and in major ways clinically with a person who wanted to take on that persona as a way to deal with other people in their life. It is not healthy.

WEST: I have been more of a researcher than a clinician and I have the feeling that clinicians sometimes go a little overboard in not wanting to find out whether the information that they are given is fantasy or reality. I know that it was at one time a psychoanalytic approach to take entirely what the patient says because that is what they are worried about, whether it is true or not, does not matter; and one goes on to deal with patient's problems arising from what experiences they think they have had. Now, in quite a different context this approach has been severely criticized. People will know that Freud assumed that a lot of the stories he had from his women patients about childhood sexual abuse were fantasies and he went on elaborating on that assumption.

He has since been criticized by J.M. Masson[5] and by others for making that assumption against evidence to the contrary known to him. It now appears that there is a very big difference whether the abuse was real or fantasy. I think, that the same probably applies to psychic experiences. As a researcher I am really more interested in what was the actual nature of the experience and was it real, than its effect on the person concerned and what they believe about it. I think one gets the same kind of conflict among anthropologists who visit different cultures and observe all sorts of magical beliefs and routines for communication with spirits and communication at a distance. Whilst reporting all these things and discussing how these beliefs fit into the social, political, and religious systems of the communities and how these particular beliefs make for stability, they never ask whether the beliefs are founded in reality, whether these phenomena actually occur. That is the question which I am interested in as a researcher rather than a clinician.

HARARY: I think that that is a very good point. But unlike Freud, I am not assuming that the psi experiences people report are always imagined or always involve real psi. The trouble is that when you are dealing either as a clinician working with people who are reporting experiences or as a researcher working with people who say they have had certain experiences, you have stepped into, a convoluted psychodynamic malaise of utter confusion about what we mean and what we are talking about when we are discussing reported psi experiences. Clinically you have so much to deal with before you can ask if a particular experience involves real psi. At some point you will want to ask if this person is hallucinating or if they are reporting something that really is going on. The worst thing that can happen is when something real is going on and the psychiatrist or the social worker or the therapist tells a person, "You are a nut. Such things do not happen. Why do you have to imagine these things?" I have actually had that experience, too. And it is awful. So at some point, yes, particularly experimentally, we want to know what is real and what is imagined. The trouble is that given the current state of psi research, we know very little about what is going on except that there is this process that we call psi or extended abilities and it seems to manifest on a widespread basis in people's lives. A lot of the problems that come up for people have to do with how we, as a culture and as scientists, respond to that situation. Even in talking about it, it is hard to know where to begin. Sure, we all want

---

[5] Masson, J.M. (1984). *Freud: The assault on truth*. London: Faber.

to know what is real and what is not. If somebody comes into your lab and says, "Look, I am experiencing all these wonderful things." The first thing that occurs to an experimental researcher is, "Holy cow, this is an opportunity for research. I better do some experiments on this person before they get away." That is not always the healthiest approach for the person who is confused and looking for answers. You want to find out how the individual is going to deal with that experiment, even the very concept of being in the experiment, how they are going to deal with that whole encounter when they go out in the world, and especially with what they think that encounter means about them. It would be nice to do experiments in a vacuum where we say, "We just want to know what is real and if it is real, then we will see it." I know you are not saying that, but we also have to deal with what being in the experiment means in the lives of the people who participate, how they are going to deal with that involvement vis à vis what we tell them it means, and what they are being told that it means in the culture at large. On a clinical level, however, asking whether or not an experience involves "real" psi is not the most important question. The most important question is how the individual will deal with this real or imagined encounter—which means this real experience—in the context of his or her own life. It most certainly is extremely helpful, in making that determination, to know if genuine psi is involved. But we do not always know the answer to that question.

WICKRAM: I found that refreshingly disarming. It is an interesting hypothesis that regarding psi as a normal human function increases the probability of the event or is the more heuristic way to investigate the phenomena. But, is there any empirical evidence that regarding psi as a natural or normal human function rather than as some laboratory constrained phenomena leads to any increase in the probability of the event?

HARARY: First of all there is evidence to show in a laboratory, for example SRI, that people who have done particularly well in experiments are not particularly unusual. The most experienced remote viewers at SRI were given all kinds of psychological tests and there was nothing particularly startling about the results except that the remote viewers looked like normal people, perhaps a little more intelligent than the population at large. But what would you expect to find at a major scientific laboratory? With the help of the Parapsychology Foundation, Darlene Moore and I have been doing research with people who are blind. Instead of looking for people who said they had a lot of psi experiences and abilities, we went out and knocked on people's doors. We found a lot of blind people who were isolated or who needed some money or who wanted to do something interesting. We just knocked on their doors and said, "Look, you may think this is crazy. I am Keith, this is Darlene, and we want to do something interesting with you and it will be fun. You will learn about yourself and it does not mean anything about who you are except that you might experience an additional way of relating with the world." This is a little subjective on our part as researchers, but making the process very normal for people appeared to make them very comfortable with it. We have some wonderful video tapes of people doing as well as anything I have ever seen in the laboratory, and not people who would call themselves particularly psychic. It is just that we said to them, "What we are talking about here is extended perception." We deliberately did not even use the word psychic. And they said, "Extended abilities? What do you mean." "Well," we said, "it might be perception, it might be communication, we are not sure, but look, you can learn to tap into this ability and we will show you how. We are developing specific techniques for training people to do this." Making the process very normal seemed to make the perceivers comfortable with it. So, we did not encounter a lot of the trauma that you might see when someone says, "Well, holy cow, what does this mean about who I am? Look at how well I did! My God, you know, I cannot even see and I was describing this place where I am going to be taken." I realize, however, that it is not quite fair that I am telling you something that is not yet published. In the remote viewing research at SRI, and after SRI, a lot was done with ordinary, everyday people. By not telling them that they had to be particularly special to do something, they did very well. In fact, taking that approach makes your life a lot easier as a researcher because all you have to do is say, "Look, we are studying this creative process and you do not have to deal with all the burdensome questions regarding what participating in this research means about who you are." If you start out right at the beginning taking that approach, being clear about the fact that how people perform in your experiment does not mean anything about who they are except that maybe they can express this normal ability, the whole experience can be much more pleasant and productive for everybody. So subjectively in the research, it does seem to be helpful to just approach psi as a very normal, down-to-earth kind of function. I have not seen any bad reactions to that approach and people seem to do pretty well. I think that assessment is more than just a subjective one because you can see the data obtained in the research and it is pretty solid.

TIERNEY: It is just an observation on something that you said earlier. Few of us, certainly I do not, act autonomously with a patient or a client; usually one is part of a team and the person has either seen a psychiatrist or a psychologist beforehand or, and will afterwards. Given that, it seems to me that we should be directing our attention to our colleagues as opposed to the patient or client. Particularly if they are using very rigid categorization such as DSM-III, the patient is likely to be labeled and he is likely to get the impression the there is something wrong, yet we are saying that this is a normal experience. The message that they will be getting from others is that it is not. Do you have any comments on how one can get around the problem of dealing with colleagues?

HARARY: Yes, it is very important. With colleagues, your attitude is crucial and this is where we need to effect some change by communicating what we do in the field of psi research. If your colleagues think that you are talking about parapsychology, they tend to build up a lot of resistance. Your attitude, the way you approach the experience or the ability, is really crucial. What you have to do is broad scale education in the culture at large. Present papers at places like the American Psychological Association that do not charge psi with all kinds of pregnant meaning or imply that someone who is having this experience is automatically crazy. Talk with your colleague about someone you know who is perfectly normal, and it may be even yourself, provide a model for responding in a balanced and positive way. Introduce your colleagues to people who have psi experiences and who are leading fulfilling lives. If the only people you see are people who are very upset by what is happening to them, then you will automatically assume that people get upset or are already upset when they have psi experiences. It depends on the language you use and on what your colleagues are exposed to in the clinical setting and everyday life. Do not forget that your colleagues, like most of the human race, have probably had their own experiences. If you can in a non-charged setting get your colleagues to open up about some of the things that had occurred un their own lives, then maybe they will feel more comfortable with it. There are all kinds of little things that you can do rather than to approach this as a problem of "them" versus "us" in which we have to convince them of a certain viewpoint. Psi researchers sometimes come at people who are either resistant in the society at large or in the scientific community, or at other clinicians and say, "Look, this is true. I know it is true. I have got it figured out. I am onto something here. You better buy it. Let me tell you what it is. Let me tell you why your worldview is screwy and mine is right." If you do that, forget it. If you start out, instead, by saying, "I do not know what the universe is all about but . . ." this might be a more comfortable approach.

NEPPE: It seems to me that we are dealing with an extremely difficult area; an area that has both semantic implications, in terms of terminology, as well as clinical implications. Just briefly, from the semantic point of view, one of the things that I perceive as relevant is the differentiation between prejudicial and non-prejudicial terms and this has a chronologic framework to it. Presumably the terms psychic and psychical were in no way prejudicial at the turn of the century. For many of our fellow scientists, the terms have clearly become prejudicial and we utilize other terms like extrasensory perception, extended experience, or anomalous instead. Using this framework we must realize that there is a major difference between subjective and objective experiences that have anomalous attributions put to them. Ideally, at an experimental level, we may seek a population of people who were having genuine anomalous experiences of so-called psi kind. At a subjective level we want a completely different subgroup who have certain experiences which one can verify subjectively according to outside criteria. This would imply a new subpopulation of subjective paranormal experients whom we could investigate. These two populations obviously merge and come together, but at this point, it is simplistic to deal with additional interfacing terms. We may have several overlapping populations with possibly special state or trait phenomena.

HARARY: I agree with you. The problem with the terminology is that we have to find terms that are not loaded and sometimes we wind up tripping over our own feet in doing it. But we have to find terms that do not automatically trigger a reaction in other clinicians or other scientists or just regular everyday folks. I think it would be fascinating to find the kind of population you are talking about, but any population is going to, in some way, have been seriously affected by the attitudes of the culture, of the scientific community, even the psi research scientific community, and of clinicians toward those experiences. So, we almost cannot find a pure, unadulterated group. Some people have looked at primitive cultures for that, but even they are affected by the beliefs of their own culture. You cannot find a pure experience, untouched by everything that people believe and have ever said about experiences like it. At some point maybe you can peel off all of the layers that have been laid on the experience and try to get to the core of it, realizing of course, that the person doing the peeling also is experiencing his or her own biased attitudes toward that which is being examined.

THE EXPERIENCE OF SIGNIFICANCE

Ian Tierney

Introduction

During the last two years I have been one of two people with a
clinical training (clinical psychology) who has been available to see individuals who have contacted Professor Morris at the University of
Edinburgh seeking help as a result of experience which they perceive
as being relevant to parapsychology. The only criterion that we established for offering some sort of clinical counseling is that the person
must report a sense of unhappiness or distress resulting from their
experience.

We have counseled a number of people living locally, but in most of
the cases the person has lived at a considerable distance from Edinburgh. Initially, we attempt (by telephone or correspondence) to analyze
the experience for psi-relevance. If it does seem relevant then we advise
such people to seek advice from parapsychologists known to us in their
area. When it seems unlikely to be psi-relevant we explore the experience with the individual in an attempt to place the experience in some
normative framework which may help the person to assimilate the experience into normal experience (e.g. hypnogogic or after-image experience). If we believe that there are psychopathological implications,
we have attempted to steer the person to an appropriate source of
counseling, either a mental health professional or religious counsellor
(preferably with a parapsychological interest) or to their general medical
practitioner.

This paper arose out of a feeling of disquiet in the author that while
the behavior of many of these individuals readily justified the DSM-
III-R diagnosis of schizotypal personality disorder, it could be argued
that their social difficulties, to a greater or lesser degree, arose from
their unusual, eccentric, view of the world, which in turn seemed to
be the result of unusual experiences. The possibility that these experiences might have a basis in reality, albeit one that acknowledges the
possibility of psi-mediated events, raises questions about how such in-

dividuals might be helped to deal with such experiences. This paper, therefore, explores the hypothesis that the effect of genuine psi experiences, for certain individuals, may be the development of delusional systems. Because delusions tend to have social consequences, this could result in a stigmatization of the individuals.

The Formation of Delusions

Most of the individuals who contact us in distress seem to want confirmation of a parapsychological "explanation" for their experience. Usually they claim that such an explanation is the only type which fits the facts of their experience. They seem to believe that, as we are known to have an interest in this area, we are the only people who can help them. In responding to such approaches one of my concerns has been the possible effect of appearing to collude with a delusional system, even in the mildest way by showing an interest. Particularly when communicating with the person on the telephone, the professionally "safe" statement might be (couched in sympathetic terms) to the effect that "although we are interested in such experience, our knowledge about the nature of such experience is so rudimentary that we are not yet in a position to comment on the value of any parapsychological explanation". Is this all we can or should say?

An influential theory for the development of delusional thinking has been proposed by Maher and Ross (1984) and further discussed by Maher (1988). Maher develops a classification of delusions first proposed by Southard (1916) in which delusions might be classified in accordance with the moods of grammar that their form reflected.

> Grammarians of his day distinguished between four moods in which a sentence might be formed in English: the subjunctive, the indicative, the imperative and the optative. The first of these, the subjunctive, expresses a proposition conditionally, that is, with the implication of truth, but not the certainty of it—in brief, in a form or mood typical of empirical science. (Maher, 1988, p. 18)

Southard suggested that delusions fall into two categories: the first characterized by subjunctive statements, and the second by imperative (delusions of grandeur) or optative (wish fulfilling delusions of bizarre or fantastic nature) statements. Delusions were not associated with the indicative mood.

In brief, Maher's model suggests that:

1. Delusional thinking involves cognitive processes in which the logic is the same as those involved in the formation of non-delusional beliefs.

2. Delusions are theories that provide meaning for empirical data obtained by observation.

3. Some observations are both surprising and puzzling, and therefore significant.

4. Significant puzzles *demand* explanations.

5. A satisfactory explanation results in marked feelings of relief and reduction of tension.

6. Subsequent data that contradict the explanation create cognitive dissonance. Data that are consistent with the explanation reduce dissonance and are given particular status in the explanation.

7. Furthermore, theories will be judged delusional by others if (a) the judges do not have access to the original, puzzling, data, or (b) the data are available but do not appear puzzling or provide the same sense of significance to the judges.

8. The experience of surprise-significance is assumed to have a neural locus in the C. N. S., and it is proposed that various neuropathologies (outlined in stage 9) effect "spurious" experiences of significance in the deluded patient, which results, as in normal people—including scientists—in extreme resistance to giving up the preferred theory.

Maher's psychopathological model for the development of delusions rests heavily on both the notion of a neural locus, and an arousing function, for the experience of "significance" (increased alertness and tension—"search mode") produced by the puzzling events. Importantly, he claims that puzzles *demand* explanations, which, if satisfactory, produce the subsequent feelings of relief and reduction in tension. The concept of relief from noxious stimuli, is familiar to psychologists as negative reinforcement which increases the frequency of the contingent behavior. If it can be shown that the tension and uncertainty associated with the puzzlement are noxious, then indeed an understandable process for the development of delusions, similar to that for compulsive behavior and avoidance behavior in anxiety states (i.e. anxiety reducing) is complete.

While the description of the neurophysiology related to the experience of significance is limited, there is a relatively consistent body of electrophysiological evidence which suggests that the P300 component of the event-related potential is associated with (a) the phenomenological experience of "meaningfullness" or "significance," and (b) reflects the theoretical concepts of the "search mode" or "orienting response/ reflex." Polich (1989) discusses his evidence for suggesting that the same fundamental mechanisms underlie both constructs because both "are thought to result from a mismatch between external events and an internal neural model (of the environment)" (p. 20). It is typically elicited by an "oddball" type of paradigm, when a train of identical stimulus events is interrupted by a single different stimulus. The P300 component is a large (ca. 10–20 V), positive-going potential with a latency of approximately 300msec. when elicited with a simple auditory discrimination task in young adults, and is of maximum amplitude over the midline central and parietal scalp areas. Polich notes that "while the origins of the P300 are still being sought, depth-electrode recordings and magnetic field studies in humans suggest that at least some portion of the P300 is generated in the medial temporal lobe, most likely including the hippocampus and amygdala structures—brain areas associated with learning and memory." Recent evidence (Le Doux, 1989) suggests that these two structures (the limbic system), once thought also to be jointly responsible for the regulation of emotion, may fulfill cognitive (hippocampus) and emotional (amygdala) functions independently, and in such a way that an emotional reaction may be elicited prior to a cognitive one. As yet, I can find no explicit studies of the effect of emotional significance of stimuli on the P300 component. If the emotional content of stimuli could be shown to affect characteristics of the P300 component, particularly by increasing resistance to habituation, then this might lend support to Maher's contention that puzzles or surprises demand explanations.

To test the significance of the P300 component in the development of delusional beliefs, it would be possible, in theory, to compare the psi-beliefs of a group of individuals who have abnormal P300 reactions to novel stimuli, such as the abstinent sons of type 2 alcoholic fathers (80% of whom have abnormal P300: Begleiter, Porjesy, & Behari, 1987) with the beliefs of a suitable control group, such as the abstinent sons of type 1 alcoholic fathers. With large enough groups, and assuming a random distribution of psi-experience, the beliefs of the groups should be different if the P300 component does represent the experience of significance, and this experience is important in the formation of beliefs.

Assuming that Maher's model is veridical, what are the implications for parapsychology, which is dealing with data which are not necessarily available to all, or indeed to anyone other than the subject? For "normal" individuals, if one or more psi experience results in stage 3 in Maher's model (i.e. one is puzzled by observations which are surprising, and therefore significant), what is to prevent the development of a "delusional" system? This is a question implicit in the criticism of the model made by Chapman and Chapman (1988).

The Chapmans present evidence from their longitudinal study of 162 college students who scored at 2.0 or more standard deviations above the mean on two questionnaires, their Perceptual Aberration

Scale and Magical Ideation Scale. Unfortunately for our interests, which are the subject of the second scale, "because the two scales correlate around .70 and identify similar subjects, we treat high scores on either of the two scales as a single group. . . ." (p. 168). Half these subjects qualified for a DSM-III diagnosis of schizotypal personality disorder. Using a modified version of the Schedule for Affective Disorders and Schizophrenia-Lifetime Version (Spitzer & Endicott, 1977) they re-examined their subjects (and 158 controls) 25 months later. Three of the subjects, but none of the controls, had received "treatment for psychosis." The direct relevance of this study to the present hypothesis is difficult to determine, as the symptoms discussed in the paper are predominantly of the auditory hallucination (perceptual aberration) type. With reference to the Maher model the Chapmans state: "If delusions are reasonable interpretations of anomalous experience, subjects with similar experiences should have similar beliefs" (p. 174). I would suggest that this is illogical, ignoring as it does the effect of prior idiosyncratic knowledge and experience on the interpretation of the experience. Having set up what is, in my opinion, a "straw man," they knock it down with this interesting observation:

> We found some cases in which delusion was a clear result of an anomalous perceptual experience because acceptance of the veridicality of the experience demanded, or almost demanded, a delusional belief. Other subjects reported delusional or aberrant beliefs that had no apparent relationship to any unusual experiences. Still others reported delusions that had some relation to their unusual experiences, but yet were not necessary, or even reasonable, interpretations of those experiences. (p. 174)

The first and third categories are consistent with Maher's model, but the second would be a clear contradiction of it. However, one might question how the authors could be certain that second group had not, in the past, had some such experience.

The Chapmans' own formulation for the genesis of delusions is "that delusional patients focus more often on stimuli that are strong or prominent by normal standards, neglecting weaker stimuli" (p. 180). As they themselves point out "there is a danger of circularity in this formulation in that we infer a difference in strength of stimuli from choice of stimuli to which schizophrenics respond" (p. 181). It is noticeable in the above that the term "patient" and "schizophrenic" is used, suggesting a relevance to a more clinically serious part of the delusion continuum (if it is such) than that addressed in the major study they report. Leaving that aside, the concept of strong and weak stimuli leads to questions of definition of stimulus strength. The Chapmans define this in terms of "a person's own emotional responses to the environment," "immediate," and "personally salient by normal standards." This sounds very similar to Maher's concept of "significance."

The Chapmans conclude their paper with the following:

> In summary, delusions of psychosis are often more deviant versions of aberrant beliefs that were held by patients before they became psychotic. The relationships between delusions, anomalous experience, and thought disorder can reasonably be construed as ones of mutual augmentation. Among patients who have all three of these abnormalities, each of the three seems to enhance the other two. None of the three uniformly occurs first in a causal sequence. None of the three seems necessary for the occurrence of another; instead, all three are probably direct expressions of the psychosis. (p. 182)

To summarize the above discussion: in the Maher model anomalous experience leads by reasonable logic to delusional beliefs, which may in turn lead to psychosis; in the Chapmans' formulation both, along with thought disorder, are the symptoms of psychosis and may occur alone or in any combination with the others. That having been said both theories appeal to a concept of "significance" or "salience" as an explanation of delusional focus.

My criticism of the Chapmans' formulation, and to an extent the Maher model, is that they construe the anomalous experience happening to people without any kind of previous unusual experience or thought. Understandably, this appeal to previous experience can be viewed as an unhelpful reductionist approach. In practical terms, however, it may be that beliefs based on psi-mediated experiences involve early (possibly childhood) beliefs, interests, and experience in what constitutes reality. If, as parapsychologists, we are becoming increasingly confident about "what psi is not" (Morris, 1986) it may be incumbent upon us to disseminate this information more widely, countering some of the more harmful effects of childrens' (usually harmless?) preoccupation with witches, ghosts, etc..

What variables are likely to affect the experience of significance? Intuitively, without any real evidence (other than high levels of anxiety in relevant clinical states), I suggest that one important factor may be the degree of generalized anxiety. It is likely that the experience of significance (of increased arousal), in individuals with already high levels of motor tension, autonomic activity, vigilant scanning and apprehensive expectation, and who have already learnt to use avoidance measures to control anxiety, will make more likely the development, and maintenance, of a "delusional" explanation for a disturbing anomalous experience. Using measures such as the State-Trait Anxiety Inventory (Spielberger, Gorusuch, & Lushene, 1970) it would be possible to test for a positive correlation between the trait value and the fixity of psi-related belief. The high levels of autonomic activity, vigilance and apprehension that a high anxiety trait score would imply should increase the value of the experience of significance as a reducer of cognitive dissonance and uncertainty. Although there is reasonable evidence for a positive correlation between scores on manifest anxiety (but not Cattell's anxiety factor) measures and ESP performance (Palmer, 1977), I can find no studies investigating a relationship between manifest anxiety and the fixity of (sheep/goat) belief.

In counseling individuals reporting distress after psi experiences, one might wish to pay particular attention to those individuals who report high levels of generalized anxiety prior to the experience, as such levels of anxiety may promote the heuristic necessity of the explanations, delusional or otherwise.

Social Consequences

In one sense it could be argued that there is no need to be concerned about the development of specific and circumscribed delusions as a result of psi experiences. In most societies there is an apparent tolerance of eccentricity providing there is no attempt by the individual to involve others in the delusion. However, as Rush has pointed out, a "notable characteristic of psychic experiences is their strangeness . . . (frequently) together with strong emotions of awe and sometimes terror" (1986, p. 5). Particularly if the psi experience is of a type which demands communication to others (e.g. crisis telepathy, or precognitions of crisis), then there is likely to be an urgency or proselytizing quality in the subsequent behavior which may reduce the tolerance shown to the individual. At worst, individuals who develop strong beliefs of this type may become socially isolated.

It is this possible consequence of delusions formed on the basis of psi-related experience that concerns me most. Many such individuals report a strong need to talk about such experiences. This, combined with the fear of the irrational or insanity common in many of their potential audience, will almost certainly affect their social contacts, and possibly their social behavior.

Schizotypal Personality Disorder

The holding of "bizarre" beliefs and reporting recurrent "illusions" are central to a DSM-III-R diagnosis of schizotypal personality disorder, as opposed to the otherwise somewhat similar criteria for a diagnosis of schizoid personality disorder (or indeed Asperger's Syndrome, which, it has has recently been suggested is a distinct syndrome, separate from the other two: Tantam, 1988). It is suggested by the DSM-III-R Manual that 3% of the population have this disorder. The criteria for schizotypal personality disorder in DSM-III-R mean that three out of the nine criteria (only five of which need be indicated to make the diagnosis, providing the criteria for schizophrenia are not met) are directly relevant to psi experience. These are: (1) odd beliefs or magical thinking, for example, superstitiousness, clairvoyance, telepathy, "6th sense," "others can feel my feelings" (in children bizarre fantasies or preoccupations); (2) ideas of reference (excluding delusions of reference); and, (3) unusual perceptual experiences e.g. illusions, sensing the presence of a force or person not actually present (e.g. "I felt as if my dead mother were in the room with me). Four of the other six criteria are based on social behavior, namely: (4) social isolation; (5) constricted or inappropriate affect (e.g., aloof, cold, rare reciprocation of social gestures); (6) suspiciousness or paranoid ideation; (7) excessive social anxiety. The last two criteria concern mannerisms: (8) odd or eccentric behavior or appearance, and; (9) "odd speech" (without loosening of association or incoherence) for example, speech that is digressive, vague, overelaborate, circumstantial, or metaphorical.

I would not wish to argue that these criteria, or indeed the clinical concept of schizotypal personality disorder, are not useful, but that a differential loading, giving more weight to the social and mannerism criteria, may be required. To illustrate this point, I will compare two examples of referrals to me. The first is of a man complaining about strong sensations of being caressed erotically by "something or somebody independent of me." On a superficial assessment this man impressed me as being normal in every other way. He was middle-aged, intelligent, articulate, well dressed with an apparently open social manner. He was genuinely puzzled by the experiences and was open to the interpretation offered by a psychiatrist, to whom he had been previously referred, that these were probably psychogenic in origin, the result of some marital difficulties (of a not too extreme nature) which he reported. He had contacted us in the spirit of open intellectual curiosity to see if another, psi-related, explanation was possible. He reported no other experiences which could be construed as anomalous. In the course of a long discussion he gradually disclosed that: (a) he was in extended and acrimonious debate with a number of individuals, and jokingly referred to occasional feelings of paranoia; (b) he complained of extreme levels of physical tension a great deal of the time (excessive sweating etc.); and, (c) he mentioned that his wife complained that they had no social life. As he was disclosing these facts, two other behaviors became apparent: (d) his verbal behavior, which initially had appeared to be concise and articulate, became discursive to the point that he apologized for it but could not control it; and, (e) an odd mannerism which was both a mild torticollis and blepharism became increasingly evident.

The second example is a woman in her late twenties who contacted us with complaints about experiences which disturbed her and which had "followed" her when she moved house. She complained that she both felt and fleetingly saw, "out of the corner of my eye," presences which moved rapidly about the rooms she occupied. On one occasion, which particularly disturbed her, she saw a vivid green face of a threatening nature appear "out of a wall." This lady spoke in a flamboyant, excited, manner, frequently not completing a train of thought. She had many friends, and an apparently stable relationship with the boyfriend with whom she lived. She dressed in an unusually striking, possibly eccentric, way. She maintained with considerable vehemence that she had experienced many and varied psi-related events throughout her life. She knew that on occasions she was clairvoyant, she frequently knew what people were thinking before they spoke, and that she could project her thoughts to others, particularly her boyfriend. She believed that apparently coincidental events, such as the appearance of an unusual word on television, in the paper, and in a friend's vocabulary, all on the same day, was "meaningful." According to the DSM-III-R, both these individuals show behavior which fulfill the formal criteria for a diagnosis of schizotypal personality disorder. Nevertheless, I suggest that while many clinicians might agree that this diagnosis is a useful formulation in the first example, I doubt whether many would want to apply it to the second example. However, had the lady in the second example shown any evidence of being socially withdrawn then, again, this formulation might appear more useful. That she did not was due, in my estimation, to her expressed attitude of "not giving a damn what other people thought." These personality factors, of assertive self-reliance, may be ones which others, with similar experience, do not possess.

The suggestion that the DSM-III-R criteria for schizotypal personality disorder, applied without some differential loading, could lead to stigmatizing individuals who have experienced genuine psi-related events, might be viewed as a "straw man": an idea which has no relevance to everyday clinical practice. Clinicians with whom I have discussed this proposition tend to dismiss it, saying in effect that they would know from experience when it was relevant and when it was not. If pressed, however, they have difficulty in articulating how they would do this in practice. There is evidence that schizotypal personality disorder is associated with schizophrenia. The four criteria which are commoner in the relatives of schizophrenics than in the relatives of controls are emotional detachment, unsociability, suspiciousness, and odd speech, but not the liability to perceptual illusions or "magical thinking" (Kendler, 1985). If the schizotypal personality disorder is applied to an individual, primarily on the basis of their beliefs and experience, rather than their social behavior, this may have implications for their employment possibilities, treatment, and most importantly their view of their own psychological well-being. It would be as well to avoid such stigmatization.

It would be interesting to make a comparison of individuals diagnosed as having an schizotypal personality disorder on the basis of psi-related beliefs and experiences with a group so categorized principally on social or manneristic criteria. Are the groups demonstrably different in other important ways (such as Maher's suggestion that one could look for associations between personality attributes and delusions of particular logical structure), would there be group differences in the differential diagnoses, or in the principal diagnoses if the diagnosis of schizotypal personality disorder was denied to the assessing clinicians?

Conclusions

This paper has looked at both Maher's model and the Chapmans' formulation of the development of delusional beliefs. It is suggested that they are very similar propositions, both of which rely on the experience of significance or stimulus strength. A case, based on the Maher model, can be made that experiencing anomalous events of a psi-related kind may produce, in otherwise normal individuals, beliefs and social behavior which could result in such individuals being stigmatized by the clinical diagnosis of schizotypal personality disorder, with the association with schizophrenia that this implies. It has been suggested that certain individuals, particularly young people with high levels of generalized anxiety and/or low self-reliance, are at particular risk.

What are the implications of this view for clinicians, sympathetic to the possibility of psi, assessing or advising individuals who report distress as a result of an anomalous experience(s)? Our difficulty, as individuals with a neutral-to-positive belief in their veridicality, is that that those we counsel have to exist in an environment which is not tolerant of such belief. The Chapmans comment that their Magical Ideation Scale

is designed to measure belief in forms of causation that by conven-

tional standards in our culture are invalid, such as thought transmission, psychokinetic effects, precognition, and the transfer of
psychic energies between people. The Magical Ideation Scale
has obvious face validity for identifying persons with delusional
beliefs . . . (p. 168).

Quis custodiet ipsos custodes?

Our specialist interest in, and knowledge of, "what psi is not" should
be helpful to us and our clients. Indeed it could be argued that this
information should be more widely communicated to all clinicians
dealing with apparently deluded individuals. If the hypothesis examined
in this paper has substance, it increases the importance of the clinical
investigation into the way the person normally forms beliefs, or tolerates
uncertainty. Does the person rely solely on the emotional reaction of
"visceral certainty" and, if not, how does the person test the veridical
value of such experiences? It is possible that the single most important
way in which such an individual can be helped is by offering him or
her strategies for testing the truth of the experience, strategies based
on "what psi is not." This may involve a detailed discussion of the
relevance of counter-evidence, does it clearly apply, possibly apply, or
not apply at all? Can predictions be made on the basis of the belief or
counter-evidence? In his concluding comments, Maher (1988) comments that "early detection of developing delusions, and the presentation of counter-evidence, before the 'solution-relief' experience has
been reached, would seem to be more likely to succeed than later in-
terventions" (p. 31). I will not go further into this aspect of the problem
because I am aware that other speakers at this conference have given
considerable thought to the ways in which people may be helped to an
accommodation with what appear to be genuine psi phenomena. This
paper may have emphasized the need for such clinical guidelines.

REFERENCES

Begleiter, H., Porjesy, B., & Behari, B. (1987). Auditory brainstem potentials in sons of
alcoholic fathers. *Alcoholism: Clinical and Experimental Research, 11*(5), 477–480.
Chapman, L. J., & Chapman, J. P. (1988). The genesis of delusions. In T. F. Oltmanns
& Maher (Eds), *Delusional beliefs* (pp. 167–183). New York: John Wiley & Sons.
Kendler, K. S. (1985). Diagnostic approaches to schizotypal personality disorder: A his-
torical perspective. *Schizophrenia Bulletin, 11*, 583–553.
Le Doux, J. (in press). *Cognition and Emotion.*
Maher, B. A., & Ross, J. S. (1984). Delusions. In H. E. Adams & P. B. Sulker (Eds.),
Comprehensive handbook of psychopathology. New York: Plenum Press.
Maher, B. A. (1988). Anomalous experience and delusional thinking: The logic of ex-
planations. In T. F. Oltmanns & B. A. Maher (Eds.), *Delusional beliefs* (pp. 15–33).
New York: John Wiley & Sons.
Morris, R. L. (1986). What psi is not: The necessity for experiments. In H. L. Edge,

R. L. Morris, J. Palmer & J. H. Rush, *Foundations of parapsychology* (pp. 70–110). Boston: Routledge & Kegan Paul.

Palmer, J. (1977). Attitudes and personality traits in experimental ESP research. In B. B. Wolman (Ed.), *Handbook of parapsychology* (pp. 175–210). New York: Van Nostrand Reinhold.

Polich, J. (1989). Habituation of P300 from auditory stimuli. *Psychobiology, 17*(1), 19–28.

Rush, J. H. (1986). What is parapsychology? In H. L. Edge, R. L. Morris, J. Palmer, & J. H. Rush, *Foundations of parapsychology* (pp. 3–8). Boston: Routledge & Kegan Paul.

Southard, E. E. (1916). On the application of grammatical categories to the analysis of delusions. *The Philosophical Review, 25*, 424–455.

Spielberger, C. D., Gorsuch, R. L., & Lushene, R. E. (1970). *The State-Trait Anxiety Inventory.* Palo Alto, CA: Consulting Psychologists Press.

Spitzer, R. L. & Endicott, J. (1977). *Schedule of affective disorders and schizophrenia—lifetime version (SADS-L).* New York: New York State Psychiatric Institute.

Tantam, D. (1988). Lifelong eccentricity and social isolation. I: Asperger's syndrome or schizoid personality disorder. *British Journal of Psychiatry, 153*, 783–791.

DISCUSSION

HARARY: I think the focus on social skills and social relationships is really essential. Sometimes I have the idea that if you think of those little scratch and sniff cologne ads, if you scratch and sniff the psyches of most normal people, and you really get into some of what they think about reality, you will find there is some pretty strange stuff going on just beneath the surface. But there is a certain skill in knowing when to shut up, and when to not share your inner self with other people. Maybe the people who are diagnosed as having real problems are the people who don't know when not to tell people, particularly psychiatrists, what is really going on in their heads. I found when I was studying diagnosed schizophrenic patients in a mental hospital in North Carolina, a lot of what was described in their charts as being wrong with them and with what they thought about reality was similar to the ideas of a lot of people outside of the hospital who were footloose in society. The problem was that the psychiatric patients couldn't keep their thoughts to themselves and could not control whether or not they acted on those thoughts at a particular time. In fact, in Maimonides Medical Center the psi laboratory was in the basement and the inpatient psychiatric ward was on the second floor. In the elevator, I would often see a lot of inpatients and I would say, "Good morning" to whomever happened to be in the elevator but they would often ignore me and be off into another world. When you talked to them, often they didn't make a lot of sense. The surprising thing was that many of those non-communicative, incoherent people were the psychiatrists who were working there rather than the patients. One more comment, and that is, some people try to rationalize their withdrawal from other people, their inability to relate, on the basis of trying to describe their own strange reality. For example, they might say, "I'm really a special, unusual person and that's why other people don't like me." So it's not that they withdrew after having certain experiences, it's that they were trying to explain why they couldn't connect with other folks in the first place. Does that make some kind of sense?

TIERNEY: Yes, indeed. The group that bothers me is the people who have had one experience and who contact us saying, "What is this?" My concern is that unless they are dealt with sympathetically, they may develop a delusional system. Now, I'm quite willing to argue the case that this is highly unlikely, that in fact, the important thing here is the psychosis and the delusions that result in psychosis. But I just wanted to explore the possibilities. Are there any formulations in the literature which would suggest that a single experience, or a number of experiences close together, might produce a delusional system? And if so, what's the consequence of that? We are used to thinking about the development of, say, depression as a result of our normal thinking. Why stop at depression? That's my other point.

DIERKENS: I am perhaps just a borderline case, I don't know. I wish to tell you what I have learned in my own practice. For about 15 years, I was very concerned about the differences between hallucination, delusion and psi events. I thought that there could be some telepathy between mother and child. I asked a professor who was the head of the World Health Organization and he said that the problem is not why the telepathy exists between mother and child, but why does it stop because telepathy is evident. From that moment on, I tried to see problems in reverse. Aren't we just in a paranoid society, absolutely delusional, denying the evidence, so we are merely half deaf or half blind trying to tell those who hear well or see well, they are perhaps delusional or schizophrenic? When you use that kind of thinking, everything that you said may be just reversed; we share that delusion in a general way. I think it is sometimes interesting, especially for us who most probably have had some experience, because I don't believe that people would spend their lives concerned about events that they never saw. So, why are others not open to it? Why is our society closed to it? If you go to Africa, or to India, it is evident. Perhaps the delusion is different. I think for people who have that "opening" it is very difficult to relive. For little children, when they see an apparition of their grandmother, most probably the family would say, "Well you're tired,"

"Well, that's just fancy," "Well, you are probably ill," or "You have fever." Instead of saying, "Well, that's perhaps one reality, but there's another too." If we could follow some adolescent, who experiences some huge spiritual emergency, as Grof said, in ESP or Spiritualist sessions, they are absolutely normal, years and years afterwards. So I think that we should not insist so much about the delusion of those open to ESP, but perhaps more to the delusion of the scientists who are not open to it.

TIERNEY: I completely agree with you. The point I was making was how do we encourage the people who write things like DSM-III-R to consider the possibility that our concerns may be relevant, because at present I suspect there is a lot of harm being done.

PARKER: I think it was excellent that you highlighted the contribution that psychologists have now made to this field. Previously it has been the territory of psychiatrists, so it is now an opportunity for psychologists who have come with their own theories. I'm not sure that we have at present much in the way of a major contribution, but it is certainly worth examining the kind of detail that you presented. I would like to say something about some of the contradictions that I think are still inherent in this approach. As you pointed out, Maher's concept of delusional assistance is that first there is a perceptional oddity that occurs and then the thought disorder comes afterwards. You tried to relate it to experience of significance and that certain people, because of their anxiety or attention span, they doubt that these perceptual oddities are to be given extra significance. But, I think we must think of the examples that Donald West gave earlier, that it is perhaps quite heterogeneous how people attribute significance. There are those that have these unusual experiences and do become quite affected by them, and develop delusional systems. Others just dismiss it as an oddity and don't know what it is. There are others who put the label ESP or psychic experience to it. I'm not sure that you can draw the line straight across and say that they all have this sort of anxiety trait, or attentional difficulties, whatever. I think personality in the sense of those earlier mentioned defense mechanisms can be important when the experience is threatening to the personality functioning. I think that what really has to be taken into account is whether it is experienced as invading the personality. Of course, this brings up a major problem. Do schizophrenics who have delusions or thought disorder, have any basis for it? Certainly, I think we have to fit in the psi model to the whole thing if one takes psi seriously. How does it fit into these perceptual oddities? I think that really needs to be worked out.

TIERNEY: Can I concentrate on the first point? I think we are just using different terminology. For defense mechanisms, I would say "anxiety reducing strategies". I don't think I was suggesting that the experience of significance was the same across the board. In fact, I'm perhaps saying the opposite, that there will be some people for whom the experience of significance in relation to some psi related event is extreme. And those for whom, the psi event doesn't matter, in fact there is no experience of significance. It is just an oddity that one forgets. So I was saying, it is for this group of people for whom, probably with high state anxiety or trait anxiety, where the experience of significance will have some function, and therefore will tend to reinforce the anomalous belief. It is difficult to call it a delusion but that is what it will be interpreted as by the people, our colleagues, who think of it as a delusional belief.

NEPPE: I have several comments to make, both from the framework of this discussion on the schizotypal personality disorders, as well as the framework of significance. In relation to schizotypal personality disorder, I really am coming from both sides, as a consultant to the Diagnostical Statistical Manual Three Revision, and now to DSM-IV, and also as someone highly critical of the current DSM framework. First, a critical aspect being missed in this presentation is the fact that the *n* criteria for schizotypal personality disorder, also include the larger subject of the criteria for personality disorder itself. Criteria for personality disorder are well formulated within the framework of DSM-III-R and relate to a maladaptive pattern of coping behavior over a prolonged period of time. When examining individual symptomatology, it is rather ludicrous to take them out of context. Second, I am fully in agreement with the absolutely appalling mess that has been made with schizotypal personality disorder, particularly in the concept of magical thinking and unusual perceptual experiences which clearly integrate and include the vast majority of a population, based on several surveys of incidence of subjective paranormal experience. In my own study of a captive population, we found 95% of elderly women over the age of 40 had admitted to at least one such experience. So the framework of using such general criteria in DSM-III-R schizotypal personality disorder is ridiculous unless one looks at the whole context. The whole context involves what are called polythetic criteria. In this instance, one needs three of nine criteria to be present. Two of these— magical thinking and unusual perceptual experiences—are easily present in many people who experience subjective paranormal experiences (SPE). The fact that many people who have SPEs might not perceive these as magical experiences, is beside the point. However, one still needs other pathologic criteria. To me, the major pathologic criterion is reference. Ideas of reference that you mentioned are not necessarily delusional. They may be ideas relating to events which the person is interpreting as having significance for themselves, but do not necessarily have a delusional quality to them. That may well be the distinguishing component between normality and abnormality. Third, I was interested in your hypothesis of anomalous experience being one kind of experience of significance and this ultimately leading potentially to some kind of psychotic break. I will be mentioning this briefly tomorrow in the concept of subjective paranormal experience psychosis which seems to be an entity, albeit rare. Fourth, it seems to me that we have to differentiate between experiences that are subjectively significant—that have a subjective meaning for the individual—from those that the average, respectable member of the culture would perceive as significant. These are two dichotomous directions that may well have a meeting point with some experiences, but unless we subdivide them at the outset we may well be interpreting chalk as the same as cheese.

TIERNEY: To take the first point, I think you are making my point in the sense that I will agree that if we had some loading on those criteria, it would be helpful. To take two of the required three ideas for magical ideation is not a good idea. I take the point that one should bear in mind the idea of a personality disorder which includes the degree of insight and the ideas of reference. But, what bothers me is that though that condition may arise after, and as a consequence of an anomalous experience, it depends when the person is being accessed. If they are being accessed 10 years after the event, having developed all of this, then a lot of the criteria may be a consequence of the original experience. That is my only point.

WEST: I want to make a very simple point. The kind of people that I was thinking of who report numerous psychic experiences, certainly the vast majority of them, do not become psychotic. In fact, if you have experiences over 10 or 20 or 30 years, and this was going to be related to becoming psychotic, you would have become psychotic long before. Looking at it the other way around, when you are confronted with very well developed psychosis, people who have extreme preoccupation with paranoid experiences, hearing persecutors talking to them through the wall or via the radio, one would like to know whether these are people who have had, before they became ill, what would generally be called the kind of psychic experiences that we are interested in. I don't know the answer to that. The very few people that I have known, both before and after they had developed a frank psychosis, have not been people who have reported psychic experiences before they became ill. I would really like to know whether that is a general experience.

TIERNEY: I would not make any comment on that other than I completely agree. Perhaps it is the basis of some research.

WICKRAM: I found the concept of unassimilated subjective psi raising the baseline anxiety level, an interesting concept. I call it subjective psi because we have no way of verifying the objectivity of these verbal reports. You have generalized anxiety at this level, but it cannot be fit into the person's life so it generates more anxiety, unless they can find an expression that then supposedly reduces anxiety. That is a psychological presentation of a distress. Have you observed any somatization in people, for example, who are doubters who cannot fit it in? Are they more repressed? Are they more apt to somaticize the experience? Have you noticed or kept track of, not only the psychological consequences, but somatic consequences of reported subjective psi?

TIERNEY: No, I haven't.

WICKRAM: Has anyone?

TIERNEY: Not to my knowledge.

HARARY: Just a quick follow up to what I asked you earlier. On a practical level, assuming that we have some idea of what we judge as everyday reality and what is a real deviation from that, how do you treat a person, in your opinion, without invalidating, a possible genuine psi experience? How do you treat the delusion or do you even treat the delusion? Does it matter if a person is having delusions if they are otherwise able to cope with daily life? Let's say, they are having delusions and you decide this is not good for them. How do you work on that problem without totally invalidating something genuine that may be going on? Because if you invalidate what is genuine, and they later find out that it was real, then aren't they likely to fall back into the delusion?

TIERNEY: It is as you said before, one should not get involved in the meaning of this. The way I would approach it is to suggest to the person alternative strategies they might like to try out, to test the explanation they have for the anomalous experience. I would not want to be getting involved, at that stage, to talk about delusions or anything else. I just want to know whether they have any framework for testing this? So, in the future they can say, "Well, it's an experience and it means this," or "That's an experience that means that."

HARARY: So, you allow them the freedom to have their genuine experience, and you just approach the interpretation of it?

TIERNEY: Yes, their interpretation.

HARARY: Do you offer them alternative explanations?

TIERNEY: It would be one way of doing it, in a way that would appeal to me. Not that they should then take those explanations, but perhaps use them as a way of testing.

HARARY: What would be an alternative explanation? Let's say, that I decided that I was having psychic experiences and spirits were in communication with me indicating I was the reincarnation of Joan of Arc. And they were giving me other information, by the way, which turned out to be true.

TIERNEY: Well, that would be excellent. One would test that by saying, "Well, tell me the next time this happens to you and we'll test out what they tell you to see whether it's true or not."

HARARY: OK. Let's say the information tests out. Does that mean that I'm the reincarnation of Joan of Arc?

TIERNEY: If it's true, it would depend on the nature of the test we set. If it was clear-cut with no outs, it would mean that something was going on here which we could take as part of your explanation, but not the whole thing.

HORIZONTAL AND VERTICAL CLAIRVOYANCE WITH SPIRITUALISTS AND MEDIUMS

Jean C. Dierkens

When working with their clients, mediums quite often for ask an object owned by the deceased from whom a message should be given. Suppose a medium gives true information, with all bias due to sensory clues (subliminal sensory clues included) suppressed, the problem remains to analyze the *origin* of the information: does it come from the object itself (by "horizontal" clairvoyance, pure psychometry), from the subject's mind (by telepathy) or from the supposed disincarnate ("vertical" clairvoyance, the object being only a link to that non material entity).

This problem of the origin of the message is a very important one for scientific spiritualism, because proof of survival can only be given with real "vertical" information, and not by any "horizontal" one.

But any object given, through its own specificity and shape, gives sensory clues. Any research in that field should therefore use tokens which shape is completely independent of their meaning, for instance, the content of a letter written in a foreign and unknown language. The research described here should test the possibility of pure "horizontal" clairvoyance concerning the content, not the form of a message, that is, the meaning of unknown signs independently of their shape.

Procedure

We used as subjects, 41[6] spiritualists and mediums (some were professional ones) attending the International Spiritualist Federation (ISF) International Convention held in London (August 87). All of the subjects were convinced of the reality of survival and of the possibility of spiritual communication.

In Mons, we had very carefully prepared "unknown" signs to be put in new opaque and sealed envelopes. By "unknown", we meant those

---

[6] For the second phase of the experiment, only 31 subjects were present, due to the near end of the Convention activities.

signs that could not be known by the subjects nor by myself, and that
their shape was such that even when openly seen, their meaning could
not be decided. They were picked at random from different cultural
sources, all of them quite distant from the subjects: one series (22 ideograms) from a Classical Chinese dictionary, another series (9 hieroglyphs) from an Egyptian grammar, two other ones (8 and 12 signs)
from dictionaries of "occult" signs (mostly Middle Age and Renaissance,
but some of them were still used in the 18th century). I did not know
which signs were chosen and, of course, what they meant. Of each of
those signs 10 photocopies were made, sometimes enlarged, so that
their shape would be approximately of the same size.[7] In my suitcase
for London, I had thus 510 small sheets of paper in 4 groups (80, 90,
120 and 220) which I mixed cautiously, face down, keeping however
all the papers of each origin in the same group. I put them at random
in numbered envelopes: envelope Number 1 received A sign taken out
of Occult I series; envelope Number 2, an Egyptian one; envelope
Number 3, a Chinese sign; envelope Number 4, a sign from Occult II;
and envelope Number 5, a Chinese sign again. By chance, the Chinese
envelopes (Numbers 3 and 5) could have the same sign.

I prepared 45 series of envelopes; 41 were used in the experiment.
It was impossible for me to know which signs were in the envelopes.

The subjects coming in two groups depending on the Convention
activities were asked to sit in comfortable chairs. They were asked to
write down everything coming to their mind concerning the *meaning*
(I insisted in saying again "not the form, not the shape") of each sign
put in the envelopes, which, of course, remained closed. They received
sheets of paper where they wrote their name.[8] No time limit was given.
When they had written down or drawn all of what they felt, each time
with the number of the envelope used, they gave their sheets and envelopes back to the experimenter.

The subjects knew that the "signs" or the "symbols" put in the
envelopes came from varied sources and that everyone had different
signs which were taken by chance so that it could happen that the same
sign was in two envelopes. They knew that the shape would not give
them any clue to the meaning.

They wrote[9] down their feelings, hesitations included; some added

---

[7] The papers were approximately 8cm/12cm, the signs 4cm/4cm.
[8] We replaced immediately after the experiment all the names by numbers so that
everything could be made anonymously, which excluded an eventual bias.
[9] Some were Scandinavians or Continental. They wrote sometimes in their own language. I needed translations and this is a bias for the constitution of the "occasional
dictionary."

drawings, more to confirm what they had written than to give new information. Nearly all the subjects took the envelopes in the order mentioned.

The day after these settings, I drew (without having opened the envelopes used), the 51 signs on standard size sheets of paper[10] and wrote a summary of the meaning of the signs as I could read in the dictionaries. I posted them up side by side on the wall of a convention lecture hall and the subjects were asked to write down, on a sheet of paper, which signs they thought they had received. They could mention as many drawings as they wanted and add any comment they wished.

The envelopes were absolutely new and never manipulated, except for the experiment itself. The signs were impersonal photocopies. I (or any other member present) could not give any telepathic clue. Even if someone would get some hints through the opaque envelope, the shape would not help. Every subject had different signs; no one could cheat looking to his or her neighbor.

Positive results would present a problem: from which origin could correct information be issued? General ESP? Akashic memory? Reincarnation unconscious memory? Spiritual guides? But if it were so, there should perhaps be a different result out of the different cultural groups of signs: an Egyptian guide, for instance, should give wonderful information about the hieroglyphs, but probably nothing specific to Chinese ideograms.

I must confess that at the onset, I was nearly convinced that this task was impossible. I admitted that the shape would be "perceived," but not a completely unknown meaning. Probability to get a hit was nearly nil because of the nature of the signs chosen (different culture and unknown signs). Indeed, it was an impossible test to succeed!

The day after, I began to analyze the results, but the real analysis was made quite a few months later (87–88 academic year). I then thought that I needed control groups to get rid of all possible bias.

The first control group consisted of 46 students in their last year in Psychology at Mons University. I asked them to try rationally to give the meaning of the 51 signs which were shown on a screen, one by one. With this group, I wanted to verify that the shape could not give any clue to guess the content.

The second control group consisted of 44 students in their last year of Philosophy or History of Art at Brussels University. I asked them to give spontaneous answers to "what could be 5 signs put in envelopes

[10] This was the very first time I could really look at the signs, and, indeed, I could not personally infer their meaning without reading the pages of the dictionaries!

in a preceding ESP experiment" which I briefly described. I wanted to see if my own personality or the test instruction would not give clues as to the contents of the test. I could compare the group of concepts given by the "ISF subjects + envelopes and signs" with the "students + nothing".

The third control consisted of the 205[11] answers given by the ISF group matched at random to the 51 signs taken at random.[12] I wished to test here if the large paradigm of the answers and of the signs (though these had more precise meaning) would not give similar results if the answers were just by chance joined to the signs.

These three control groups were made and analyzed during the 88–89 academic year.

Experiment

The subjects did not like the rigid experimental set-up which they did not understand at first hand, but no one went away. Most of the subjects were puzzled and even disappointed with the second phase (trying to recognize the signs they thought they had received), because they had not expected such symbols and signs.

When at the end of the convention I explained the aim of the experiment, quite a few subjects did not understand the value of it although I told them that this test could improve the probability of the existence of real "vertical" information if it were established that "horizontal" information was irrelevant.

When I counted the different signs slipped at random in the envelopes, I saw that their frequency range was normal. All the signs were present at least once. Two subjects received the same Chinese sign. I could see later on that there was no link between the quality of the answer and its frequency in the envelopes.

There was no link between this frequency of signs slipped in the envelopes and the frequency of the signs chosen by the subjects for recognition in the second phase of the experiment.

Results

The answers were analyzed by myself and two other "judges," both of them clinical psychologists. We had to give the following values:

---

[11] 41 subjects and 5 envelopes. I should be noted that each "answer" consisted sometimes of more than one specific guessing. The paradigm of each answer is therefore larger than what could be expected if each subject gave only one concept as answer.
[12] The random choice was made through 6 Turbo-Basic programs seeded every time with another at random start number.

0 to an irrelevant answer (no link with the sign concerned);

1 to an answer which "perhaps but doubtfully" gives some link to the sign;

2 to an answer which showed clearly a link with the sign, without being considered as a "hit";

3 to a "hit", which for us meant that, if given in a psychological test of recognition (for instance, in a very short time projection on a screen), we should consider that the subject, consciously or unconsciously, got the general concept linked to the sign.

There was only one point difference between the scores given by the judges, except for very few of them, mostly because one judge gave more importance to the symbolic meaning of the sign than the other ones.

To make things clear, I considered only three groups and out of them, I think that the two extreme groups are beyond subjectivity.

—one was for the *irrelevant* answers (from 0-0-0 to 0-0-1),

—one for the *doubtful positive* answers (from 0-1-1 to 1-1-2),

—one for the *hits* (from 1-2-2 to 3-3-3).

The results were the following ones:

146 answers	(71%)were irrelevant;
41 answers	(20%)were "doubtfully" positive;
18 answers	(9%)were considered as "hits".

No sign appeared significantly "difficult" or "easy." The Occult II was the worst guessed. No subject was "extraordinary" (more than 6 points for the 5 guesses) but 14 subjects gave 1 point or less.

For one subject who got twice the same Chinese sign, the answers were linked positively to the concept of the sign.[13] For the other subject with a duplicate Chinese sign, he wrote during the test "Again,[14] the Roman Period. Racing of the chariot," but he mentioned envelopes 2 and 5, and not 3 and 5; the content was irrelevant.

Some answers were very stimulating, because they mentioned in a precise way the infrequent content of the sign (Occult II. 12 ("Mark of a Mason, Master printer" of the 16th century), for instance, with "drifting far away. Perhaps in time rather than geographically. Scrolls, or lettering associated . . .").[15]

---

[13] Chinese "2" has a double meaning: one is linked to medicine (to heal the plague), the other one to exorcise and religious ritual. The answers were (abstracts): ". . . Energy, Protection, Mysticism, Initiations . . ." and Needle, Pin, Medicine, Peace, Relaxation, Knowledge, China, Korea."

[14] The frequency of words as "again" is very low; only 5 occurrences in the 2644 words given.

[15] As mentioned in footnote 1, it is impossible to give more details on this paper already somewhat too long.

The five subjects known as professional mediums gave a somewhat better score in general (total of the points given to the answers), but the result was not statistically significant. A better result was also given by them in the recognition phase. We can't however give a true analysis of these specific subjects, because some good mediums are not "professional" and were not counted in the group, and because every professional medium did not declare that he or she was. To be able to appreciate the specificity of the hits, an "occasional" dictionary was made out of all words written in the answers.[16] The total amount was 2644 words. The length of the answers varied from 0 (only drawings) to 236 words.

Because of the translation problem, it is impossible to match the frequency to the usual frequency dictionaries, but let us give the frequency of the 39 most frequent words: I(176), as(49), impression(48), with(42), to feel(42), to see(36), me(31), not(29), very(26), symbol(22), something(22), to be able(22), but(20), in(19), color(18), big(18), envelope(17), my(16), water(15), hand(15), to come(15), warmth(14), fire(14), light(14), image(12), sensation(12), towards(12), tree(11), two(11)l peace(11), sign(11), may be(11), much(10), blue(10), red(10), circle(10), force(10), sun(10), to receive(10).

What might be interesting for a linguist is the apparition with about the same frequency words which could be linked: red-blue (the most frequent colors mentioned); warmth-firelight; to feel(42); to see(36); image-sensation. The frequency of one element of duality should also be interesting to analyze, giving a general dictionary of values for the ISF Group: "bright, light" 19 times in comparison with "darkness, dark" 4 times; "high, above, on" 21 times against "low, under" 5 times; "strong, strength" 15 times against not one "weak"; "inner, in" 28 times against "outer, out" 7 times. We can't however use these features in our research.

We then tried to match the frequency of the concepts linked objectively to the signs with the frequency of the concepts used in the answers. We isolated 86 concepts for the signs and 534 for the answers. No correlation may be considered, except for the concept of Nature (air, sky, earth, water, etc.) which was the most frequent one in the answers (64) and in the envelopes (14). As for the cultural origins mentioned, the subjects gave "Far-Eastern" 20 times, in comparison with "Egyptian" 9 times; Greek or Roman, 7 times; Continental, 5 times, Anglo-

---

[16] Articles, pronouns other than linked to "I", auxiliary verbs, prepositions other than very specific ones were not counted. Remember: for quite a lot of subjects, English was not their maternal language.

Saxon, 5 times; American Indians, 3 times; and Indian and Middle-Eastern, 3 times. The "circle" was the most frequent shape.

But we can't make much out of this finding in this research: all those elements mentioned were *not* linked with the quality of the answers. There were no concepts more linked to a specific group of signs, even not Chinese for the Chinese signs, or Egyptian for the Egyptian signs.

First Control Group: Rational Guessing of Signs' Meaning When Shape Is Clearly Visible.[17] From the answers, no real information concerning the meaning was given, except for the Occult I.5 where the moon was mentioned 12 times. If we use the same scoring system, we find 0.5% of positive answers (instead of 9% in the ISF group). Indeed, shape was more confusing than helpful. Let us give as examples the three first signs:

Occult I.1 : 17 answers were centered on "barbed wire" instead of the Goddess of Water;

Occult I.2 : 27 answers mentioned "water", "boat" or "waves" though the sign meant the planet Mars;

Occult I.3 : 31 mentioned "cock", "bell tower" or "weathercock" when the meaning was Quicklime-powder and calcination . . .

The occasional dictionary (3415 words) was totally different than the ISF one and entirely based on the shapes seen. We may conclude that even if shape was seen through the opaque envelope, it could not give any positive clue to the meaning.

Second Control Group: Pure Imagination Without Any Target.[18] By the instruction the subjects were more inclined to draw than in the ISF Group (20% were only drawings). There were only 6 answers which could eventually match to the signs: lotus, gnosis, mystery, Hermes,[19] tears, shouting.

The number of elements of answer to analyze was 382. The subjects were quite short in their descriptions or drawings (more geometrical forms than any other ones). The occasional dictionary was poor, completely different from the two other ones and had no relation with the objective signs. We may conclude that my personality did not give clues to the ISF group.

Third Control Group: At Random Matching Group. Through very careful random procedures, 51 signs were matched with the 205 answers of the ISF Group.

---

[17] 46 students, 230 answers.
[18] 44 students, 220 answers
[19] My students know my personal involvement in Pythagorean and Hermetic traditions.

The answers were analyzed through the same procedure (scores from 0 to 3) and ended in the following results:

178 misses   (instead of 146 in ISF Group),
19 doubtful answers   (instead of 41 in ISF Group),
3 "hits"   (instead of 18 in ISF Group)

The mean score of each "subject" (total of the 5 signs scored from 0 to 3) was less than the half of the mean score of ISF Group: 1.0 instead of 2.4.

Out of the 41 "random subjects", 26 scored 1 or less (14 for ISF Group) and 2 "random subjects" scored more than 3 (13 for ISF Group).

Through this quick analysis, we already may conclude that the ISF Group is different from chance expectation.

Recognition

Out of 114 choices proposed by the subjects, 13 were correct, but no one was correctly justified: all of the added comments were irrelevant.

There was perhaps one interesting finding. The professional mediums did better than the rest of the group. The group of signs which was the best recognized was the Occult II, though this was the worst "guessing" group; and the Egyptian one was the least recognized though they were quite "well" guessed.

To be absolutely confident in the results of recognition, I should be absolutely sure that no small subliminal sensory hints were available. I took quite a lot of precautions, but I must confess that I was not too concerned by small perception of the shape, because of the independence of the meaning. I may, of course, suppose that the ESP way of guessing is based on different mechanism than ESP recognition. But I can't seriously make that assumption now.

Conclusion

The results showed a small but significant link between the meaning of unknown signs taken from a far removed culture and answers given by clairvoyant technique, without telepathic channel or any "psi" charge. Sensory clues and telepathy being excluded, the possibility of direct clairvoyance of the meaning as an intervening factor in communications with supposed disincarnate entities may not be neglected. The information however was not conscious and clear enough to explain the usual psychometry of meaning, as mediums show in their practice.

Signs with very short definitions.

OCCULT I. GETTINGS, Fred. "Dictionary of occult, hermetic and alchemical Sigils". London, Routledge and Kegan Paul, 1981.

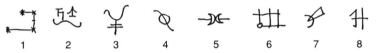

1. Dina, Goddess of rain. 2. Planet Mars (magic). 3. Quicklime powder; calcination. 4. Bronze. 5. Moon (Byzantine). 6. Tin; Jupiter. 7. Silver paint (alchemy). 8. Herb (shape very near of a Hermetic sign).

OCCULT II. SCHWARZ-WINKLHOFFER & BIEDERMAN. "Das Buch der Zeichen und Symbole". Graz, Verlag für Sammler, 1972.

1. Hermes. 2 and 3. Sulfur. 4. Conjunction Jupiter-Saturn. 5 to 11. Operative Masonic signs. 12. Signe of 16th Century Printer Paul Sohn.

EGYPTIAN HIEROGLYPHS. GARDINER. "Egyptian Grammar". Oxford.

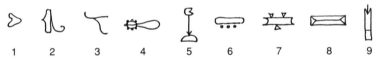

1 & 2. Parts of udjad eye. 3. Tongue of an ox. 4. Animal's belly. 5. Lotus. 6. Alluvial land; mystery. 7. Road and shrubs. 8. Garden pool. 9. Column.

CHINESE IDEOGRAMS. WIEGER, Léon. "Caractères chinois. Etymologie. Graphes. Lexique". Taiwan, Kuangchi Press, 8th edition, 1972.

1. Shouting. 2. Chasing plague' spirit. 3. Small. 4. Crab. 5. Flower; beautiful; dissolute. 6. Wheat ear. 7. Reliable man; send a message. 8. To inquire. 9. Tired eyes. 10. Bamboo mat. 11. Anguish. 12. Yijing hexagram. 13. Law. 14. Crying. 15. Sundial. 16. Core. 17. To burn. 18. To reach. 19. Steep. 20. Brave. 21. Much. 22. Bad quality jade.

DISCUSSION

NEPPE: If one wants to replicate this, what would you advise us to do now? In other words, how would you, given a "retrospecto-scope," change your experiment?

DIERKENS: I would eliminate the recognition phase. The second phase is useless, it gives a lot of hope and afterwards a lot of disappointment, because they were so convinced they saw those signs but, nine out of ten, were not able to do it. Perhaps I would not take all those Masonic signs; that is something which did not provide much. But the other signs were signs of Polish families, and I could not really see if that was right or not. What would be best is perhaps if somebody else would choose the signs and try not to take useless signs.

NEPPE: They would have to take a whole new series of signs presumably, being now familiar with these.

DIERKENS: Yes.

NEPPE: That is very exciting.

VON LUCADOU: For me there is still one possibility for theoretical implications which is the observational theories. My question concerns how the judges evaluated the results. The observational theories say, that to some extent, it is important what judges observe and that, if they find a hit, that these are the people who produce the psi effect. That is the essence of the observational theory. Of course, one can doubt it; but from this point of view, it becomes very important to know what the instruction to the judges was and whether they could recognize the hit immediately or not. What feedback and what information was given to the judges?

DIERKENS: In fact, for the judges, if I could do what I like, I would not give the judges the answers with the signs. I would give the judges the work of doing the 10,455 matching of the items, not knowing which one was taken. But it's quite a lot of work to see 10,000 items. The judges had to give a score of zero if they thought that the answers had nothing to do with the sign. One, when something was doubtful. Two, when there was something but something was missing. Three meant they thought it could not be said that it was not a hit. The judges did it quite independently. I myself did it many months later to see if I changed my scoring. In fact, I did change some of them, about six or seven; a zero became one or one became zero. Only one became two, no two became three, and no three became two. So, that is something. Perhaps, the old series should be given twice to the judges, but, there is always time to do it. But if you ask the judges to do all

10,000 items that would lessen your concerns about the observation theory. No?

VON LUCADOU: The observational theories would say that is a theoretical question. Your subjects, the clairvoyants, probably have not produced the effect, but the observers checking the symbols hit the items. Now, can you say something about the judges? Were they good psi hitters? Have you controlled for this in an independent experiment?

DIERKENS: One is a good psi hitter, but the other two were not.

IREDELL: I just query your definition of psychometry because, to those of us who have been in the subject a long time, any object for psychometry should bear an influence and it is that influence which is allegedly tapped by the percipient, whether professional medium or not. The instances you gave are more comparable, in my estimation, to the book tests, where a person with perception can tap-in at a distance to written or drawn figures and give that to a percipient. I wonder also if I might ask you why you discount discarnate entities? Can it not be with many thousands around that they are in fact operating through your percipients?

DIERKENS: I agree with you that psychometry is produced by an object which has a charge and a history. But sometimes people say that the mediums give hits not because of that influence, but because they are able to get, through ESP, the information needed. I thought, therefore, that using mediums in this experiment, would not get results because they are not using psychometry. The other thing, of course, is it always possible that some deceased entities or guides would help. But then, you would most probably have some more information about that deceased person or that period in which they lived. In the Chinese letters about two-thirds are used now and one-third are no longer used, so I could match the ancient and the new ones. I would have thought, for instance, that a medium who has a good Chinese guide, and one of the mediums has one, would get better results in the Chinese series. But, she did not and that is a question for me. She knows she is a good medium and she gave a lot of very good information. You have to understand, it is not to prove that they are there; I know they are there, but where do they come from? You see? If the results were no percent or one percent, I could say, "Well, I'm almost sure that in psychometry it comes from only the deceased person." But now I have to say, some hints may be given by another clue.

IREDELL: If I could just come back to one thing: it doesn't surprise me in the least that you get the failures from these so-called successful people, because the great factor that comes in so much in all influences from discarnate sources, is boredom: boredom and the difficulty in sustaining any concentration. There is a tendency suddenly to be fed up, or feel they can't continue.

ELLISON: I remembered Rupert Sheldrake's modernized version of the Akashic records, his experiment on the Turkish nursery rhyme and the nonsense rhyme that sounded just like it. I haven't looked at the statistics carefully, but it appears to have been shown that the real Turkish nursery rhyme could be learned much more quickly than the other by people who did not know any Turkish. In other words, Sheldrake's view (which is just a modernization of the Hindu idea of the Akashic records) is the "memory of nature." It would appear to fit with your research quite well, because these symbols were perhaps familiar to generations of Egyptians and Chinese and others down in the unconscious. The successful subjects then, would not know where the information was coming from. Now human beings, particularly scientific human beings, could almost be defined as mental model building creatures. Couldn't we? When we have built our model, as I said earlier, we defend it by almost impregnable psychological defenses. I was interested to hear this morning how almost everyone, with a few exceptions, was taking a very simplistic realism model of reality as perfectly obvious and self evident. If you go back a long way, particularly to the Hindu ideas, an alternative idealism paradigm is perfectly respectable. It would not show any difference in dealing with ("explaining") ordinary science, but it would give the possibility of modifications of the idea pattern, the thought form, which we call the physical world.

DIERKENS: If I have to put a label on it, I would say that I definitely have a Spiritualist paradigm. But, I don't forget my other parts. So I really thought more about the Spiritualist hypothesis than any other one. I am not against Akashic memory. I used what is called the super-ESP hypothesis because I don't know what could explain it. I have no explanation. It puzzles me.

ELLISON: We have no explanation. Surely what that means is, we are unable to describe this paranormal phenomenon in terms of some model we have in our minds which represents it. That's all it means, isn't it? There is nothing but models in our minds. The raw experiences are in our minds; the models which pattern them are in our minds. One such model is realism; another model is idealism. Understanding and explaining means having the ability to describe—no more than to describe—a phenomenon in terms of the model that the speaker and the listener have in their minds.

VON LUCADOU: I have only a short remark which just came into my mind, because if I correctly understood, the symbols were hidden in an envelope when they were presented to the subjects. So, what seems rather interesting to me is the fact that this is something different from the normal ESP experiment where you have a symbol which is hidden in an envelope and you have to guess the real symbols, say the Rhine cards. Now, this seems to me a very productive way because, if you look into history, you find a similar phenomenon. Take for example the experiments which had been done by Mary Craig Sinclair, the wife of Upton Sinclair. She often reported something strange. She said that she could get a certain impression and she tried to redraw a drawing which was sent by her husband. Very often she did not grasp the meaning, but she did grasp the form. Sometimes she grasped the meaning, but she did not grasp the form. So it seems to be that the ESP does not work in a direct way, that we could get better results in an indirect way. In other words, if we do not use it in a direct way to get a direct answer, but something which is hidden behind it. It is very often apparent in spontaneous cases, that we do not get the direct target, but something hidden. I think that your symbols are good examples for something which is hidden by an object.

IVANOVA: First of all, for many years we have been terribly fed up with the words materialism and idealism. We simply can't hear them any more. For us, what is right is right. We think that these expressions, perhaps, should not be used at all. That is our impression, it is our understanding in our country. Perhaps in your country it is different. I think we should not stress this part. Because if it is energy and if some information exchange is going on, it is some form of matter too, but we don't understand how it works. Everything is matter. The highest scientists know it, but not everything is substance, so that is a little different. Another thing what I wanted to say, do you accept that psychometry is a certain form of clairvoyance?

DIERKENS: If you wish to call it so, you may.

IVANOVA: Is the dermal-optic effect connected with your experiment? Perhaps, not fully because you don't have the meaning of the signs so there is a difference.

DIERKENS: The difference is that here nobody knew or could read the signs.

IVANOVA: You stress the help by discarnate entities. I completely agree, and I don't find anything unscientific about it. But, we cannot say if this is a discarnate entity, that, is a person who lived on earth, died, and exists in the form of energy, or if it is perhaps an entity from other dimensions which never was incarnate on our plane, or if perhaps there are supposed extraterrrestrials which exist too in some energy form. It is very difficult to distinguish what is really happening. We can't say because "they" have not passports. We can't see them. We don't know. We can only feel and that is still not considered scientific.

DIERKENS: Maybe I can answer that very quickly. You said that everything was matter, but you can still say that everything is consciousness, as the Hindu says, "There is *chitta* and everything is consciousness." Then it comes into what we call matter and something else.

IVANOVA: I am very glad to hear you say that.

DIERKENS: Now, about the discarnate source, you remember that I said the deceased person or "guide" that means I do not know if guides are deceased people or were never incarnate.

PSI MANIFESTATIONS IN MULTIPLE
PERSONALITY DISORDER

ROBERT L. VAN DE CASTLE

The unusual mental states present in dissociation have always held special interest for parapsychologists. Dissociation is an unconscious defense mechanism which involves the segregating of mental or behavioral processes from conscious awareness. Dissociative processes are considered to underlie such phenomena as mesmerism, hypnosis, hysteria, fugue, trance states, mediumship, possession, and multiple personality disorder (MPD). In his 1896 Lowell Lectures at Harvard, William James devoted a entire series of lectures to dissociative phenomena and their implications for psychology. He summarized his first lecture with the statement that "the mind seems to embrace a confederation of psychic entities" (Taylor, 1982, p. 35). He expressed his personal conviction that "super normal cognition and super normal healing" could manifest in such states, but also noted "alternate personality, the tendency of the self to breakup, may, if there are spirit influences, yield them their opportunity. . . . If there are devils, if there are super normal powers, it is through the cracked self that they entered." (Kenny, 1981, p. 341). Examples of dissociated states and psi phenomena are frequently described in the literature of mesmerism. Justinus Kerner, a German poet and physician who discovered botulism, or food poisoning, also had a strong interest in parapsychology and in magnetic therapy. When he encountered cases of possession, which he called a demonic-magnetic disease, among his patients he used a mixture of exorcism and magnetism as therapy. In 1829, he published the first psychiatric monograph devoted to an individual patient, Friedericke Hauffe (Ellenberger, 1970, p. 81). This uneducated woman, at age 19, suffered the double trauma of an undesired marriage forced upon her by her parents and the simultaneous death of a preacher she greatly admired. She became extremely ill physically and imagined she was in bed with the preacher's corpse. Friedericke gradually improved with magnetic treatments and although she subsequently spent considerable time in magnetic sleep, she claimed to be "more awake than anybody" on these occasions.

In this state, her facial features were described as "illuminated," her voice as musical, and her manner as full of feeling when she gave advice or gave elaborate discourses on the nature of man and the spiritual world. Many noted philosophers and theologians came to visit her in Kerner's home, and it was reported that she gave evidence of seeing distant events, foretelling the future, and psychokinetic moments of objects occurred in her presence. She claimed to receive messages from discarnate spirits about personal and general matters and spoke frequently in an unknown sonorous language which she said was the original language of mankind forgotten since the time of Jacob. She eventually became known as "The Seeress of Prevorsto" in Kerner's widely read book about her. In her magnetic trances, the "seeress" successfully prescribed which medications would be useful for her and when their effect would be observed. She also devised a "nerve-tuning" apparatus in one of her dreams which Kerner constructed according to her instructions and which was reported to be effective. The "seeress" also effected cures of several people.

The first objective study of MPD appeared in a monograph published in 1840 by Despine, a French physician. He described an eleven-year-old Swiss girl named Estelle sent to him with a severe paralysis and excruciating pains which he eventually treated with magnetic therapy. In her magnetic sleep, a comforting angel, whom she named Angeline, appeared to Estelle and they engaged in lively conversations. Angeline became a co-therapist and indicated how treatment should proceed. Estelle remained paralyzed in her normal state but was able to move and walk in her magnetic state if gold were present on her body. The child could only tolerate a few foods in her normal state but was able to eat large quantities of varied food in her magnetic state. Observing this psychophysiological discrepancy, Despine commented that it seemed as though she had two stomachs. Her normal state alternated every twelve hours with spontaneous magnetic states. During the subsequent year, Estelle predicted that she would visualize a big ball that would burst and great improvement in her condition would follow. Two weeks later she was finally able to take a few steps in her waking state and within two months her normal and magnetic states gradually fused (Ellenberger, 1970, pp. 129–131).

Many examples of dissociative states and MPD were reported later in the 19th century and the early years of the 20th century. Prominent investigators included Janet, Charcot, and Binet in France; Frederic Myers in England; and William James, Boris Sidis, and Morton Prince in the United States. Morton Prince wrote in 1906 his classic work *The Dissociation of a Personality* which described his use of hypnosis to uncover several different personalities of Miss Beauchamp. Another famous investigator was Walter Franklin Prince (no relation to Morton Prince) who studied the Doris Fischer case. Intensive investigations of Doris by Walter Prince (1915, 1916) and James Hyslop (1917), both prominent psychic researchers, were published in the *Proceedings of the American Society for Psychical Research*.

Prince (1915) reported several examples of paranormal phenomena associated with various personalities of Doris. He described an instance when the Margaret personality told him about a letter he had recently written and indicated its contents, to whom it was written, and also described some thoughts he had while writing it but later decided against including. These announcements were always made after she gazed steadily into his eyes. Her responses were always related to something that he had recently been thinking about and she claimed she saw "not what I was consciously thinking of at that moment, but what was 'passing like a parade down underneath'" (p. 58). Her accuracy was apparently impressive as he stated "she never made any incorrect announcement of this kind" (p. 58). Both the Margaret and Real Doris personalities displayed clairvoyant abilities. Real Doris was particularly sensitized to tuning in on her mother's actions whenever Real Doris was away from the house.

For reasons that will be clear later, I was impressed with the personality or state of consciousness called Sleeping Margaret (S. M.). Although S. M. stated that she was constantly aware and never slept, she seldom talked except when her eyes were closed. Her facial expression was described as displaying "philosophical calmness." She disclaimed any identity with Doris or her body. S. M. made predictions about the development of the case which where usually quite accurate and would warn or advise the Real Doris personality of any impending emergencies. Prince acknowledged, "She was my chief coadjutor in the cure" (p. 43).

Hyslop (1917) attempted to determine more about S. M.'s identity. She said she came when Doris was 3 years old and had been sent by someone higher up than she was. Her assignment was to insure that Doris did not get hurt or lost and that she had to take care of Doris until she was released. S. M. indicated "I can see the thoughts that she thinks all day. They look to me what a moving picture does to Doris" (p. 240). She claimed to be able to see thoughts that happened years ago. The higher-ups were white light but not seen very often by S. M. who professed that she also was white light when she was out of the body. S. M. indicated that she was called *the* guard and there was considerable diversity of functioning among the community of guards who acted as go-betweens and communicated by thoughts.

Reports describing cases of MPD declined markedly after the early 1900's. Several explanations for this trend have been advanced. The theory of dissociation proposed by Janet which involved a splitting or division of conscious contents and processes lost favor as Freud's theory of repression gained greater acceptance. Although repression could explain how early childhood emotional identifications could alternately "seize hold of the consciousness in turn," it did not account for the phenomena of co-consciousness often found in MPD. In coconsciousness, an alter personality has total awareness of its own identity and existence while simultaneously experiencing the thoughts and feelings of another personality. Freud insisted that co-consciousness was not possible. Since hypnosis was frequently utilized as a tool in uncovering the existence of alter personalities, Freud's dismissal of the therapeutic benefits of hypnosis decreased the opportunities of encountering MPD. A significant increase in the use of schizophrenia as a diagnosis also served to short-circuit more careful consideration of symptoms which might be indicative of MPD (Rosenbaum, 1980). Such symptoms could include hearing internal voices, displaying regressive childhood behavior, experiencing a sense of depersonalization or having a feeling that someone else had control of the patient's mind.

During the past few decades there has been a remarkable resurgence of interest in MPD. One stimulus has been the heightened interest created by the appearance of several popular books on the topic. *The Three Faces of Eve* published in 1957 became a best seller and Joanne Woodward won an Academy Award for her movie portrayal of Eve. Another popular book and movie describing the case of *Sybil* was published in 1973 (Schreiber). Simultaneously, some significant shifts in clinical attitudes were also taking place. Hypnosis had been gaining increasing scientific acceptance and innovative research in this area was being published. Ernest Hilgard (1977), in his book *Divided Consciousness*, advocated a "neo-dissociative" theory of hypnosis and described the operation of a "hidden observer." His work provides important information about the multiplicity of consciousness. A clear statement of the phenomenology of the experience was provided by a young female subject:

> The hidden observer is analytical, unemotional, business like. The part of me that was hypnotized was off on a tropical island. The hidden observer is a portion of Me. There's Me 1, Me 2, and Me 3.

Me 1 is hypnotized, Me 2 is hypnotized and observing and Me 3 is when I'm awake . . . The hidden observer is cognizant of everything that's going on; . . . like being awake in a dream and fully aware of your actions . . . The hidden observer sees more, he questions more, he's aware of what's going on all of the time but getting in touch is totally unnecessary . . . He's like a guardian angel that guards you from doing anything that will mess you up. (Crabtree, 1985, p. 32)

More recent research has discovered that there can be *multiple* hidden observers within individuals (Beahrs, 1982). If a subject is placed in a number of distinct hypnotic states, each one can have its own hidden observer with distinguishable personality traits. These findings suggest there may be an almost unlimited number of potential hidden observers or 'personalities' within an individual.

The concept of dissociation has also been rediscovered by mental health personnel encountering post-traumatic stress disorders among a large number of Vietnam veterans. Disturbing memories of combat atrocities that had been blocked off and creating amnesia often flashed back into recall when these veterans were in a safer hospital environment. Another critical factor contributing to greater recognition of MPD was that clinicians finally began to pay serious attention to accounts of childhood sexual abuse. Accepting Freud's earlier pronouncements on this topic, psychoanalysts had for seven decades been dismissing such accounts as merely fantasies developed by young children to provide gratification of wished for activities. Accepting that such traumatic activities had, in fact, occurred, enabled clinicians to recognize that dissociation was the coping technique that allowed bewildered childhood victims to initially shut out these painful memories from awareness.

As a result of all of these convergent influences acknowledging the central role of dissociation in producing unusual mental phenomena, cases of MPD began to be reported with increasing frequency in the literature. Official recognition of the disorder was provided in 1980 when the American Psychiatric Association established specific criteria in the third edition of the Diagnostic and Statistical Manual of Mental Disorders for diagnosing MPD. The revised edition of the DSM-III in 1987 defines MPD as follows:

A. The existence within the individual of two or more distinct personalities or personality states (each with its own relatively enduring pattern of perceiving, relating to and to thinking about the environment and one's self).

B. Each of these personality states at some time, and recurrently, takes full control of the individual's behavior.

The First International Conference on MPD was held in 1984 and annual meetings have been held in Chicago each fall since that time. A comprehensive bibliography published in 1983 (Boor & Coons) required revision within two years (Damgaard, Van Benschoten, & Fagen, 1985).

The number of personalities present in MPD may range from 2 up to nearly 100, although the median number is around 8. The diagnosis is given for women nine times more frequently than men, perhaps because instances of sexual abuse are reported in 80% of all MPD cases. Since depression and suicide attempts are frequently associated with MPD, these symptoms of aggression turned inward may bring women more often into contact with mental health professionals, while male MPDs may more frequently direct their aggression outward toward others and therefore show up in penal institutions. Most MPDs have received a large number of previous psychiatric diagnoses and been in the health care system for more than six years before they are appropriately diagnosed.

Many mental health personnel still have difficulty in accepting this disorder. Dr. Paul Dell undertook a survey study of clinicians' responses to MPD and presented his findings at the Third International Conference on Multiple Personality Disorder held in 1986 at Chicago. In his survey of members who had treated cases of MPD, he found that 77% had encountered colleagues who were upset or incensed by the diagnosis of MPD and one third of the MPD therapists had been told bluntly by colleagues that "there is no such thing as multiple personality." In speculating upon the possible sources of this "narcissistic rage" toward MPD, Dell comments that "multiple personality is an uncanny, and upon first encounter, often a deeply disturbing and even threatening phenomena. MPD appears to threaten not only the hegemony of the personal ego, but also the currently prevailing Western views of the self, the individual, and even personal responsibility." The challenge posed by MPD to our professional serenity is summarized by Kluft as follows: "Multiple personality disorder delights in puncturing our generalizations, revels in shattering our security about our favorite techniques and theories, and exhilarates in the role of gadfly and disturber of the peace."

What are some aspects of MPD that create such chaos in our conceptual schemes and strain our credulity as to its genuineness? Despine's comments in 1840 about Estelle seemingly possessing two stomachs could be considered a precursor to recent psychophysiological investigations (Putnam, 1984) which indicate that various alter personalities may differ markedly in food preferences, allergies, medication responses, and sensory acuities. In an NIMH survey of 100 recent MPD cases carried out by Putnam, Guroff, Silberman, Barban, and Post (1986) it was reported that 75% of all cases had at least one personality under 12 years of age, 50% had alter personalities of the opposite sex, and over a third exhibited changes of handedness from one alter personality to another. Changes in heart rate, blood pressure, and regional cerebral blood flow in multiples have been observed when they switched personalities, and differences have been reported in cerebral dominance, EEGs and Average Evoked Potentials between alter personalities. Some alter personalities whose initial job may have been to "take the pain" are capable of demonstrating anesthesia to current pain. One female multiple was abused by family members putting out lighted cigarettes on her skin and when the personality that received burns took over during therapy, the burn marks would reappear on her skin and last for several hours. Several accounts in the literature suggest that multiples can heal more quickly than others and there are cases where cuts, bruises and third degree burns healed with extraordinary rapidity. The whole issue of mind-body plasticity and interaction could undergo a major reformulation on the basis of what is emerging from current research studies examining the neurological, physiological, and endocrinological aspects of MPD.

Might parapsychology also benefit from a more thorough study of dissociated states and might some new paradigms emerge for understanding the conditions under which psi manifestations occur in conjunction with MPD? My answer to these questions would be a resounding "Yes." Experimental work involving normal subjects experiencing modified internal states such as hypnosis (Honorton, 1977) or dreams (Van de Castle, 1977) has produced relatively consistent and significant psi results. The anecdotal accounts of psi functioning in MPDs gleaned from biographical material are quite provocative.

Christine Sizemore, the MPD anonymously described in *The Three Faces of Eve* later collaborated on an autobiographical account entitled *I'm Eve* (1977). She described an incident when she was a child and her little sister fell into a creek and subsequently developed a mysterious illness. Sizemore reported that Jesus came to her in a dream and told her that her sister had diphtheria. When she gave this information to her parents, they sent for a doctor who confirmed that it was diphtheria and ordered life saving serum from 100 miles away.

As an adult, Chris reported many precognitive experiences. One involved the vision of her husband being electrocuted at work. She urged him to stay home with her and the man who replaced him on the job that day was electrocuted. On another occasion when pulling their trailer through a mountainous area, she demanded that her husband stop the car and check the wheels because she had a vision of one of the rear trailer wheels flying off. He stopped and discovered to his surprise that one of the rear trailer wheels was actually loose and would shortly have dropped off the vehicle. The following comments about Chris's psychic abilities appear in her co-authored book:

> Being unable to explain these sorts of phenomena, the civilized world turns away in half-embarrassed silence from the serious account of such events, and truly they are strange; but Chris never appeared to attach to them more than a mere passing interest. They were simply another confusing facet of her already inexplicable existence; and she did not question this unusual aspect as she did not question her whole incredible condition. (p. 337)

For Henry Hawksworth, an MPD who was a real-estate salesman in northern California, his psychic talents represented something "more than a mere passing interest;" they enabled him to rescue himself from awkward financial circumstances. As the result of the antics of one of his destructive alters, Hawksworth would sometimes find himself inexplicably in Los Angeles with no money. A child personality called Peter would emerge and give psychic readings for people visiting bars in nearby Venice Beach. Hawksworth describes these experiences in his autobiography *The Five of Me* (1977).

Billy Milligan received wide public attention when he was charged as the rapist terrorizing Ohio State University in 1977. Several examples of his psychic ability when he was a young boy to know when his sister was in trouble are described in *The Minds of Billy Milligan* (Keyes, 1981). He also had unusual talents in xenoglossy. One of his 24 personalities was an Englishman, Arthur, who spoke with a British accent and also read and wrote fluent Arabic. Another male personality, Regen, read, wrote, and spoke Serbo-Croatian. Regen was a karate expert able to display extraordinary strength because of his ability to control his adrenalin flow. The personality responsible for the rapes was Adalana, a 19-year-old lesbian.

An additional case of xenoglossy is referred to by Mayer (1988). Troubled by some apparent metaphysical aspects of an MPD case he was working with, Mayer sought consultation from a psychiatric colleague, Dr. Densen-Gerber, who had had more experience with MPDs. This is his description of that consultation:

I have the same problem, she said. Judi told about a patient who had claimed to have a reincarnated fifteenth century Welsh poet living in her body. This personality could even speak a strange tongue that a linguistic expert confirmed was a fifteenth-century dialect although the patient had never been to Wales or studied any of its dialects, past or present. Judi had no explanation for it. She also told me about another patient who had claimed to have a demon living in her body. (p. 161)

Another psychiatrist prominent in the clinical treatment of MPD is Ralph Allison who has personally treated over 30 cases of MPD and has seen approximately 60 cases in his clinical career. Perhaps because his family "has produced a long line of ministers," Allison feels that religion and mental health are compatible and is comfortable discussing the psychic and spiritual facets of MPD.

In his book, *Minds in Many Pieces*, Allison (1980) stated, "In my role as explorer, I witnessed parapsychological phenomena for which there is, as yet, no satisfactory explanation" (p. 5). When interviewed by Scott Rogo (1987) about how many victims of MPD possess psychic abilities, he answered:

Everyone of them. This is a sort of sine qua non that goes along with it. It may be the primary personality that has some ability to tell what's coming up in the future for her kids, or accidents they're going to get into. That happens quite frequently. They may not mention it unless you start asking. If the patient has a lot of personalities, there will be one who is very psychic, and the others will have average ability or no particular abilities. (p. 253)

Later on during this interview, Allison speculated that "when you get into those patients with a multitude of personalities, there is a lot of pathology in the use of psychic abilities for dangerous activities" (p. 255).

One of these dangerous activities can involve possession. Allison (1980) wrote "Repeatedly I encountered aspects of entities of the personality which were not true alter personalities . . . I have come to believe in the possibility of spirit possession" (p. 183). Allison proposed a continuum of possession divided into five grades. Grade Four is control of a person by the deceased spirit of another human being. Grade Five is control by a spirit that has never had its own history and identifies itself as an agent of evil. This would correspond to demonic possession.

Allison speculated that a negative or rageful alter personality would sometimes willingly call for the assistance of some available demonic entity to carry out an act of revenge toward a perceived enemy or persecutor. Their intense reservoir of hatred can serve as a magnet to attract a demonic presence who is more than willing to possess a receptive MPD victim. Allison acknowledged that he sometimes selectively engaged in rites of exorcism to vanish such demonic entities.

M. Scott Peck is another prominent psychiatrist who has reported his involvement in exorcism. Peck's participation is discussed in a chapter entitled "Of Possession and Exorcism" in his popular book *People of the Lie* (1983). Beginning with a skeptical attitude, Peck requested referrals of cases that might purportedly represent possession. On the basis of his personal involvement with two cases elicited in this manner, Peck became convinced of the reality of demonic possession. He said he felt he had confronted and experienced Satan, not as a material creature with horns and hooves, but as a non-material spirit of malevolence that was able to manifest in supernatural ways once it was incorporated in a human body. The lengthy exorcisms were successful in both cases because there was "the presence of God in the room" that was evoked through the loving dedication of all the team members. Peck was so impressed by what he had witnessed that he made a serious attempt to have an "Institute for the Study of Deliverance" established and urged that a centralized data bank be set up where case reports and video tapes of exorcisms could be sent.

Possession states are not rare events (Crapanzano & Garrison, 1977; Montgomery, 1976). They occur in many exogenous cultures (Mischel & Mischel, 1958; Osterreich, 1974; Yap, 1960) and are also not uncommon in contemporary America (Pattison & Wintrob, 1981). Some form of exorcism is generally employed to expel the invading spirit (Goodman, 1981; Martin, 1977). A particularly dramatic account of a three day exorcism involving a sixteen year old North Carolina girl is given in *The Devil and Karen Kingston* (Pelton, 1977). The author claimed that Karen twice levitated off the ground for extended periods of time and several instances of macro-PK events occurred such as vases flying and spontaneous combustion. These events were witnessed by several clergymen, a psychiatrist, clinical psychologist, general practitioner and three nurses besides the investigative reporter. Marked positive changes in the girl's appearance, behavior, and IQ level followed the exorcism. In the experience of the British psychiatrist and former surgeon, R. K. McAll (1982), he finds that a history of past experimentation with the occult is often found in cases of demonic possession. McAll discusses several forms of possession and uses prayer and the Eucharistic rite in cases where departed spirits and demonic possession are involved. An excellent collection of cases in which presumptive spirit possession was involved can be found in the book by Adam Crabtree (1985) entitled *Multiple Man: Explorations in Possession and Multiple Personality.* Crabtree is a Catholic priest and psychotherapist in Canada.

Krippner (1987) reviews how MPD cases are conceptualized among three spiritist sects in Brazil. Although accepting that some MPD cases may be attributable to childhood physical or sexual abuse, other cases are considered to arise from past-life experiences or spirit possession. A team of mediums may be utilized to help diagnose MPD or to treat it by having one of the mediums temporarily incorporate the unwelcome spirit and then expel it. Ebon (1974) described an "exorcism" performed by Eileen Garrett, the famous medium, through having her 12th century Arab physician "control," Abdul Latif, engage in a psychic battle with the possessing entity. An excellent review and thoughtful analysis of the relationship between mediumship and MPD is provided by Braude (1988).

I would now like to review some material which suggests that MPD cases are often found to be accompanied by the presence of an entity or energy system which utilizes paranormal abilities to facilitate life enhancement and integration in MPDs. The current interest in the healing and stabilizing role attributable to a spiritual entity in cases of MPD was stimulated by the same Ralph Allison discussed earlier in connection with spirit possession. In Allison's 1974 article entitled "A New Treatment Approach for Multiple Personalities," he introduced the concept of an *Inner Self Helper* (ISH). He observed remarkable progress in one of his MPD cases when an unusual "personality" component that he named Beth emerged. Beth knew what the other current personalities were thinking and doing and clarified the patient's total history for Dr. Allison. He considered Beth to be his co-therapist. This is what he wrote when he was trying to comprehend "who or what really was Beth?"

> Was she just another dissociated personality, or something quite different? She had no neurotic conflicts, she was always polite and gracious, she always knew what to do in any situation, and she knew God.
>
> Experience with five subsequent patients with multiple personalities, all of whom had an equivalent of Beth, and all of whom found that they could get well only by listening to their Beth, has convinced me that this is the manifestation of a higher part of the personality which is a derivative of the Soul, a part called Inner Self. (p. 30)

How unique was Allison's experience in discovering that dissociated and fragmented aspects of MPD could be unified if the patient attended to this higher source and the therapist honored the information supplied by a spiritual co-therapist? Examples of apparent ISHs can be discerned in the earlier historical accounts I gave about the Seeress of Prevorst, the Angela entity associated with Estella, and the Sleeping Margaret aspect of Doris Fischer.

The concept of the ISH is fairly well accepted by most contemporary therapists working with MPDs. M. Ann Adams mailed a 44-item questionnaire on ISH characteristics to 100 therapists who had worked with MPD patients. An ISH was defined on the questionnaire as a portion of psychic energy within the MPD person which primarily serves as a helper in the MPD system. Her results were presented at the 1987 International Conference on MPD. Forty therapists participated in the study. All 40 had heard of the ISH phenomena and all agreed that ISHs can be valuable assets in the therapeutic process. Direct contact with an ISH was reported by 90% of the therapists, and 64% viewed the ISH as a co-therapist. Advice from an ISH was almost always considered helpful. They possessed extensive knowledge of the MPD's life experiences and would intervene in crisis situations. The ISHs described themselves to therapists as separate and different from alter personalities and presented themselves as more powerful than alters. They often referred to themselves in mystical terms. Adams concluded from the wide variety of explanations regarding ISHs by her respondents that therapists explain and work with ISHs according to their own ideological orientation. Some respondents felt that ISHs were artifactual or iatrogenic in nature, while others viewed them as completely separate entities that were mystical in nature.

In Allison's original article (1974), he indicated that an ISH will not appear if it isn't going to be taken seriously and that the therapist must call for an ISH to come out. He offered the intriguing concept that the therapist must be in good contact with his own Inner Self, if an ISH is to emerge, since his Inner Self is in constant communication with the patient's Inner Self. In Adam's survey, 50% of the respondents indicated that MPDs may have more than one ISH and 58% indicated that each unitary person (non-multiple) had a part of themselves which is similar to an ISH.

In another paper presented at the 1987 International Conference on MPD, G. A. Fraser proposed that there can be more than one ISH, but only one ISH truly is the core or central self helper. He suggested that the latter should be called the Central ISH and proposed that it was present in all cases of MPD. Fraser cautioned that it is possible to miss the presence of a Central ISH unless it is carefully investigated.

Employing somewhat similar language, Christine Comstock (1987) described the highest of the helping personalities as The Center. Comstock indicated that she envisions Centers as:

> Separate beings within a person to help them through the life time. A Center is not the unconscious mind in the Ericksonian tradition, it is not the soul and it is certainly not just another personality. A Center is more like a personified energy vortex, it has a definite individuality and has access to knowledge and abilities far beyond our own . . . Centers have no age and few needs of their own. (pp. 3–4)

Comstock described several unusual abilities possessed by Centers. Besides being the repository of all information about the MPD's lifetime, they can: begin flash backs, collapse time, blend two personalities together to provide some help to the weaker one, build inside walls to separate the personalities, grow up personalities or help a person to grow down, and they can also create dreams to provide needed insights. Comstock made reference to the unusual communication abilities of Centers and gave some examples of Center to Center communication. She states "Whatever it is called, it is present, useful and mysterious" (p. 11):

> The replication of physical sensations or feelings of the multiple in the therapist is another mysterious communication . . . In session a therapist may feel light headed, have a numb hand, an ache, feel sudden fear or any other feeling. All these feelings are important clues as to what is transpiring within the multiple. (p. 12)

In her paper at the 1987 MPD conference, Comstock indicated that she had worked with 65 MPD clients. She described another interesting example of Center to Center interaction where the therapist could offer energy for the Center to take when the Center was temporarily fatigued. Her own technique involved "imagining that I take off the top of my head and the bottoms of my feet to allow a golden-white-iridescent light to flow through me unimpeded. The Center does whatever needs to be done to take the energy." As is evident in Comstock's remarks, a very special relationship can develop between a therapist and the Center of an MPD. Allison (1978) has remarked: "There is no human to human relationship with which to compare this partnership. It is so unique a relationship it has to be experienced to be believed" (p. 12).

Acceptance of the ISH phenomena has become extensive enough so that a recent text book, *Diagnosis and Treatment of Multiple Personality*

Disorder, by Putnam (1989) devotes three pages to what he calls the "Internal Self Helper." He indicates that the importance placed on identifying and working with the ISH varies with different therapists. Putnam's own view is that he tries to incorporate the advice of an ISH if he feels he is talking to a genuine ISH, but cautions that there can be "ISH impostors" who can give misleading or destructive advice. He says:

> It is important to listen to these voices of inner wisdom, but it is a mistake to view them as all-knowledgeable or all-powerful. When one is struggling with a difficult patient, one often wishes for some miraculous intervention, and I think that this wish is what leads some therapists to ascribe omniscience to ISHs. (p. 204)

A fascinating description of an encounter with a Center "trinity" is given by Robert Mayer in his recent book *Through Divided Minds* (1988). Several of his MPD cases are discussed, but his major attention focused on a female patient called Toby. Mayer was becoming extremely frustrated and desperate because he felt he was not making much therapeutic progress. He had recently read Allison's book *Minds in Many Pieces* and began to develop some hope that Allison's description of ISHs might prove to be beneficial in his own treatment of Toby. He inquired if such a helper were available inside. A few weeks later he was confronted by a voice which declared: "We are the Dark Ones." They claimed that there were three of them, interchangeable but different, but that they spoke as one. He devoted an entire chapter to "the Dark Ones." He provided some examples of dialogue between him and the Dark Ones. When he asked where they came from, they replied that they came from "beyond." When he asked who they were, they indicated that they had been sent to help Toby. Below is an excerpt of one exchange between Mayer and the Dark Ones:

> "Who sent you?"
> "We were sent by the Archangel Michael. We suspect that you know who he is."
> "You mean to tell me that you are some sort of angel or spirit that lives in the spirit world?"
> "That is correct."
> "Are you assigned specifically to her, or do you float from one person to the next?"
> " 'Float' is trite and shows a lack of understanding of the spiritual world. We are assigned to her, but we wish to caution you, we are not part of her, so do not think about integrating us."

I felt that they had read my mind. I had been talking about integration with Toby from time to time and was just thinking about what I will do about the Dark Ones when it came their time to merge. "I don't understand," I said.

"Haven't you ever heard of guardian angels? You have one also."

"I'm not aware of it."

"That is because your spiritual awareness is that of a flea."

"What happens when Toby dies?"

"We are assigned elsewhere."

Our conversation went on like this for a while. I was chided for my lack of spirituality. They argued that in dilemmas of this nature in which one has to make a leap into faith. They held Buber and Kirkegaard up as models for me. Hadn't I ever prayed to God for help? they wondered, implying that I knew of a God but that I thought of him as a Santa Claus. What did I think happened to the soul after the body dies? They treated me with patronizing disdain. (pp. 158–159)

The Dark Ones explained that they had been around since Toby's childhood and that they had created the machinery that Toby used to create other personalities to help absorb the pain from her numerous childhood traumas and abuses. The Dark Ones continued to help Mayer in his therapy and Toby eventually achieved integration. Mayer came to rely heavily upon them and actually urged them to stay around for a year after integration to make sure that Toby was really all right. They told him they would be available if they were ever needed and encouraged him to develop his spiritual side so that he would be more accessible to his own Dark Ones. He reported that although Toby was Jewish, whenever she passed a church she felt compelled to enter and light a candle for one of the archangels.

Another account of a mysterious source of guidance can be found in *When Rabbit Howls*, a book written jointly by the 92 personalities who collectively call themselves "the Troops" of Truddi Chase (1987). The therapist working with them, Robert Phillips, Jr., reported numerous instances of feeling that several of the personalities could read his mind. When he inquired about how they did this, he was told, "We don't read minds. We get right into them. We've been in yours" (p. 393). Reference is also made to various electrical disturbances occurring such as fuses blowing and appliances stopping when certain mental states of the patient appeared (pp. 296-297). The therapist would sometimes find his belief system challenged by one of the alter personalities, as in the following passage:

But have you ever wondered how real your world actually is? As you sit there, you perceive things in a certain way and assume all of it is real. That's only natural; it's your frame of reference. But how can you be sure that somewhere another world doesn't truly exist wherein your reality, as you perceive it, is just as ridiculous, or at least as strange, as your perceive ours to be? (p. 358)

The Center was called Ean, an ancient Irish warrior, who introduced "the woman" to an experience of timeless, spaceless, brilliant white light on one occasion and who provided lively and humorous philosophical discourses on the meaning of life. The therapist was clearly challenged by what he had witnessed and in the epilogue raised this question:

Who is Ean, really? He seems to be part of the Troops—yet also is separate from them. It is said that Ean sits "above." He works powerfully behind the scenes to choreograph the comings and goings of the Troops, and he emanates great energy. It is also said of him that he is not only of this time but also timeless. The power of Ean appears to be beyond this time and place, but what does that mean? Are we seeing into the realm of what modern persons call psychic phenomena, or are we viewing the vestiges of past lives? Perhaps we are peering into a world of which we cannot conceive, and are privileged to go beyond our senses into the world of the spiritual. (p. 412)

My own challenging firsthand experiences with the world of the spiritual and psi manifestations in MPD began in August 1987 when I first met Susanna. She had been admitted as a psychiatric impatient to our hospital and remained there for five weeks. After discharge, I worked with her professionally for nearly a year and then continued to see her regularly on a friendship basis after her insurance was canceled. During this two year interval I witnessed and experienced an endless number of psi experiences.

Most of the psi manifestations were associated with Katherine, who presented as a spiritual entity sent from The Source to facilitate eventual integration of Susanna's personalities. So far I have encountered 11 personalities. Two are child personalities, one is an adolescent, and the others are adults. One is a male and one is an apparent discarnate spirit. Katherine insists that she is not a part of Susanna and I do not include Katherine as being one of the personalities, as it has become abundantly clear to me that her existence is definitely not bound by any physical parameters and her origin cannot be accounted for by any psychodynamic factors, as can the other personalities.

Katherine, who speaks with an unusual accent, has explained that she was sent to facilitate Susanna's integration because Susanna will carry out important service work that will benefit many others in the future. Although significant progress has occurred, Susanna is still a long way from integration. Katherine was Susanna's confirmation name and Katherine says she selected it for herself because of its spiritual significance to Susanna.

As would be expected from any respectable ISH or Center, Katherine has total awareness of every facet of Susanna's past and current life and often makes predictions about her future actions which are always extremely accurate. Availability of such detailed personal information about Susanna's personality might be explained along non-parapsychological lines but Katherine apparently also has total awareness of every facet of my life.

She has described numerous details of my past life which would be unknown to Susanna and precognitively knows what topics I wish to discuss with her before I introduce them into our conversation. Katherine gently chides me whenever I do not offer a full and honest self-disclosure in discussing my current attitudes or behaviors. Her sensitivity for detecting half truths has forced me to be more candid about myself than I have ever been in any other interpersonal situation, including my own psychotherapy. She has said that it is important for me "to develop knowledge of Self" so that I can grow individually and also better assist Susanna with her growth.

Katherine has also given me valuable non-judgmental insights about the character of people that I interact with in various settings and has also given me accurate information about the future actions of others, such as members of Susanna's family, that might have implications for Susanna's welfare. If someone has been particularly helpful or supportive to Susanna, Katherine has occasionally been willing to provide brief consultations, which have always been described by that person as yielding significant personal insights.

When it was important for Susanna's therapy, Katherine has been able to mentally intervene and arrange events so that therapy can proceed. The first such example I encountered was while Susanna was still an inpatient. The staff had made arrangements for Susanna to have skull x-rays taken at a hospital five miles away one afternoon. I had hoped to spend that time in therapy with Susanna. Katherine came out and indicated that the therapy time would be more important that afternoon and told me she "would take care of" the scheduled neurology appointment. I began the therapy session expecting we would be interrupted at any minute, but we never were. The neurologist had phoned to say that he had decided to change his examination until the following day. I thought that perhaps it might have been a happy co-incidence, but there were many subsequent occasions when Susanna was suddenly given unscheduled days off from work which allowed she and I to proceed with some timely and important phase of therapy that Katherine had indicated should be a priority. When I asked Katherine how she accomplished this, she said that she was able to enter into the employer's or other significant figure's mind and simply redirect their thinking so that it would be compatible with our plans. Instances of this type became so numerous that it was impossible to think of them as happy coincidences.

I can't determine whether my own chain of thoughts has ever been directly influenced by Katherine, but there have been many occasions when I subjectively experienced marked changes in my moods or energy level. During times of great anxiety, I would suddenly experience a tremendous feeling of peace and tranquillity emerge or I would feel an enormous surge of energy and laser beam concentration for some important task if I had been sleepless, physically exhausted and de-spairing about my ability to successfully accomplish the task.

Dreams are another mental landscape which Katherine can influence. Susanna, along with one adult and one child alter personality, have reported dreams to me in which they saw and experienced Katherine. She was described as being of indeterminant sex, often in a flowing gown, radiating bright light, and providing soothing feelings of peace-fulness to the dreamer. They said they sensed a flow of love emanating from Katherine which created a sense of joy and hope for them. Ac-cording to Katherine, dreams are a channel which are often used by spiritual beings to send imagery which will facilitate spiritual awareness and personal growth.

I observed several examples of psychokinesis which were impressive to me. On one occasion, while walking with Susanna on a recently storm-ravaged beach still displaying large hills and gullies of sand, I casually dropped a thin flat seashell type object somewhat resembling a silver dollar that I had been looking at. It began to roll along on its edge, down through the gullies and up over the hills and continued to roll for a distance of 50 or 60 feet. There were strong cross currents of winds still blowing at the time which made the balancing and forward progress of the object against the wind even more impressive. I kept exclaiming "Wow" to myself over and over as I observed this phenom-enon. At the conclusion of the object's long journey, Katherine came out, smiled at me, and said, "I thought you would enjoy that." Another occasion involved a small rectangular strip of spongy plastic used in an electric dryer for softening clothes and reducing static. I was sitting in my living room talking to Katherine when suddenly this object appeared on the chair. It was tied in an extremely tight knot. I have tried several times to tie one of these small strips into a similarly tight knot and have been unable to succeed. Katherine was smiling at my puzzlement and made a comment that the perception of reality held by human beings was a very limited one and that many things were possible which would be categorized as impossible from a material viewpoint. These and other similar PK demonstrations were apparently intended by Katherine to stretch my boundaries of belief as to what was physically possible. My boundaries were definitely stretched and I came to realize how much we are prisoners of our narrow conceptions as to what is or what can be.

In addition to my contact with the positive healing energy emanating from Katherine, I have also encountered the negative destructive energy associated with demonic possession. One of Susanna's alter personalities, Susy, became very guilty and self-punitive and on several occasions sensed a threatening presence that she felt wanted to enter her. Her dog would act erratically at these times and eventually slink out of the room. Since Susy prided herself on not being afraid of anyone or anything, she felt this "creature" was challenging her for control and she accepted the challenge by allowing it into her body. That turned out to be a bad mistake and this evil entity gradually began to take increasing control of her and also of Susanna. This situation escalated to a dangerous level and Katherine said an exorcism would be necessary and told me she would help me with it. I assembled some volunteers who were willing, out of altruistic love, to assist me at what turned out to be an extraordinary six day event in an isolated rural setting. This entity displayed knowledge of a surprising amount of personal, embarrassing information about each team member and used this knowledge publicly to exploit each individual's points of vulnerability in an effort to discourage their further participation. This ordeal was exhausting for everyone involved and turned out to be successful after the key personalities eventually accepted God.

At the conclusion of the exorcism, Susanna's body was horribly bruised after having been tied to the four corners of a bed for most of the time while being subjected to violent thrashing and twisting during possession. In between bouts of possession, Susanna would be allowed time out of bed, but she would fairly quickly become possessed again and team members would be violently assaulted. It would require at least three team members to wrestle her back into bed and place her wrists and ankles in restraints. While restrained, she would often manage to bite her arms and shoulders and team members who came too close were often also bitten or scratched. It seemed as if almost all of Susanna's body contained huge black and blue or yellowish-brown bruises. She was very concerned about her appearance because she was afraid it would frighten her children when they saw her. Katherine, who had provided critical guidance during the exorcism, told me that she would offer Susanna "a gift" which would enable the bruises to disappear by the end of the next day. Ordinarily, it would take close to a month for one of Susanna's bruises to heal, but as Katherine had promised, Susanna's body was free of bruises by the end of the next day.

My experience with the paranormal abilities demonstrated by the evil or demonic spirit have emphasized for me that consideration has to be given to the goal for which psi is utilized. Psi does not appear in a vacuum; it can be used for growth and healing or it can be used for destructive purposes. The issue of intent is of paramount importance. Psi can facilitate personal integration or personal disintegration.

I think MPD offers a definite challenge to parapsychologists. There is ample anecdotal material to suggest that a treasure chest of psi riches is available to the explorer who is willing, in an "Indiana Jones" fashion, to encounter one frightening opponent or risky situation after the other in pursuit of the treasure. One of the potentially sinister assassins lurks in the abyss called the unconscious. Everyone, parapsychologists included, dreads too direct a confrontation with this fire breathing dragon that resides within the investigator as well as in the subject, but it cannot be avoided since there is a wide consensus among parapsychologists that psi has its origin in the unconscious.

Parapsychologists seem to generally prefer experiments in which there is only a hint or whisper from the unconscious detectable in their results and they are ingeniously clever in developing experimental designs that will have no meaningful personal consequences for the experimental participant. Perhaps the researcher may get a publishable paper from the results, but the experimental subject can expect nothing more than a "thank you" for his or her involvement. By way of contrast, the unconscious appears not with a whisper, but with a loud shout and sledge-hammer directness in cases of MPD and the eventual stakes are either life threatening or life enhancing for them. Will their existence remain that of surviving as broken glass shards throughout their lifetime, or will they discover some force or helpful source of energy that will enable them to someday look into the mirror of self-reflection and perceive only a single, solitary figure with observable dimensionality visible to them? Will healing light eventually shine into the previously

dark and undetected chambers of a tortured mind or will the door
blocking that light remain permanently bolted?

I don't feel it's necessary to engage in a protracted discussion as to
whether the source of the light comes from a distant power station or
whether it is produced by an internal generator. In my view, which
has certainly changed during my 35-year involvement with organized,
professional parapsychology, the analogy of psi and light is a comfortable one or, to make a forced pun, an illuminating one. Psi helps us to
see and guides us in our efforts to achieve wholeness or individuation
and also facilitates our developing fuller and more satisfying relationships with others, if we have a deep and sincere intent to do so. The
force field or atmosphere through which this light travels is love, and
if love is not present, psi can be used to produce alienation.

I recently rediscovered Rhea White's Presidential Address delivered
in 1984. There are many themes that she presented in it which strike
a very resonant chord for me. She felt it was time to abandon the
procedures pioneered by Rhine and to discover ways of developing
what she called a "depth parapsychology." She proposed that psi is
most likely to be encountered in situations where change is imminent
such as in stages of relationships of lovers to each other, the creator
with his or her product, or in the therapist/patient relationship when
a new level is about to be reached (p. 171). I particularly like her
speculative comment: "It is my guess psi happens where there is growth.
It feeds on, it may even flourish under, the conditions of growth" (p.
184). She reminded us that "We hardly ever 'sit down like a child'
before the data nature has given us" (p. 179). White also encouraged
investigators "to stand for their experiences" (p. 174).

I feel I am attempting to display both of the postures advocated by
White. I have sat as a child before the intriguing data that nature has
given us in cases of MPD and made an effort to comprehend it in a
fashion that makes sense for me and I am also "standing for my experiences." When I first encountered Katherine, it was a very bewil-
dering and unsettling experience for me. Before it occurred, I could
never have imagined that I would be sharing the type of information
that I am presenting in this paper with you, but these experiences *did*
happen and I "stand" for them.

REFERENCES

Allison, R. (1974). A new treatment approach for multiple personalities. *American Journal
of Clinical Hypnoses, 17*, 15–32.
Allison, R. (1978). A rational psychotherapy plan for multiplicity. *Svensk Tidskrift fur
Hypnos, 3–4*, 9–16.

Allison, R. (1980). *Minds in many pieces.* New York: Rawson, Wade.

Beahrs, J. (1982). *Unity and multiplicity.* New York: Brunner/Mazel.

Boor M., & Coons, P. M. (1983). A comprehensive bibliography of literature pertaining to multiple personality. *Psychological Reports, 53,* 295–310.

Braude, S. (1988). Mediumship and multiple personality. *Journal of the Society for Psychical Research, 55,* 177–195.

Comstock, C. (1987). Internal self helpers or centers. *Integration, 3,* 3–12.

Crapanzano, V., & Garrison, V. (Eds.). (1977). *Case studies in spirit possession and multiple personality.* New York: Wiley.

Crabtree, A. (1985). *Multiple man: Explorations in possession and multiple personality.* New York: Praeger.

Damgaard, J., Van Benschoten, S., & Fagen, J. (1985). An updated bibliography of literature pertaining to multiple personality. *Psychological Reports, 57,* 131–137.

Ebon, M. (1974). *The devil's bride. Exorcism: Past and present.* New York: Harper & Row.

Ellenberger, H. (1970). *The discovery of the unconscious.* New York: Basic Books.

Goodman, F. (1981). *The exorcism of Anneliese Michel.* Garden City, N.Y: Doubleday.

Hawksworth, H. (1977). *The five of me.* Chicago: Henry Regnery.

Hilgard, E. (1977). *Divided consciousness: Multiple controls in human thought and action.* New York: Wiley.

Honorton, C. (1977). Psi and internal attention states. In B. B. Wolman (Ed.). *Handbook of parapsychology* (pp. 435–472). New York: Van Nostrand Reinhold.

Hyslop, J. H. (1917). The Doris case of multiple personality: Part III. *Proceedings of the American Society for Psychical Research, 11,* 5–866.

Kenny, M. G. (1981). Multiple personality and spirit possession. *Psychiatry, 44,* 337–358.

Keyes, D. (1981). *The minds of Billy Milligan.* New York: Random House.

Krippner, S. (1986). Cross-cultural approaches to multiple personality disorder: Therapeutic practices in Brazilian spiritism. *The Humanistic Psychologist, 14,* 176–193.

Martin, M. (1977). *Hostage to the devil.* New York: Bantam Books.

Mayer, R. (1988). *Through divided minds.* New York: Doubleday.

McAll, R. (1982). *Healing the family tree.* London: Sheldon Press.

Mischel, W. & Mischel F. (1958). Psychological aspects of spirit possession. *American Anthropologist, 60,* 249–260.

Montgomery, J. W. (Ed.). (1976). *Demon possession: A medical, historical, anthropological, and theological symposium.* Minneapolis: Bethany House.

Osterreich, T. K. (1974). *Possession and exorcism.* New York: Causeway.

Pattison, E. & Wintrob, R. (1981). Possession and exorcism in contemporary America. *Journal of Operational Psychiatry, 12,* 13–20.

Peck, M. (1983). *People of the lie.* New York: Simon Schuster.

Pelton, R. (1977). *The devil and Karen Kingston.* New York: Pocket Books.

Prince, M. (1906). *The dissociation of a personality.* New York: Longmans.

Prince, W. F. (1915). The Doris case of multiple personality. *Proceedings of the Society for Psychical Research, 9* (Part I), 1–700.

Prince, W. F. (1916). The Doris case of multiple personality. *Proceedings of the Society for Psychical Research, 9* (Part II), 701–1419.

Putnam, F. (1984). The psychophysiologic investigation of multiple personality disorder: A review. *Psychiatric Clinics of North America, 7,* 31–39.

Putnam, F. (1989). *Diagnosis and treatment of multiple personality disorder.* New York: Guilford Press.

Putnam, F., Guroff, J., Silberman, E., Barban, L., & Post, R. (1986). The clinical phenomenology of multiple personality disorder: A review of 100 recent cases. *Journal of Clinical Psychiatry, 47,* 285–293.

Rogo, D. S. (1987). *The infinite boundary.* New York: Dodd, Mead.

Rosenbaum, M. (1980). The role of schizophrenia in the decline of the diagnosis of multiple personality. *Archives of General Psychiatry, 37,* 1383–1385.

Schreiber, F. R. (1973). *Sybil.* New York: Henry Regnery.

Sizemore, C. & Pittillo, E. (1977). *I'm Eve.* New York: Doubleday.

Taylor, E. (1982). *William James on exceptional mental states: The 1986 Lowell lectures.* New York: Scribner's.
Van de Castle, R. (1977). Sleep and dreams. In B. B. Wolman (Ed.), *Handbook of parapsychology* (pp. 473–499). New York: Van Nostrand Reinhold.
White, R. (1985). The spontaneous, the imaginal and psi: Foundations for a depth parapsychology. In R. White & J. Solfvin (Eds.), *Research in parapsychology 1984* (pp. 166–190). Metuchen, NJ: Scarecrow Press.
Yap, P. M. (1960). The possession syndrome: A comparison of Hong Kong and French findings. *Journal of Mental Science, 106,* 114–137.

DISCUSSION

PARKER: I thought your presentation was most fascinating and most enlightening. There's a book coming out in Britain, if I remember correctly, by R. Aldridge-Morris[20] who claims that no multiple personalities have been found in Britain. Having interviewed psychologists and psychiatrists, he compares the situation with the United States and he tries to come up with an explanation in terms of cognitive theory and social identity theory. It seems as though there is a skeptical branch in the research in this area. How would you explain that there are those that don't apparently encounter the same sort of phenomena as you encounter?

VAN DE CASTLE: I received very little training in this area. I'm a clinical psychologist, but I encountered nothing with regard to anything to do with MPD in any of my graduate training or in any of my professional work. There certainly is some definite skepticism. We have a large psychiatric inpatient unit, 40 beds, at the University of Virginia which is a very prestigious medical school in the United States. We've been running those wards for many years. When Susanna was admitted, they would not accept that it was a diagnosis of multiple personality disorder—borderline personality, fine; hysterical personality, fine, anything but not multiple personality. So it wasn't until several of the personalities emerged and proceeded to get the staff rather upset that they eventually did accept it and the discharge diagnosis was multiple personality disorder. I tried within this paper to review the whole history of dissociation and it has not been a very popular topic. It dropped out after Janet and after Freud came in with the notion of repression. Freud ruled out that there could be such a thing as co-consciousness. I know that there is such a thing, in my experience, there is co-con-

---

[20] Aldridge-Morris, R. (1989). *Multiple personality: An exercise in deception.* London: Lawrence Erlbaum.

sciousness, certainly working with Susanna. One of her alter personalities, Susy, always knows exactly what's happening with Susanna as
well as what is happening with herself. She is able to speak to Susanna
internally and they can carry on a dialogue. So, co-consciousness can
exist. There are lots of statements that Freud has made that I would
not agree with, but I think because the notion of repression held sway
for so long, dissociation fell out of favor. I think it is coming back now,
because of post-traumatic stress disorder. Lots of Vietnam veterans
are manifesting symptoms that are simply explained by dissociation. I
think the remark made earlier today about Freud is relevant here.
Stories from female patients, who reported having been sexually abused
as young girls, would always be dismissed because this was their wished
for desire but it never really happened. We find that with MPD; about
80% of all MPDs report a history of sexual abuse as children, and a
higher percentage would be of physical abuse. If you have seen and
encountered an MPD, it can be a very extraordinary, and for many
people, a very uncomfortable and disarming experience. So I think if
when you trained, none of your professors accepted it, you've never
seen it, you've never had a chance to do rounds and encounter it, I
don't think you're as skillful about asking the right questions. If you
ask about black outs, for example, "Have people started to talk to you
as if they knew you and seemed to have some previous interaction, but
you don't know who they are?" By asking similar kinds of questions
you find that it is, I think, more common. So, in the United States
there are now three or four standard text books, Putnam's and others,
that have come out on it. Ever since 1984 there has been an Annual
International Conference in Chicago. Last year 1,000 people attended
it. In the United States, the estimates would be that there are at least
30,000 MPD patients. Usually in our country, things go from California
across the country; maybe eventually, it will move from the United
States to Britain. I don't know. I can say from personal experience,
it's there; it's very real, and it definitely exists.

NEPPE: Do you have any feelings about whether or not those patients
with multiple personality disorder who have previous histories of
marked sexual abuse, for example, have any different kinds of presen-
tations from the perspective of possible psi experiences? Do these people
also exhibit the same kinds of control that you were talking about, or
are we talking about a completely separate group? I have several questions, but that is my first one.

VAN DE CASTLE: I don't know that anyone has ever tried to break
it down along those lines, Vernon. It's accepted that most cases, not
every, but most cases of MPD have had childhood sexual abuse. So,

because it's such a high percentage you more or less have to make the statement that most MPDs are going to present in that fashion.

NEPPE: The second question is the differentiation between multiple personality disorder and patients with some fragmentation of personality. I have seen several patients whom I would regard as multiple personality disorders, but I also see patients who I would tend to label as having "fragmented personalities" and many of these people have underlying temporal lobe dysfunction. Have you got any comments in that regard?

VAN DE CASTLE: The DSM-III-R has very specific criteria. They try to narrow it down, to make a much narrower window as to what the criteria are to grant an MPD diagnosis. As far as fragments, if you have a multiple personality disorder, the average number of personalities with the multiple would be about 15, but that's the mean. The median would be about eight. The reason it gets to be as high as 15 is because there are some like Truddi Chase who claim 92 personalities, so those boost up the average. But if you get very many personalities, say beyond 10, some of those are likely to be very fragmented, very specific. They could manifest to carry out one particular, limited activity. It could be just a work personality or one to deal with a very narrow life issue for them, and they don't have a whole, full, rich complexity of detailed memory and a more autonomous ego. They seem to come up in response to a limited situation, operate during that time, and then do not manifest very much after that.

NEPPE: Now, how would you differentiate those personality fragmentations from mediumistic experiences, trance-like experiences, or dissociative experiences, where the person may or may not be manifesting differences in behavior? You may be asking, "Is that personal? Is it some kind of entity?"

VAN DE CASTLE: Good question, and a difficult one. I guess if I were to try and answer it, most mediums would seem during their usual daily routine to have a sense of individualized ego. When it comes time to do a reading or to go into trance, they would then, at that point, voluntarily, consciously, go through whatever their induction procedure would be. Some may recall the content of what they said, generally they do not. It seems that those trance personalities that come through don't really assist them very much with life maintenance behavior. In the case of a multiple, the different kinds of personalities each seem to have some function. One which is a minus function over here, is taken as a plus function by another. They are needed throughout the day or they are needed whenever the occasion would call for it. It isn't as if the main or host personality gives them permission to do it. Often the main personality is taken over unwillingly, and does not wish to have that happen. So, the difference would be the control aspects of mediumship; a time and place is chosen by the medium and what happens during the mediumistic trance does not influence the general overall everyday behavior. Whereas in MPD a personality would come out in response to whatever would be the stress and would be necessary in order to provide the ability for the MPD to survive by having the different facets represented.

NEPPE: The final part of this question relates to my limited experience. I have seen two different kinds of multiple personality disorder. The one seems to be the dissociative kind, where the splitting seems to be a splitting down the middle of cognition, affect, and volitional functions all split together. The other is the kind that seems to exist within the framework of a schizophrenic history and a schizophrenic diagnosis. Would you think that this differentiation is a legitimate one?

VAN DE CASTLE: Probably so, because having a diagnosis of MPD is often not an exclusive one. Many of them will carry a secondary diagnosis of some type: an eating disorder, a diagnosis of borderline personality, or schizophrenia. So it is not a nice, clean pigeonhole to place people in. Some of those with schizophrenia could seem to have that kind of a presentation, but I think the vast majority of MPDs would not be considered to come under the schizophrenic label. There are marked differences between the personalities, as I tried to bring out in Putnam's NIMH study, in terms of what their characteristics are, what they can do, and the differences in brain wave activity. But, within each personality, their view of reality is appropriate and congruent with the organizing mode for that personality.

WEST: I'd like to follow up on a previous question. Is there an analogy between spontaneous multiple personalities and the induced experiences of recollections of previous lives produced by hypnosis? I have heard it suggested that in actual cases of spontaneous multiple personalities, the use of hypnosis might, in fact, increase the dissociation and produce still more personalities than existed spontaneously. I have a second comment on this question of child sexual abuse and various psychiatric conditions, I have to tell you that I can hardly find any psychiatric condition these days which is not allegedly associated with child sexual abuse. I have read recent reports suggesting that 90% of both male and female prostitutes have been sexually abused as children. There is a researcher in Cambridge who finds sexual abuse in the histories of schizophrenics. We have reports of the same thing in eating disorders and also in addicts. I have also recently read an interesting American study which suggests that at least 50% of rapists in prison report that they had been sexually abused by women when they were boys. I just think that one has to regard the association of multiple personalities and child sexual abuse in the same light as one regards all these reported links.

VAN DE CASTLE: Concerning the first comment on hypnosis, this has been one of the counter claims made against MPD, that it doesn't exist, that it is iatrogenic and is created by the therapist utilizing hypnosis. Hypnosis is generally the preferred treatment modality for MPD because with hypnosis you can go back and regress, and frequently encounter the traumatic material which they can then re-experience, have the catharsis, and subsequently incorporate and integrate it. There have been several studies, such as those by Kluft, Putnam, and others, indicating they feel this would be an extremely small percentage; my impression is that certainly under 5% of any of the kind of MPD phenomena could be attributable to the therapist engaging in hypnosis and creating the personalities. The other comment about the widespread reports of sexual abuse, I don't think we should negate it with MPD. In both Kluft's and Putman's theories about why people develop MPD, one of their criteria would be that the person has to have the biological predisposition towards dissociative phenomena. Then, if there is a traumatic experience, which would be the sexual abuse, and there is no benign consistently supportive available figure during those times, MPD may eventually be created. So, you have to have the necessary preconditions—the tendency toward dissociation. You also find a large percentage of people in pain management clinics who report sexual abuse as children. So that, if you somatize and you were abused, then you will develop these other kinds of somatic disturbances in response to the abuse, because they may not have the ability to dissociate. So, someone would have to have a dissociative tendency as a precursor in order for the MPD pattern to follow.

KRAMER: I was interested in the relation between MPD and psychic abilities. During your lecture you said that one of the personalities possessed psychic powers. Do you know of any similarities between those personalities who possess psychic power? For instance, do they have the same personalities, or, do they have the same behavior, or, perhaps do you find the same facial expression?

VAN DE CASTLE: I don't know of any work that's been done on that. To my knowledge, this is the first time a paper has been presented specifically on the psi aspects of MPD. There have not been any at any MPD conferences because I think when you're carrying a big basket of eggs in one hand, you don't want to simultaneously take on another big basket of eggs in the other hand. MPD is controversial and psi, in some quarters, is controversial. So trying to carry both of those baskets at the same time is not going to help to win the popularity contest of the year. One of the possibilities that might lead to MPD is that very often, you'll find that the host personality has a rather idealistic view of their early life, of their family, and of people in general. They will be unacquainted with any of the details of the childhood abuse. Then you'll usually find an alter personality who has exquisite memory of each and every one of those abusive incidents. That alter personality learns very early on to develop very sensitive antennae because they never know when something is going to happen that is physically or emotionally painful for them. They have to learn to pick up on the slightest little twist of the lips or look to the eyes, because that may mean they are going to get struck or whatever would be the trauma. It may be that they have so sensitized themselves to try and tune in for self survival, that they can become aware of cues ahead of time, so they can hide or do some other sort of self protective maneuver. In other words, they may have had to develop whatever may be the latent psi ability that we all possess. But I don't know of any studies that have ever tried to look at it because as I say, outside of Arthur Ellison's comments, some that I'm making today, and a few that I've included in the paper, it has been a totally neglected topic.

KRAMER: When a client has 10 or more personalities, do you find that there are one or two personalities who have psi abilities, and do they differ in the amount of psi abilities? For instance, do you find one personality has slight psi abilities, and another personality has strong psi abilities?

VAN DE CASTLE: If I exclude Katherine, because I don't feel she is a personality, I feel that the description by Comstock of an energy vortex makes more sense to account for her, then I would say in connection with Susanna, that it would be Susy who had the knowledge of the abuse, who seems to have a psychic talent. I would say that there are no psi manifestations with any of the others. Susy claims that she can look into your eyes and tell you about your character. I have come to accept that because I tend to be too trusting, which always frustrates her. Several times she has looked into somebody's eyes, and told me she sees something undesirable. I have learned to pay a lot of attention to that. That doesn't necessarily mean it's psychic; it could be these minimal postural and facial cues that I have not been sensitized to reading.

KRAMER: Is it possible that you can put it the other way around, that when people have a paranormal experience, they will have a short multiple personality?

VAN DE CASTLE: My understanding of it would be that this type of a spirit guide would be available in cases where the abuse had been very, very intense, but not every multiple would have this kind of a presence available. This presence, if we do some kind of metaphysical stretching here, doesn't seem to operate in the same ways and views of Western reality that as a scientist I had always used. I have found that I have to read other material such as *Seth Speaks* because Seth makes more sense to me than my fellow parapsychologists do. I can read it and find principles and possible explanations that get me more turned on and seem more congruent with what Katherine has said to me of what is the kind of ultimate reality. One quote that I didn't have time to read to you is in the book *When Rabbit Howls*. One of the alters comes through and addresses the therapist, "But have you ever wondered how real your world actually is? As you sit there, you perceive things in a certain way and assume all of it is real. That's only natural; it's your frame of reference. But how can you be sure that somewhere another world doesn't truly exist wherein your reality, as you perceive it, is just as ridiculous, or at least as strange, as you perceive ours to be." I think it's a very, very good question, and I think if you really stretch it that way, as I think that Arthur Ellison was saying earlier, if it doesn't fit with our particular conception, then it's automatically strange or weird. So, if there is this other kind of level of reality or other worlds, or an other kind of energy system that we're only getting hints about through parapsychology and maybe through contemporary physics, then it could well be that these multiples who have that energy available will eventually achieve integration. It won't necessarily be that quick. Katherine has told me that she could integrate Susanna instantly but it would be pointless because she would not have learned the things she needs to understand in this lifetime. Tomorrow it could fall apart again because she has not truly gone through the hard work and the pain of sorting out all those discrepant experiences that have caused her to be so fragmented. So it can still take a long time. I feel absolutely confident that I could look this audience in the eye and say, "Susanna will be integrated one of these days. I have absolute total faith because Katherine has said that." There have been several times I have had to literally risk my life, but have been willing to do it if Katherine says, "This is what you need to do." There has never yet been a single statement that has been inaccurate. With that kind of a track record, if she says, "This is what you have to do," I'm willing to put my life on the line.

NEPPE: How many statements has she made?

VAN DE CASTLE: Three hundred, I don't know. It is one of those things that I don't expect this group here, even though you are fellow parapsychologists, to accept. It was mind bending for me but after a while, it got through to me, and I finally said OK, I believe. Now, I would have thought as a parapsychologist I would have believed a long time ago. I was fairly successful as a telepathic dreamer at Maimonides and was able to select the correct target picture to a statistically significant degree, which is the big thing as far as parapsychologists are concerned. If you have a significant p-value, then it is something. If it is a personal experience, it is a nothing. I would have thought that the Maimonides experience would somehow have opened up the door but it didn't. I'd say that the door is wide open now. After being repeatedly bombarded with these kinds of experiences with Katherine, all I could do is just say, "I believe, I accept." I find that the group that gets most threatened by such statements are parapsychologists. I agree with some of Rhea White's statements that many parapsychologists are closet goats. I also agree with some of Keith Harary's comments today about a lot of clinical psychologists. If you look at their backgrounds, you find they have gone into the field because they have had serious questions about their own emotional stability and they have tried to intellectually work through that by a career in clinical psychology. I think a lot of parapsychologists are kind of intrigued, or as Keith suggested today, threatened by it. Just as the clinical psychologist attempts to do the intellectual exercises to deal with it at arm's distance across the therapeutic desk, I think a lot of parapsychologists attempt to deal with their phenomena as long as it's across the laboratory room. But when it comes too close and hits home, they don't like it.

I'm firmly convinced if I could now levitate, pass around this room six feet above you, and then pass out a sheet of paper for validating signatures, not many people are going to be willing to sign that you've really seen legitimate psychic phenomena. I really don't think we would get that many people willing to sign it. And if you did today, and you had the chance to think it over tonight, you might want to cross your name off tomorrow.

WICKRAM: I think your paper is a model of intellectual courage and of existential work. This kind of work seems inevitably reactive. You just can't leave it out there because it changes you as you investigate it. The question is, are there any models as a theoretical question? Are there any explanations or attempts to explain multiple personality in terms other than dissociation?

VAN DE CASTLE: There are a lot of models. One that was proposed and seems to be more in vogue in England is a role playing model: there's the one that Donald West suggested that it is all iatrogenic; it's all created purely by the hypnotherapist. There are others, Kenny who is an anthropologist, suggests that it is somehow a function of the particular culture, so that in his article on MPD and possession, he said that that is why psychical research is not very popular now because it was a passing fad, culturally accepted around the turn of the century, and it is now on the way out. MPD was popular in the last century. Many cases of it were reported, and is now on its way up. If you look through the accumulated literature, and you examine the 200 papers being presented at the International Conference each year in Chicago, these other theories don't seem very compelling.

WICKRAM: Most of those suggestions could be incorporated within different theories of hypnosis. Are there any neurological or psychophysiological theories of MPD?

VAN DE CASTLE: There have been some. I don't feel neurophysiologically sophisticated enough to try and capture them, but Bennett has done a survey article in which he tries to point out all the different types. One person who does a lot of work with hypnosis suggests that because they are such superb hypnotic subjects, they are, without realizing it, engaging in lots of self-hypnosis and creating all of these personalities themselves. So, one theory is the therapist is doing it. The other one is that they are doing it to themselves because of their extreme ability for self-hypnosis.

GENERAL DISCUSSION
DAY ONE

BENOR: Relating to Robert Van de Castle's work, healers and many mediums say that every person has an inner self helper and I'm wondering if you would consider that a possibility. Perhaps the people who have multiple personality disorder are very susceptible to hypnosis and maybe that inner self helper can be accessed more easily.

VAN DE CASTLE: I feel that probably all of us have an internal self helper. It gets to be a problem with definitions because sometimes the term ISH or inner self helper, is used to refer to a higher ego, an executive capacity within the personality. In that sense, we all have times when we function fully, totally, crisply, and with laser beam concentration. So sometimes in MPDs this higher executive capacity would be available as a more knowledgeable, more comprehensive memory system available within the MPD. Others talk about an ISH as being an energy vortex from outside that comes in a role similar to what we might call a guardian angel—to be there for the purpose of facilitating integration. That is why I like the term center as proposed by Comstock, because that, at least, in some way differentiates it from the ISH. So I would rather leave the ISH as being internally inclusive and try to reserve the term center for this additional energy vortex which is not a part of the personality but does have very comprehensive information and knowledge that seems to far transcend our usual means of communication and knowledge acquisition.

RONEY-DOUGAL: From what I can gather most of you here are working within psychiatry and psychotherapy. In the last two years, I have been teaching classes in parapsychology and quite a few of the people who come to my classes are actually suffering from clinical depression *and* they have psychic experiences. For me, as a teacher and as a parapsychologist, it is very difficult to know how best to help them integrate their psychic experiences as a normal psychological function. Some people experience it strongly and others do not. I have known people who suffered severe psychosis, there has been the seed of psychic experience behind whatever the delusion was. You can't deny the whole delusion because there's a seed of truth, a core of truth in it. But, what can I say to these people so that they can fully integrate the whole of that personality, including the psychic, so that their ability can be used most beneficially within our society? I look at the anthropological literature and I see that there are cases whereby somebody had an epileptic fit or psychotic breakdown, and would be trained to become a shaman. They used their ability within the society. I think psychiatrists and psychotherapists are our Western culture's shamans or witch doctors. What can be done to try to bring the positive out of very sensitive people? From what I can gather, these are supersensitive people, which is why their reality system is so different from this reality system. The reality system, as defined by Ian Tierney, is suffering, it seems to me from what I have called the white middle class male reality. The problem is, people really need help and where can they go to get it? What can we do to help them?

TIERNEY: That is really the question behind my paper—what do we do when we are faced with people who had this experience and are asking for help. My feeling, which is obviously changing with experience, is that all I can do is ask them about their experience and try and help them put it into some framework which they feel happy about. I'm not going to be involved in the nature of that framework, but try to help them find some way of accommodating it. I would probably use a system for testing their experience. In other words, suggesting that if A is the case, then how can we produce the situation again, so that it occurs again, that way we can be convinced that this is the case. To just collude with their belief, I feel, is probably dangerous.

NEPPE: It's a very difficult question, and there's no easy answer. I think one of the things that one has got to be certain about is the fact that any kind of psychotherapeutic intervention can be as much poison as food. In fact that psychotherapy is not all good. You use the phrase, "How can I get them to integrate their personalities?" Who says they should integrate their personalities? Who says they should be functioning at anything but the level that they are functioning? And every single patient needs to be individualized and evaluated appropriately so that it's logical to say, "They ought to be referred to a health care professional." The only problem with that logic is many health care professionals may perceive pathology where pathology does not necessarily exist and will not be able to handle those aspects of pathology that might exist. In other words, they may perceive as abnormal things that the person is experiencing as a normal phenomenon. The ultimate answer relates to education. But, this involves a far broader framework than just being able to give a pat answer.

RONEY-DOUGAL: I think it is dangerous to collude and also what you're not taking into account is that quite often the delusions, or whatever we care to call them, are causing a lot of people to suffer intensely during their lives because of things that they think are happening around them.

NEPPE: This is why I emphasize the need to individualize and refer the person out to the appropriate health care professional and not give a pat answer.

KRAMER: I'm afraid I cannot give you a clear-cut solution to your problem. The only thing I can say is that your question is recognized by me. I'm from Holland and we have the same problem over there. People turn to classes in parapsychology or become members of a parapsychology society seeking answers to personal problems. The problem is, where can you get them the counseling they need? The only thing I can say is that I think it is not a good idea to try to do counseling inside the classes, because I've learned that some teachers have tried to do that and it always brings out more problems than they can handle. I think it is wise in those circumstances to simply say that it's going too far and that it is better for them not to be a student with you anymore. Because it's not good for them, it's not good for you, and it's not good for your classes. They should try to find some professional help for that matter.

DIERKENS: The problem is frequently posed to us with youngsters. In fact, my wife is speaking in Brussels about how to help children and adolescents who have psi experiences because it is a problem. We find that small groups are good, and when they are youngsters, to try to involve the family. For instance, we try to see the father, the mother, and the child together, to speak with all the family members and not speak only to the youngster, or only to the wife, or only to the man because it is very often problems inside the family.

TIERNEY: In Edinburgh, we tried to use group methods for treating people with generalized anxiety and our experience was that it produced more problems than it solved. There were certain elements that you could approach that were common to these people, but in the main, most people had individual problems and they had to be dealt with individually. That's the flavor that came out of your comment and I think you would raise more problems than you would solve.

ELLISON: Two fairly quick questions for Robert Van de Castle. Katherine reminded me strongly of Jung's Philemon or Socrates' Damon—maybe an archetype from the collective unconscious which enables wisdom to flow out. I wonder what you might think about the psychosynthesis model of a human being (because we are all using mental models of human beings, aren't we?)—what do you think of that model of a human being? It is of course also a model of the universe if you are an idealist? Katherine is perhaps an aspect of the higher self—rather like I would describe the "Being of Light" in the near-death experience. I'd be happy to hear your views on that.

I have a much briefer question, concerning the clinical application regarding the changes in the physiological characteristics which you mentioned between different personalities. Willis Harman told me of a multiple personality case they were investigating at the University of California, in which one of the personalities was extremely myopic and needed very thick concave lenses to see, and the other personality could see perfectly well. I told a professor of ophthalmology about this, and she said, "Have they done a refraction?" Well, I've written twice to Willis to ask him, without any response. (I don't usually get a reply when I ask awkward questions.) So I wanted to ask you, don't those differing physiological characteristics have rather important implications for the medical treatment of the two personalities?

VAN DE CASTLE: I'll take the second one first because it's easier. There have been some research attempts by ophthalmologists to do the refractory tests. Some of those papers were reported in Chicago. The marked physiological differences between alter personalities are one of the reasons why it is so difficult to accept the concept of MPD. For example, over 33% of MPDs can have shifts in handedness. You can show demonstrably different EEGs between alter personalities. It is as if you have two brain systems in there. You have these clear-cut physiological discriminators, and when integration begins to occur, you find these EEGs start gradually fusing closer and closer together. The differences exist in medication responses; they exists in intelligence tests and personality tests. There's definitely evidence for the ophthalmological differences which are very clear-cut and involve a fairly large number of subjects.

With regard to how to conceptualize Katherine, I have certainly struggled and struggled as to what kind a label to put on it. I'm not sure that the label is truly important. I can only say from my personal experience, I'm absolutely, utterly convinced she is not an alter personality; she is not a subpart. She has made the statement that once integration is achieved her goal is accomplished. She said that this has been the third human that she's been sent to help achieve some kind of resolution to their emotional problems. The others were not MPDs, but they were other kinds of psychiatric cases. When she's successful with facilitating Susanna's integration, she'll go back and the "Source" will send her on a new assignment. It's hard for me who has spent 35 years in parapsychology to say that I think there could be such a thing as an angel. But it seems that that's the best concept we have in English to try and comprehend this kind of an energy system that seems to be relatively all knowing, is extremely kind, and in my perception, seems to be almost radiant. Others have commented on that. Other people, when she appears, will report spontaneously feeling tears coming to their eyes. So, there is a presence about her that seems to be quite different. Remember the quote from one of the alters in the Truddi Chase MPD case, "Who's to say what the conception of reality should be." When Katherine says that our conception is a very limited one, and there are much higher levels of interaction and energy involved, I'm willing to accept it because so far the kinds of explanations I, as a parapsychologist, could come up with are inexplicable and totally unsatisfactory. I don't know whether Jung's Philemon would have involved some sort of externalized energy source that was capable of entering into Jung or not. But I think my own views of psi are emerging along the lines that it can be here to facilitate not only self-actualization as in the case the Maslow, or individuation, in the Jungian sense, but it can also allow the person to expand and grow and move toward fulfillment. As the acorn moves toward becoming the mighty oak, I think psi can help us to move toward becoming a fuller functioning human being. Each time that happens with any one individual, I think there is a sort of incremental planetary actualization that occurs. So, to me, psi is in this larger scheme that you were hinting at, and is in some way energizing planetary evolution which we desperately need. Given the way things are going in terms of the nuclear threat and the ecology, we are in for some very bad times unless something starts turning it around. I'm not sure that psi experiments, as they are now carried out, are going to be very persuasive. In Rhea White's paper, she observed that when we poll top scientists, it's not on the basis of the research evidence that any of them accept ESP, it's a personal experience. If you have had it, it can produce a very dramatic shift in your belief system and orientation toward reality. We have over 100 years of the SPR publications and I still don't see scientists sitting down and saying, "Oh, now I see, given all this evidence, it's obvious that ESP exists." The laboratory evidence doesn't do it, not for most of them.

ELLISON: No one was ever convinced of anything via statistics. I can't persuade some fellow parapsychologists to walk across the road to see something which they consider impossible. I've had lots of genuine experiences. It's the old adage of "he who seeks shall find," isn't it? You have to start seeking sometime and the right place may not be in within a laboratory.

VAN DE CASTLE: Again, I refer to Rhea White's paper when she said that if someone comes up to a parapsychologist and opens up the conversation with a challenging statement, such as, "I've had a psychic experience," the battle is joined because the parapsychologist is going to work his or her damnedest to try and convince that person they have *not* had a psychic experience.

VON LUCADOU: I think that is a rather interesting point you made, and I will connect it with another question I want to discuss. Personally, I would say I have indeed had some personal experiences and personally I have no problems in believing that ESP may exist. However, the problem is that if we are doing the experiments and we still get rather poor results, so it makes it very difficult. I want to address one remark which was made by Professor West this morning and to some extent also raised by Serena Roney-Dougal, and that is the problem of how to deal with people who have paranormal experiences. Six months ago we started a counseling project in Germany. It seems to me that there are not two groups, but three. One group has had paranormal experiences, does not understand what happened and simply wants to get information about it. The second group has had paranormal experiences, has difficulty, and gets into more problems. Then there is the third group, who have not had paranormal experiences but they believe that they have. In the discussion I think Jean Dierkens said that the psychiatric cases probably may be just those paranormal cases we do not understand. Coming back to my initial remark, I think there is indeed a criterion which seems to me rather obvious. This criterion is that true paranormal phenomena have a different color or a different appearance than the pathological. They say that they always get these influences, these influences are constant, they never go away, and they are very much disturbed by them. Whereas those people who have real paranormal phenomena say, "Well, we feel something spontaneous. We cannot repeat it willingly. We cannot just push a button to produce these things; nevertheless they are there." I think from a theoretical point of view, the spontaneity of the paranormal effects might be the reason why it's so difficult to get them in experiments, because we want to push a button and that doesn't work.

VAN DE CASTLE: It may be tough to get them in experiments. I don't think it's that difficult to get them in experience, if you take the paradigm that I was proposing—that it has to be done in a loving context. If it's a growth related phenomena, then both parties have to grow from their participation, both experimenter and subject. I don't think our subjects grow from any of the kinds of experiences that we provide. I'll give you a model of one where I think that could operate. I think there is a strong case that can be made for demonstrating telepathic dreaming. The Maimonides protocol and the subsequent results, give very good evidence that you can have ESP in dreams. When I was a subject at that time, my goal was a purely narcissistic, egotistical one; I wanted to be the best damn dreamer they had ever had. Now, I don't think that really accomplishes much. But, if you could say, "OK, we accept that ESP occurs in dreams, how can we do an experiment so that everybody is going to benefit from it? How can we turn it into some kind of service that is helpful for all of us?" Henry Reed and I have devised what we call a dream helper ceremony. Rather than having a target picture, which someone is going to try and dream about, we have a target person. To be a target person one has to be willing to acknowledge that he or she has some emotional problem and would like help with it. We ask them not to give us the slightest clue as to the nature of the problem because we are going to discover it through our dreams. We then gather together about eight people that we call dream helpers. They sit with the person that night and then there would be some exchange. For example, if we were doing it and I was going to be the target person, I might let you wear my watch tonight. We try and provide the dream helpers with something containing the target person's energy. Then we would do something to try and unify the group. You could sit quietly; you could hold hands; you could pray; you could chant; or, you could do whatever you wish to somehow get the group together. Then all the dream helpers would go to bed that night and say, "I am not going to have my dreams tonight. I dedicate my dreams to X. I will not have any personal dreams tonight. My dreams will all be for this person." It's a great way to improve dream recall because you will cheat yourself out of your own dreams, but when these are not your dreams, and they're the other person's dreams, you won't cheat them of what you promised. When you get together the next morning, all the dream helpers start sharing their dreams. What you find if you listen sensitively, is that there's an interwoven fabric that develops, a warp and a woof that goes back and forth. You find certain things building up and building up. The target person is under no obligation to disclose anything but is usually overwhelmed because these eight people have been working all night long by getting up and writing down their dreams. They gave up something which is priceless; it is a unique contribution from each individual. The target person is the recipient of this love and of this personal gift from eight people. They frequently get tears in their eyes, they are so overwhelmed by this caring. The dream helpers like it because if it's more blessed to give than to receive, they have given this very special and unique part of themselves to another person. Everybody seems to benefit in that they frequently tune into what the problem is, and they can also tune into what may be the possible answer or solution or suggestion to it. Then they get the further benefit because obviously this was just a game, saying, "I'm not going to have my dreams tonight" because the dreams are still going to be colored by their own personal problems. If they find out what the emotional, traumatic issue was for the target person, and now go back and look at their dreams, they see how they approached this problem area and learn something important about themselves in the process. The dream sharing is analogous to the blind men with the elephant; one feels the tusks, another feels the tail and everybody comes out of it enriched. The target person with has this generous flow of information and knows that other people can share their problem; the dream helpers have given this special dream gift and they also get some important clues as to how they relate to the target issue. Statisticians are going to have a difficult task if they try to assign specific p-values for the event. The important thing is, once you've participated in it, you don't care about the p-values because you now know psi exists and you've experienced it in mutual loving atmosphere. Trying to do something helpful with psi and being open to it will turn you on more than guessing whether a card shows a square or circle and coming out with a high score.

VON LUCADOU: I totally agree with you, but there seem to be different notions of what we call a psi experience. One is from our scientific point of view because we want to prove a scientific anomaly. The other is what happens in real life. In real life you do not switch off or disconnect from the different patterns and actions which are important for our lives. I think this is the reason why the so-called isolated psi events are so shy and so elusive; this is the reason why we have a problem with it. On the other hand, we should not throw out the baby with the bath water because it's indicating something from a theoretical point of view—that psi cannot work like a normal information transfer or like a transfer of energy. This is a theoretical model and we could discuss it. If this is true, and there are some experiments indicating this, it would at least give us a way to distinguish real anomalous events which cannot be understood under the present paradigm from those that could be understood. I think it is also important to know that there are people who are not pathological, not psychiatric cases, who have these anomalous experiences which are shy and elusive.

WICKRAM: We can very reliably select a control group and systematically manipulate the P300, somatosensory evoked potential. We can manipulate the P100 both somatosensory evoked potentials and visually evoked potentials. We can change electrophysiology. We can cause inhibition and increase gastric secretion in high hypnotizables. The point is, we don't have to necessarily invoke the concept of multiple personalities to account for the manipulation of physiological parameters. We can produce these in people who are non-pathological. This does not take away from what Robert Van de Castle was saying, it only says that in a non-pathological group we can identify a subset who can reliably manipulate all these things including the construction of memory.

RECENT EXPERIENCES WITH PSI COUNSELING
IN HOLLAND

WIM H. KRAMER

Introduction

As long as people have reported paranormal experiences there must have been many who have suffered from these experiences. Since as a rule parapsychology and paranormal phenomena have been neglected by the established sciences and by medicine, the emotional problems related to such paranormal experiences were not recognized and often classified either as exaggerated behavior or as part of traditional psychiatric patterns and hence treated accordingly.

Traditionally parapsychologists are research oriented and consider as their main goal to "isolate" and to obtain control over psi phenomena. Parapsychologists work hard to find the necessary conditions for a repeatable experiment to be able to demonstrate the reality of psi. In testing psychics the emotional feelings and needs of the subjects are often considered merely a disturbance for the scientific efforts. When a psychic's personality or emotional needs becomes too manifest the parapsychologist might conclude that it is not possible to continue further experimentation and perhaps advises the psychic to see a psychiatrist to deal with the emotional problems.

In the 30s J. B. Rhine and his collaborators pointed to the importance of psychological conditions in order to make a subject perform optimally in a Zener card ESP test. In the Netherlands it was W. H. C. Tenhaeff who frequently stressed the importance of "the person behind the psychic." Tenhaeff had many sittings with psychics. He was convinced that in the case of gifted psychics clinical and psycho-diagnostical analyses could teach the parapsychologist a lot about the personality patterns of these people and its relation to and effect upon their psi-functioning.

There has been comparatively much interest in the personality patterns of psychics (Heymans, Tenhaeff, Schmeidler, Rao, & others) but like Tenhaeff mostly with the intention to find an answer to the question: "Which personality factors are psi enhancive and which are psiinhibitive?" Psychiatrists like Eisenbud and Ehrenwald have done some research on the role of telepathic communication during psychotherapy, but here too the psi-process itself was the central issue.

During the 70s parapsychology seemed to make some quick advances (ganzfeld research and the remote viewing projects) and the public opinion became more pro-minded to the paranormal. As a consequence people started to "come out of the closet" about their emotional problems related to paranormal experiences. Every research institute in the field frequently receives calls for help. Most of these institutes, however, are not equipped for clinical counseling. Apart from some general information about paranormal phenomena the only thing they can offer is the advice that the caller should try to find a psychiatrist or a psychologist with some interest in the field who might be at least "open minded" toward the client's experiences.

An exception to this is perhaps the study of poltergeist phenomena (RSPK). It is generally accepted among parapsychologists that the poltergeist agent is a person who suffers from extreme emotional pressure and is not able to cope with this pressure in a normal way.

The Founding of the Parapsychologisch Adviesburo

During the 70s the Parapsychology Laboratory of the Utrecht University appointed a clinical psychologist (Dr. Hendricus Boerenkamp) who, as part of his job, would give information and provide some elementary counseling to people who called the lab for help. This is one application in which parapsychology can make itself useful to the general public. In the middle of the 80s, however, as a result of the extensive reorganization of the Dutch universities and the associated reductions in funding, this service came to an end because there was no longer sufficient time and money available for this kind of work.

On the other hand, during the same period parapsychology became more and more a part of daily life resulting in a vast amount of radio and TV programs and especially articles in the popular press. As a consequence the "cry for help" from the general public increased considerably and became much more intense. Not only persons seeking advice for their own experiences, but also mental health institutions were confronted with an increase of patients claiming to possess paranormal abilities. In addition employers, general practitioners, lawyers, and even the police became more involved with persons claiming that they are special in the sense that they are "gifted."

In 1983 and in 1987 the Dutch police became involved in cases lasting several months concerning the kidnapping of important captains of industry. Both times after a few weeks the case seemed hopeless and the police investigations came to an impasse. Because of the "VIP" character of the abducted persons the kidnappings remained "hot" items in the news for several months until they were solved. During that period of uncertainty in 1983 the police received about a hundred "paranormal" tips from the general public as well as from professional psychics. In the 1987 kidnapping, however, they received over six thousand of such tips.

The considerable increase in the number of paranormal impressions sent in was partly due to an offer of a considerable amount of money as a reward for anyone who could tell the police where to find the victim but it undoubtedly also reflects an increased tolerance and acceptance from the public and authorities of such impressions.

In the last case the police did not know how to handle this huge pile of "paranormal" information. They were inclined to believe that it was worthless but since their own investigations brought no solution they were willing to accept an offer made by a few parapsychologists to help them to scrutinize the paranormal impressions. For parapsychology it was the chance of a lifetime, to carry out a field study on the practical value of paranormal impressions in a real-life setting. However, in both cases the practical value of the paranormal impressions proved to be low (Neu, 1985). Surprisingly there was a large number of people who had a strong feeling of being "right" about their impression. In several cases, the police, accompanied by the "psychic," actually went to visit the spot "seen" by the psychic or intensively searched the areas indicated. In none of these cases did this have any result at all. Often the psychic reacted to the failure by saying that it was impossible that their impressions were wrong. They often had such experiences and, according to them, normally their impressions are right.

The failure was explained by them by suggesting, for instance, that the kidnappers had just left the place and "If the police only had been more active they could have catched them," or, that the place must have been "associatively" connected with the crime, although they did not know how? After the crimes where solved by the police, just by intensive police routine, several interviews in the popular press appeared in which psychics claimed that they had known "all the time" where the victims had been hidden but that they had not dared to tell the police out of concern for the lives of the victim, or that they had called the police but that the police had not listened to them or had understood their message incorrectly.

In May 1986 the Parapsychologisch Adviesburo (Parapsychological

Consulting Agency) was founded in Utrecht. Although it is a private institution it operates in close relation to the Parapsychological Laboratory of the Utrecht University. Its goal is to cover the gap which exists between the scientific knowledge about parapsychological phenomena and the problems of people arising in every day life as a result of supposed paranormal experiences. These problems can be divided into two main categories: (a) individual problems (intra-personal), and (b) social problems (inter-personal). In addition to helping persons to overcome emotional problems related to paranormal experiences the agency is actively engaged in providing general information about parapsychology. The main areas of activity in this respect are: (a) providing information to students who intend to write a paper on a parapsychological topic and lecturing in high schools and universities, (b) interviews for radio/TV and with newspapers about parapsychology, (c) providing advice in legal cases and to the police, and (d) providing advice and information to people involved in regular counseling activities, like psychiatrists, clinical psychologists and social workers.

Types of Complaints

From various investigations it appears that a number of people claim to have had one or more experiences in their life which they classify as paranormal. Boerenkamp (1988b) estimates that at least 20% of the population reports having had such an experience. The figures reported in the literature vary considerably from less than 10% to over 50%. Hence, it is safe to conclude that we are dealing with thousands of people in society who consider paranormal experiences a reality in their lives.

People approach our counseling agency with various questions and complaints related to what they consider the paranormal. The complaints can be roughly divided into four categories;

1. People with problems concerning spirits or ghosts, mysterious forces, voodoo, supernatural powers etc. They consider these forces as somehow having a negative effect on their lives and their first question in general is whether we can provide the name of a reliable and powerful medium or psychic to counter these evil forces and to neutralize them. One might say that these clients have already made a diagnosis of their problems and turn to our agency purely to obtain an effective supernatural solution. The solution they are looking for is some procedure to eliminate the evil powers effecting their lives. From sessions with such clients it appears that in general they are firmly convinced of the correctness of their own diagnosis and in their belief

in the powers of these evil forces. The suggestion of possible alternative explanations for their problems are rejected and often immediately interpreted by them as a sign that the person offering such suggestions does not know what he or she is talking about and, therefore, is considered by them as unable to provide the help they are seeking. Clients with complaints belonging to this category are often people who originally come from cultures in which the possible influence of evil spirits is generally accepted. In this group one also finds a relatively high frequency of Dutchman from the lower intellectual and social levels. These people are also the ones who are most strongly influenced by the popular radio an TV programs, currently transmitted in Holland, which give more or less the impression that ghost stories are in general true but that the government or the scientific community want to make everyone believe them to be nonsense because they are "afraid" of the phenomena themselves.

2. People who approach us for names of psychics or psychic healers in the expectation that such a person, with the help of his or her paranormal powers, is able to immediately solve some important problems they have. It appears that in general people have a much too optimistic picture about the capacities of psychics and psychic healers. It is not uncommon to find the belief that a psychic is able to "see" everything and, hence, can solve the most complicated problems if he or she only wants to. The psychic is often considered a true magician. The reasons most often given for wanting to consult a psychic are: The wish to know what is going to happen in the future, problems in relationships with other people (especially in marriage), chronic ailments, and finding missing persons or objects.

3. People with a psychiatric past who have undergone ambulant or intra-mural psychiatric treatment. Mostly the psychiatrist has given up on them and since there is no real need to keep them hospitalized they are sent back to their homes. Then they often run into all kinds of problems in society and keep on looking for help, the kind of help they didn't find in the regular institutions. In that process they might come into contact with alternative circles in which their pathological based feelings often become positively labelled so that what the psychiatrist has called "sick" is now turned into "special" or "gifted." These people have complaints about being possessed, or about the strong influence of positive or negative psychic powers regulating all their behavior and thoughts, or about a feeling of being watched from outer space or even being an extraterrestrial agent themselves. Characteristic for them is the high tension with which they undergo their emotions and the fact that they do not know to put limits to the framework of their story.

TABLE 1

1 May–31 December 1986	66	0.5*
1 January–31 December 1987	534	1.0
1 January–31 December 1988	206	0.5
Total	816	

* In 1966 and 1988 working hours were only half-time.

Everything they are confronted with is an integral part of their paranormal world and in everything they hear from others they will find a hidden message. This is the group of people among which you find people who call in the middle of the night just to tell you that somebody has stolen their astral-body and dumped it in a dustbin; but that they will send the apocalyptic horses to punish the thief.

4. People who have had certain feelings or subjective experiences which they cannot explain to themselves. This group of clients can be divided into: (a) people who believe to be paranormally gifted and are looking for a test or some other type of confirmation that they are "sensitive," and (b) people who have had unexplainable experiences which disturbed them but who do not consider themselves as sensitive. These people often call and complain about feelings of uncertainty or ask, whether the experiences are an indication that they are becoming mentally insane. Other complaints are related to unexplainable depressive moods, undefined feelings, "feeling" the pains of other people, precognitive dreams and other forms of spontaneous ESP, or the feeling that they often are in unwanted telepathic contact with someone else.

It is noteworthy that complaints are rarely related to physical phenomena, for instance, poltergeist events or other types of psychokinetic occurrences. In the few phone calls we have received in the past three years about poltergeist phenomena it was clear within a few minutes that the supposed poltergeist was merely an over attribution since the poltergeist generally turned out to be a curtain or a plant that suddenly moved, a painting falling of the wall, a fridge or central heating system making strange noises.

Once a man called and said that he owned a car with strong psychokinetic effects. During a drive all the instruments of the car would suddenly point into another direction. Since he had just bought the car he had gone back to the dealer several times to check it out. The dealer spent many hours trying to discover what was wrong with it, but did not succeed. The owner said that he was puzzled because mysteriously enough the PK only happened when he was driving the car. He asked if we would be kind enough to scrutinize the car so that he would have an official report that the car was "haunted." We said that it was impossible to tell anything about the car just by phone but that he was welcome to drive over to our agency and show the car and the phenomena. He made an appointment to do so but, unfortunately, never showed up.

Some Figures

During the period from the inception of the agency in May 1986 until the end of 1988 a total of 816 sessions with over 200 clients were held (see Table 1). Of the clients approximately 73% were female and 27% male. As the Dutch population is about equally distributed over males and females (CBS, 1988), it can be concluded that significantly more females request counseling for "paranormal" problems. This finding is roughly in agreement with two other data. One is that in the Netherlands the number of females requesting counseling for psychological problems is about 2 to 3 times larger than the number of males seeking help for such problems. The other is that in collections of spontaneous paranormal experiences the proportion of female percipients is also consistently higher compared to the males and varies between 55% and 85% (see Schouten, 1979, 1981, 1982).

The age distribution of 177 clients with whom sessions were held and from which this data is currently available is presented in table 2. This distribution is roughly similar to the age distribution of the entire Dutch population (CBS, 1988). Hence it appears that people of all ages are troubled by problems related to paranormal issues and that such problems are not restricted to certain periods in the lives of people.

Of course a lot more phone calls are made to the agency than there are clients, since not everyone who calls wants to make an appointment for counseling. On the other hand, not all questions asked can be answered by us. We found that a lot of people simply look in the telephone directory and when they see the word parapsychology they simply call because they think that every question which can't be answered by others can be answered by something which is called parapsychology. Wives call that their husband has walked away with another woman and ask if we can do something to bring him back or someone asks whether we can put a spell on someone the caller doesn't like, etc.

Most phone calls refer to problems related to the problems in categories one and two. Questions from these people are generally dealt with by phone. People with problems related to the categories three and four usually make an appointment to see us. An estimate of the number of phone calls received over the period 1 May 1986 until 31 December 1988 is approximately 2,500.

Relation Between Emotional and Paranormal Experiences

Boerenkamp's conclusion, based on his clinical experience in counseling people with "paranormal" problems and his experiences with psychics when carrying out the research reported in his dissertation (Boerenkamp, 1988), is in agreement with our experience and clinical research on psychic healers (Kramer, 1986) in that often people first become aware of their psi abilities after a major life event. In our interviews with psychic healers we found that generally healers became aware of their healing powers after they had gone through a period of deep depression or extreme emotional pressure. In general, the idea of possessing psi abilities turned out to be an important personal discovery and helped them remarkably well to overcome their emotional pressure. It opened new ways of life. Often these healers reported that after they first became aware of their psi powers they realized that they always had had such feelings, and that as a child they already felt different from other kids in that they were more sensitive to social and emotional problems. Considering this we might conclude that there is very likely a correlation between the present state of emotional functioning of a client and the experience of an alleged paranormal phenomenon. The paranormal experience has a tremendous impact on the person and often becomes "the one and only thing" in the focus of their attention. In analogy with the poltergeist phenomena we made the assumption that the experience of the alleged paranormal phenomenon is also a result of the psychological-emotional problems the client has at the time. We assume then that there is a strong and lasting relationship between psychological and emotional problems of a person and paranormal experiences. It is outside the scope of this paper to discuss the nature of this relationship. It can be assumed, however, that at a certain level of emotional instability the likelihood increases that the person will have a paranormal experience, and this experience in turn strongly influences the way people classify and handle future emotionally significant events.

Counseling Technique One

What we needed was a simple and, above all, practical approach for counseling which could be used within the limits of our possibilities. Among others these limits are that our service is not subsidized by the government. As a consequence clients have to pay their fees themselves in addition to their travel expenses. Since our agency is the only one in Holland which provides this specialized type of treatment, people from all over the country are coming to see us. Fortunately, Utrecht is located in the center of Holland so that clients never have extensive travel expenses or time consuming travel. Thus, in order to reduce the financial costs for the client, the therapy we offer has to be concluded within a few sessions. Another limit is that we needed a simple model which could be applied to the variety of problems we are confronted with. There is simply no time or money available to develop different therapeutic models and counseling strategies for all the different kinds of problems one might encounter.

The first model we formulated is based on the principle of system theoretical model therapy. In this model a functional analysis of the relation between life events and the paranormal experience or experiences must provide the key to the solution we offer the client. This implies, among others, that we are not so much interested in the question whether the alleged paranormal experience is a real or a pseudo psi phenomenon. What is important is that the client experiences it as a real psi experience. Our goal, as counselors, is not to investigate paranormal experiences, but to provide psychological help to the client. Since we can not say for sure if a psi experience is real or not we have to give the benefit of the doubt to our client and take, at face value, the experience as real, because the client, at least in the beginning, is convinced of its real character. In short the procedure for the functional analysis is as follows: We ask the client to write down at home, his first, second, last and his most important paranormal experience. During the sessions we make a short report of the client's life with an emphasis on major emotional life events. The next step is to match the life events and the reported psi experiences on the time axis. In this way clients see for themselves how in most cases generally both occur in approximately the same period of their life. What we try to make clients aware of with this procedure is that: (a) paranormal experiences are human experiences, (b) paranormal experiences can occur to every person, (c) paranormal experiences are related in time to emotional life events, (e) paranormal experiences are correlated to emotional pressure, and (e) paranormal experiences are not an indication of insanity. To put it into one sentence: Paranormal experiences are normal human experiences, they are not an indication of mental insanity per se, but can occur to everyone who at a certain stage in his or her life is suffering under extreme emotional pressure.

To summarize the goals we want to achieve with our counseling strategy: (a) reduction of the emotional tension associated with the experience, and (b) integration of the paranormal experience with the other psychological emotions and feelings the person has. The ideal is when the alleged paranormal experience is integrated by the client to become a part of his or her general psychological experiences and the client is able to cope with the idea that he or she has had, at least, one such experience and accepts that this fact doesn't make him or her any more or less interesting than any other human being.

Technique One in Practice. A client calls the agency and an appointment is set up. In the first call the client often indicates the type of problem involved. From each call a short record is made and filed away. The next step is to send the client a standardized letter providing general information about the agency (e.g. how to find it and what the fees are). Enclosed is also a confirmation of the day and time agreed upon and a request to write down a detailed account of the most remarkable paranormal experience in his or her life. The client is asked to bring this account to the first session.

At the beginning of the first session the client fills out a standard application form. This asks for some personal data and for information concerning the nature of the complaint, duration of the complaint, prior contacts with counseling agencies or therapists, use of medication, what assistance is expected from our agency, and how they came to learn about it. The first session is filled with learning about each other, starting to make the report and discussing the client's "most important" paranormal experience. At the end of this session the client receives a form to fill in at home which requests a description of his or her first, second, and last paranormal experience. In this way extensive information about the nature of the client's paranormal experiences is efficiently and with relatively little time, obtained. In general, the mixture of written and verbal interviews yields in a few sessions the information needed for the cognitive restructuring which serves to eliminate the problematic aspects of the clients paranormal experiences.

Of course, both phases, collecting information and working on cognitive reconstruction, overlap. Gradually, the emphasis shifts from gathering information to psychological integration of life-events and paranormal experience. However, in all phases of the counseling both elements are present.

Although this model has advantages in that it is easy to learn and to apply, takes just a few sessions (our goal was five at a maximum), uses no "mumbo jumbo" and is neutral in regard to the reality of the phenomenon, it appeared to have some disadvantages which make it less generally applicable than was expected:

1. It requires from the client a certain level of intelligence and the ability to abstract.

2. It turned out that even in the case that the intellectual capacities are present, people have a strong resistance to abstract and to reflect about their own feelings.

3. The approach is often considered too "psychological" and hence it is felt that the real paranormal nature of the experience is not sufficiently acknowledged or is even neglected.

4. The variety of problems is too large. Not all problems could be dealt with in a way that was meaningful and of sufficient value to the client.

Counseling Technique Two

To overcome the problems associated with the first approach gradually a more "free running" technique was developed and used from the beginning of 1987. This second type of approach is related to Rogerian therapy and aimed at the client finding his or her own cognitive restructuring at his or her own level. This means using his or her own words (level of language) and at his or her own speed (taking as much time as the client thinks he or she needs) and, most importantly, taking his or her view of parapsychology and paranormal reality as the starting point. Thus in the first technique there is "top-down" information: the expert counselor presents the framework of paranormal phenomena, whereas in the second approach there is a "bottom-up" structure: the client is presenting his or her framework and the counselor, by asking questions and making remarks, presents the client with constructive ideas on how to "put the pieces together."

An example will clarify this procedure. A young man called us and asked for a regression therapist to help him. He was convinced that he was the incarnation of the poet Dylan Thomas. He has read all the books by and biographies about Thomas and found that the life of Thomas and his ideas about life in general were exactly the same as he had. The problem was that during his life Thomas was an incurable alcoholic who treated his wife very badly. Thomas had died in 1953, leaving behind his wife in misery. Our client now felt sorry for Thomas's wife, who still lives, and since he considered himself the reincarnation of Thomas he felt that he had to see her and make up for his bad behavior in his previous incarnation. He was so obsessed by this idea that already for several months he felt miserable and was not able to concentrate on his work or his social life. He had figured out that the best thing to do was to undergo a hypnotic regression in order to find out more details about Thomas's private life so that when he would meet the widow he would be well equipped with information about his previous life.

I told him that in this case the agency could not offer him regression therapy but that it might be useful for him to make an appointment for a discussion about his experiences. He showed up with his girlfriend and with a huge pile of books about Dylan Thomas. The first thing he did was to show me a photo on the cover of one of the books and to point out his physical resemblance to Thomas. He continued with the observation that Thomas's life and his own looked very similar and that when reading Dylan Thomas's poetry he always was struck by the fact that it expressed exactly his own opinion "as if the things I'm feeling are written down in that book". I told him that the question whether he really should be considered a reincarnation of Dylan Thomas or not is of no real importance for deciding what actions he should take. If we take reincarnation for real then we can ask ourselves what the reason might be that people reincarnate? Has reincarnation the meaning of going back in time to bother about all kinds of problems which existed in the past or is reincarnation something which perhaps has a meaning for the future, for instance, in the sense that it is important that the ideas of Thomas would survive, but not his drinking habits. In the session, which took two hours, we talked about the meaning of life and the role of reincarnation. At the end of the session the young man had gathered some new insights about reincarnation and had integrated those new insights into his own philosophy.

In this case the question whether or not the client should be considered a reincarnation of Dylan Thomas was not an issue. What matters here is that his problem of how to function and how to act were solved without forcing the client to reject his feelings with regard to the reincarnation question. He came as an "inert" person with a compulsive feeling to act, but not knowing how to. At the end of the counseling session, he felt quite differently about the problems he was facing and found that the things which had bothered him at first now had turned into something which was useful for his life. From "inert" he became active, using his feelings about Dylan Thomas and reincarnation as a "guiding light." Within a few weeks I learned that he had started his own business and that he was doing quite well.

In our experience this second approach, which is less formally structured than the first one, works quite well for clients belonging to our category 4(b). In this approach counseling is something of a pleasant game, in which one does not approve or disqualify the feelings and belief system of the client. It is also a more difficult approach to work with than the first technique because the counselor must have a lot of knowledge about all kinds of paranormal or occult theories, and needs to be able to adapt this knowledge to the intellectual level and belief system of the client.

Theses

I would like to conclude with some theses which are based on three years of practicing counseling with people about their psi experiences.

1. In view of the increase of interest in parapsychology and the increased incorporation of the paranormal in society the need is growing for psychologists and psychiatrists with training in this specialty.

2. Specializing in counseling problems related to the paranormal and providing information on such topics is a legitimate field.

3. The suspicion with which general scientists consider parapsychology is, justified or not, invalid when it concerns counseling clients with problems attributed to the paranormal.

4. These counseling activities should be recognized as part of regular mental health services.

5. Most problems of clients which they consider as related to true paranormal experiences probably involve no parapsychological phenomena at all.

6. The most frequent reasons why clients attribute a paranormal character to experiences which parapsychologists would not label as such appear to be: (a) badly informed about what constitutes a paranormal phenomenon. For instance, a woman can't choose between buying a red or a green dress. She keeps thinking about that problem until she suddenly realizes that she sees many red objects and people wearing red clothes. This she labels as a paranormal sign indicating that she should buy the red dress; (b) emotional problems. We frequently observed that female adolescents escape to a self-created world of spiritualistic nature when they are in fact troubled by relationship (schoolmates, parents) or sexual (incest) problems about which they don't dare to talk to anyone; (c) pathological cases. Occasionally psychiatrists sent clearly pathological cases to us for treatment when their own approach failed. These are, of course, difficult cases but sometimes we found that at least our deviant way of encountering "weird" experiences created new possibilities with these patients.

7. For this type of counseling, knowledge of psychopathology is at least equally important as knowledge of parapsychology.

8. For successful counseling of problems related to parapsychological experiences, experience and knowledge of psychotherapy seems more

TABLE 2

X < 1925	3	2%
1925 < X < 1935	11	6%
1935 < X < 1945	30	17%
1945 < X < 1955	59	33%
1955 < X < 1965	51	29%
1965 < X < 1975	21	12%
X > 1975	2	1%
Total	177	100%

important than a profound knowledge of the achievements of parapsychological research.

9. It is essential to have good insight into the organization of both the regular counseling services as well as the alternative circles in order to help the client in his or her search for stability and well-being.

10. Do not expect that counseling clients with psi experiences brings in new cases for collections of spontaneous paranormal experiences. In counseling you have to concentrate on and to be aware of other aspects of the client's story than when you are looking for evidence of a spontaneous psi phenomenon. In theory, of course, it is possible to do both but in practice it does not work that way because people have to pay themselves for the sessions and it would not be ethical to spend time on aspects other than those directly related to the client's well-being. In addition to that, people often have to take time from their work for the sessions and therefore want "the job to be done as quickly as possible." But even if the client is willing to spend time purely for the sake of research, it often happens that the counselor does not have the time for it. This implies that combining research on spontaneous cases and counseling is only possible in a research setting where both therapist and client can take all the time they need.

11. In stories that look most like real psi phenomena you often get people who can be characterized as "borderline" personalities.

REFERENCES

Boerenkamp, H. G. (1988a). *Helderziendheid bekeken*. Haarlem: De toorts.

Boerenkamp, H. G. (1988b). *A study of paranormal impressions of psychics*. Utrecht, The Netherlands: Proefschrift Utrecht.

CBS. (1988). *Statistisch zakboek 1988*. Den Haag: Staatsuitgeverij.

Gerding, J. L. F., Millar, B., Molewijk, G. C., Neu, J. G., & Voois, W. (1989). Analyse van de paranormale tips in de ontvoeringszaak G. J. Heijn. *Tijdschrift voor Parapsychologie, 57*(1–2), 2–71.

Kramer, W. H. (1986). *Paranormaal genezers, een klasse apart?* Unpublished doctoral dissertation, University of Utrecht, The Netherlands.

Kramer, W. H. (1987). Persoonlijkheidskenmerken van paranormaal begaafden: Beknopt overzicht van onderzoek en resultaten, in *Paranormal geneeswijze anno 1987*, NVP, Utrecht, Oct 1987.

Neu, J. G. (1985). De waarde (loosheid) van spontane Bijdragen van paragnosten: Een analyse van paranormale tips in de Heineken-affaire. *Algemeen Politieblad, 134*(3), 51–59.

Schouten, S. A. (1979). Analysis of spontaneous cases as reported in "Phantasms of the living." *European Journal of Parapsychology, 2*, 408–455.

Schouten, S. A. (1981). Analysing spontaneous cases: A replication based on the Sannwald collection. *European Journal of Parapsychology, 4*, 9–48.

Schouten, S. A. (1982). Analysing spontaneous cases: A replication based on the Rhine collection. *European Journal of Parapsychology, 4*, 113–158.

DISCUSSION

TIERNEY: I would like to make two points. The first one is sort of a plea from the equal opportunities commission concerning the sex ratio you mentioned. We just analyzed the last 1,000 cases in my unit, and when you compare day versus evening sessions, the sex ratio during the day is 3:1 female to male, and in the evening it's 3:1 male to female. So, when you put them all together, you get 50:50. I suspect it is a reporting problem.

The second point is, I wonder whether you would agree with me that the term normality has been used quite a bit. Keith Harary has used it; he stressed the importance of emphasizing the normality of such experiences in the therapeutic context. It has occurred to me listening to you that the term may be being interpreted differently. If I had an experience that I found horrific and somebody told me it was normal, my immediate reaction would be, "Is it going to happen again?" In other words, the concept of normality builds up an expectation that it may happen again. Would you like to comment on that? Is there a problem with using the term normality in that way?

KRAMER: There is not because you don't use the word normality in the sense that this will happen every time. You use the word normality in the sense that every person can have such an experience. I mean, there are other things which are quite normal in our views, but they don't happen regularly.

TIERNEY: It was the concept of expectation that worried me.

KRAMER: They don't expect it because most of the time they are also aware of the fact that it is something special in the sense that it just happened at that moment. They somehow feel, one way or another, that it is something linked to that moment. There is a big difference between people who have lots of experiences and people who have only one or two experiences, in the way they think about it, and the way they react to it.

FENWICK: I think those of us who have sat in a clinic in which people come in distressed with very strange symptoms, will agree with practically everything that you have said. I have two comments and one question for you. The comments are that your description of the way that the Dutch medical profession responds to people's experiences is very similar to the way the British medical profession responds to experiences that people have had. For example, you cannot talk about near-death experiences and if you do they consider you mad. The counseling that people get is really very poor, so we have had to try and provide alternative ways for counseling people.

My next comment relates to religious experiences as a whole. You have chosen just one aspect which is parallel to psychological experiences. But the data, again from England, relating to religious experience really bears out exactly what you were saying; these experiences usually occur in a situation in which the person is under stress, and then they get elaborated. I was interested in your comment about age. We found that parapsychological experiences occurred linearly throughout the age range, but trailed off at 60. I didn't know whether this was because our sample was starting to get rather thin at 60, or whether it actually does trail off at 60. I would be grateful for a comment on that. Again, I'm raising the same question that I did for the last speaker. We can fit it all very nicely into our understanding of the relationship between personality and stress and so on. You started off your paper with a lovely description of the failure of the police in Holland to find anything at all which suggests there was anything in parapsychological predictions. Now then, you have obviously been working in this area for a long time, and so, I would like to put you on the spot, and ask, do you feel that only a reductionist model, such as we have been discussing for half the time I have been here, is sufficient to explain everything? Or do you believe that we need wider models?

KRAMER: First I'd like to make a comment on your remark that what we see in Holland is that the medical profession is divided into two groups; namely, the medical people working in the academic clinics or the official academic state of medicine, and the general practice, working in the field and having clients all day. What we find is that the official people neglect parapsychological things. The general practitioner has no problem whatsoever with it most of the time. When you compare young to old general practitioners, you see that most of the time the older ones are very strongly against it or overreact to it, saying to the clients, "It's the work of the devil. It's something you shouldn't do. You are not allowed to go there anymore." The younger ones tend to take it seriously, and are even very interested and want me to talk about it for days because they can't hear enough. Concerning your comment about experiences trailing off at 60, I'm not quite sure. I did not find that at least not in my population. I can think of one explanation. When people are over 60, the number of women will exceed the men, and at that age, people are more likely to be involved with spiritualist ideas. So I think that most of those women in Holland go to Spiritualist groups and are not inclined to go to any young doctor who will tell them what to do. That is something you see when you look into the meetings of Spiritualists, most of the people are elderly ladies. So I think there might be some sort of bias in that they simply don't come to clinicians because they think they're too old for it, or they have other ideas. The last question was?

FENWICK: It was a challenge; to ask you whether you felt that the reductionist model in science was sufficient to explain everything that you talked to us about?

KRAMER: You talked about a special topic which I could talk about for hours, the research we've done with the police about how paranormal information can be of any assistance to them. It is very difficult because you have to think in two ways. Sometimes people can say things which are from a paranormal origin, but are of no use to the police. For instance, a person is missing and the police go to a psychic and the psychic says, "Well, he is a very nice person. He is characterized as such and such, and when he was 12 years of age he had this and that illness and when he was 32 he had that kind of stuff." The police will say, "OK, that's all fine, but that is not what we want to know. We simply want to know where he is." That's the way we look at it. There has been a tremendous amount of research done in Holland, but I'm afraid there is not much published in English. Each time, however, it turned out that those people simply didn't give information which could be of any practical use by the police. I mean, they never say, "There it is." The problem we are confronted with is that there exists a lot of stories about psychics finding missing persons, but every time it turned out to be just a story. No one knows exactly but the stories are very strong, happening mostly about people who are already dead. There is a problem in how to evaluate all the spontaneous cases which are available and all the characteristics involved. When you look about the experimental things which are done, and some of them are not done in a laboratory, something like the case whereby people send in their impressions and the parapsychologists scrutinize them, it always turns out that there is nothing of any importance for the police. So, I'm not quite sure what to do with that information but the only thing that I can say when a police officer phones me and asks, "Will there be any use in getting a psychic?" is that the likelihood that they will find anything is very low, but you always can try.

HARARY: When Ian Tierney was stressing the normality of certain unusual experiences to people, you want to make sure that there is some kind of normality. If somebody calls me up and says that he or she has turned into a werewolf, I don't say, "It happens all the time. Don't worry about it". If it is widespread and common, then I say so. If it is not something I am familiar with, I then back off a little and am honest and say "I haven't heard a lot about that." The other thing is to find out why people find things horrific, you could ask them, "What is horrific about your experience?" We are so used to dealing with certain ideas and experiences, we forget how unusual it is for people. Bob Van de Castle and I have mentioned psi experiences as related to psychological growth. That doesn't mean that it is not disturbing when it happens because we are still dealing in an unsupportive cultural context. How can we facilitate that psychological growth process when people contact us?

KRAMER: It's a difficult question because as a clinical psychologist I'm inclined to draw a line between something which is called a problem area and the solution to the problem. After you've solved the problem, you can go into the growth area, but most of the time people don't do that with clinicians. Furthermore, I'd like to say that growth is not only related to paranormal experiences. I mean, everyone who has had some tremendous illness, or who has had some tremendous depression or something will say afterwards they had grown from it.

HARARY: And people who have fallen in love have had positive experiences. Psi can be a positive thing; it doesn't have to be a trauma.

KRAMER: It should not be a trauma. It's hard for me to tell how to establish that growth because I never worked with it. After we have solved the problem, people go back and grow in their own way, or they become a member of some movement.

HARARY: The movement is not necessarily growth oriented.

KRAMER: It's not necessarily, but it happens sometimes. We are not focusing on growth in our counseling. It is something which we, of course, can do. It will lengthen the counseling period, and that means people will have to spend more time and money for it.

HARARY: Can we direct them towards something such as reading books?

KRAMER: That's not a problem; when you say read these books some people really want to read about the topic. The problem in Holland is that there are no good books on the topic; they are either too academic or lousy. There are no books in the middle. The only reason that no publisher wants to publish them is because no one wants to buy a book in the middle.

VAN DE CASTLE: I just wanted to compliment you on the innovative way that you worked with the Dylan Thomas situation because I think often we are confronted with this as psychotherapists. When people come in with a belief system like this, it is important to not immediately jump the gun and make some sort of judgmental description. I'm wondering though, what that would be like when presented with ghosts or possession. Could you accept this as a theoretical possibility? I'm beginning to feel that there would be very few parapsychologists willing to accept, even as a theoretical possibility, that there could be such a thing as a ghost or possession, and would start automatically labeling rather than being willing to entertain the possibility that such energy or systems could exist. I thought the way you were able to go into that kind of philosophical discussion of the merit underlying the incarnation, was a creative way to take this particular situation and work with him from his metaphor, from his approach and come out with a very creative resolution. I obviously like that approach as evidenced by the points I've been trying to make about psi being related to a growth process. It is sort of an old dictum in psychotherapy, no pain, no gain. It may be difficult to work through these and assimilate them but you found a close correlation between the crisis or the midlife situation and subsequent psi experience which somehow facilitates and aids that kind of meaningful integration. I know I'm really being hard on my parapsychological colleagues, but if it takes this kind of a crisis to be able to activate psi, how much of a crisis is it until next Tuesday at three o'clock to show up for testing at the lab? There is no real crisis. There is no real crunch or push to motivate them.

NEPPE: Concerning the question of age and incidence of subjective paranormal experiences in the over 60s, I think that this is very much dependent on the kind of question, the focus and, in essence the culture. For example, I found 80% of subjects claimed to have experienced presences in a predominantly 40 to 70 year old female population. I believe incidence is dependent on how people perceive things and how threatened they are in terms of their responses. I'm mentioning this because if you look at the citations of deja vu and incidence relating to age, prior to my own work, there were always comments that deja vu was inversely related to age and that it did not occur very much in the elderly. This may or not be so. However, it does seem that if one goes into detail in terms of experiences, you elicit responses which are positive, which otherwise would have been negative. So, I think it's dependent on a variety of cultural and research approach elements.

The other point that I wanted to make is that I was very pleased that you emphasized the non-prejudicial approach in relation to psychological and psychotherapeutic intervention with clients who have presented with various kinds of subjective paranormal experiences. I think that this, in general, is certainly the most logical approach for a mental health setting. It's the way that I found most convenient to go. It also amplified the need for such terms as "subjective paranormal experience" where one is using a non-prejudicial approach, making no interpretations about the veridicality or nonveridicality of the person's experience. In effect, we say, "You have these special things happening to you. Let us try to deal with the problems that either may or may not be related to these things." Under certain circumstances it may imply educating the client or the patient in relation to further knowledge of the area and other times you may want to steer them off in completely different directions.

DIERKENS: I think that I should make some comment about the use by the police of some psychic information. The problems are perhaps completely different in two cases. One is when police ask the general public for some information. The police sometimes ask that because they get some sensory information that the people would not give in direct way. They prefer to say, "I have a dream, or have something in my head and I know that," because then they feel less involved with the police. The second is the use of mediums such as Croiset of Utrecht; I worked with him quite a number of times. In fact, there had to be some link between the way of death or the personality of the deceased person and Croiset himself. When they got the information, even if they were right and even if they were useful, which is not always the case, the information was sometimes given in a symbolic way so that is another problem. If someone wishes to see a wonderful case of Croiset, there is a movie on Croiset's arrival in Tokyo, it's wonderful.

Now, another point about models, I am quite conscious about the necessity to use many different models in the clinic and in research. In fact, I was a psychiatrist and psychoanalyst for 20 years in private practice, then a researcher and teacher in psychology. Having taught theories of personality, experimental psychology and transcultural psychology, I know very well that at one point, one model is useful, but that same model is not useful somewhere else. If we think to the beginning of Freud's work, he thought that the brain anatomy would give him a good model to explain his unconscious. But that brain model had to be put away, he never published it. If he succeeded in understanding the unconscious, it was because he put that brain model aside. I think that in our subject, we should do the same for all the usual realistic psychology models.

KRAMER: The police business should be a topic for a whole conference because there's so much to say about it. Of course, the police are aware that sometimes a person who is actually involved in the crime, may call them and say, "Well, I'm a psychic and I've got an idea for you." So, that's one of the reasons why they take it seriously. In the research we've done, we've left that all out. On the other hand, it is not that the police are saying to the general public, "Please send in your information." The general public simply sends in the information. In the second case I mentioned well over 6,000 people in a few months put on record their information. That means that for entire days the telephone system was completely blocked because all kinds of people tried to phone the police with their psychic information. The problem was that the communication channels of the police were completely blocked so there is another practical problem. You have to find all kinds of solutions on how to deal with that and it's very difficult.

CLINICAL PSYCHIATRY, PSYCHOPHARMACOLOGY, AND ANOMALOUS EXPERIENCE

Vernon M. Neppe

The history of psychiatry is riddled with attempts at unifying psychiatric diagnosis. More than a hundred years ago (1860), psychosis was summarized very simply by Heinrich Neumann: "There's only one kind of madness, and we call it insanity" (Neppe, 1982c). Over the next fifty years, this broad conceptualization was insufficient. Instead, numerous labels were placed onto mentally ill patients, such that psychiatric diagnosis was at its most varied and most scientifically inappropriate.

What has historically been perceived as a major breakthrough in psychiatry occurred in the 1890's: Emil Kraepelin's discovery of the term Dementia Praecox (Kraepelin, 1899). This condition was renamed schizophrenia in 1911 by Eugen Bleuler. Bleuler (1911) emphasized specific symptoms occurring at specific times, and the conceptualization of a split between cognitive and emotional functions. This differed from Kraepelin's conceptualization of a deteriorating illness occurring over many years, presenting in the young, and, ultimately, exhibiting features of intellectual deficit. These two conceptualizations of schizophrenic illness reflect prevailing philosophies pertaining to the importance of cross-sectional symptoms (i.e. symptoms occurring at a specific moment in time) and longitudinal features (i.e. symptoms occurring over periods of many years reflecting the course of illness). It was with this conceptualization in mind that Kraepelin (1922) subdivided major psychiatric illness into three, namely: dementia praecox, manic depressive insanity, and epileptic insanity.

It is worthwhile reflecting that our current classifications of psychosis are even more limited than this, and emphasize two major conditions: schizophrenia and affective (or mood) disorder (either bipolar illness or unipolar major depression). From these two major conditions arises a variety of others: for example, in between is so-called "schizoaffective disorder"; when there is suspicion of organic impairment, we talk of "organic delusional syndrome" or "organic hallucinosis"; and inability to classify these conditions under any of these broader headings results in the diagnosis of "atypical psychosis". Even worse, this term "atypical psychosis" no longer exists in the Diagnostic and Statistical Manual, (Third Edition, Revision) of the American Psychiatric Association, the bible of psychiatric diagnosis, and has been replaced by "psychosis, not otherwise specified" (American Psychiatric Association Committee, 1987). A large proportion of our current psychiatric diagnoses do not fit well into any of these Procrustean frameworks, where specific clinical criteria have been worked out, and where patients are expected to be placed within diagnostic categories which may have dubious clinical relevance. Psychiatric diagnoses today are at times a dumping ground for the diagnostically destitute.

This cynical viewpoint is based, unfortunately, on empirical experience. Some 15 years ago it was said that the easiest way to cure schizophrenia was to travel across the Atlantic. This reflected the diverging views of this condition in American and European psychiatry. (See Neppe, 1982c). Fortunately, criteria unification at the clinical level has led to more consistent diagnostic labels. But these are only very relative, and every week my colleagues and I see patients who have a prolonged psychiatric history with a variety of different previous diagnostic labels. First admission, borderline personality disorder; second admission, schizoaffective illness; third, schizophrenia; fourth, mania; fifth, atypical psychosis; sixth, maybe one of these earlier conditions, maybe organic delusional disorder. Clearly diagnostic nomenclature at this point in time, from the psychosis framework, is in difficulties, and the same applies to the more limited neurotic kinds of illness.

This emphasis on the deficiencies of current psychiatric nomenclature is made for another reason. When groups of symptoms such as anomalous experiences, or experiences which are out of the ken, the training, the knowledge base, and the conventional framework of clinical psychiatry appear, these features are perceived frequently as psychopathologic, and attempts are made to place the experience within the frameworks of one of these broader diagnoses. Thus "out of body" experience can, at its broadest psychopathologic level, be perceived as "extreme ego splitting, with marked derealization and depersonalization, and delusional out-of-touchness with reality" (Neppe, 1982b). Precognition can be perceived as a "primary delusional idea, with alienation, passivity, or reference phenomena." The same may be said for other forms of ESP such as contemporaneous clairvoyance. Telepathy can be perceived within the framework of thought-broadcasting or thought insertion, both "first-rank symptoms", outlined by Kurt Schneider, 50 years ago (1959). Trancelike states, and writing automatisms, can be perceived as extreme dissociative phenomena, or as extreme passivity phenomena within the framework of psychosis (Neppe & Smith, 1982). These symptoms may in fact be interpreted correctly under certain circumstances: Clearly patients who are psychotic may misinterpret reality, and it is not uncommon for such patients to believe themselves psychic, and to act out their delusions (Neppe & Tucker, 1989). They may well join subgroups who will accentuate such belief systems. This does not, however, imply that all subjects with subjective paranormal experience, or anomalistic experience, are psychotic, yet psychiatrists have in general attempted, without empirical studies, to insert such symptoms into the framework of psychopathology and abnormality (Neppe & Tucker, 1989; Neppe, 1984a).

What alternatives exit to this current state of affairs? We can use approaches, such as those of Robert D. Laing (1976), or Thomas Szasz (1957), and perceive the patient as not necessarily pathological. His interaction with society is damaging because of societal labeling and sociocultural misinterpretations. This, therefore, shifts diagnoses out of the framework of the psychological to the sociocultural.

An alternative is to approach diagnostic nomenclature at two levels—firstly, the functional, and secondly, the psychopharmacologic. I believe that these together form an appropriate approach. Using the functional framework, one perceives the patient in the context of his biological, psychological, social, family and cultural functioning. One perceives him as a biopsychofamiliosociocultural system (Neppe, 1989a). Defects at any of these levels producing noncoping, or non-optimal coping, can be perceived as psychopathologic. No matter how strange the patient's experiences are, they are not perceived as abnormal unless they distinctly interfere with the patient's functionality and coping skills (Neppe, 1984b). This is a good, basic, empirically-derived definition, which allows paragnosts to experience realities which others may not be able to conceive of, but which do not produce labels of psychopathology.

The second, related approach, actually fits within this first, and involves emphasizing the biologic components to psychiatric disorder (Neppe, 1989a). A great deal of research has occurred in the modern era, trying to find biological correlates for such conditions as schizophrenia and affective illness. Specific tests have attempted to differentiate these conditions —at this point, unsuccessfully.

Less emphasized, and a theme of my latest book, (Neppe, 1989a) is the marriage of psychopharmacologic responsiveness and toleration of psychotropic medication to psychiatric diagnoses. It is largely irrelevant to me whether or not a patient is necessarily labelled schizophrenic, schizoaffective illness, organic delusional syndrome, or mood disorder. If a group of patients respond to a specific medication, or combination of medications, I believe this cluster of patients is far more homogeneously expressed by this responsiveness to specific combinations of psychotropic medication, irrespective of diagnosis (Neppe, 1983, 1989c; Neppe & Holden, 1989).

Moreover, we have a very conventional, useful, underused and underemphasized diagnostic test. It is said the "normal person would not handle such crazy medications," and this is quite true: High doses of psychotropic or antipsychotic medications are tolerated only by patients who are psychotic, have severe personality disorders, have drug dependency problems, or have an extremely active liver, (allowing very rapid breakdown), or a poorly functional gastrointestinal tract (at that point allowing nonabsorption). The average person, in the vast majority of cases, does not tolerate antipsychotic doses of neuroleptic medication (Neppe, 1989b; Neppe & Wessels, 1979). This implies that we have specific biochemical diagnostic traces that differentiate normal from psychotic conditions.

Thus, two principles exist in differentiating out normative from abnormal behavior. First, the definitions of coping at a functional level (Neppe, 1984b); and secondly, psychopharmacologic toleration and responsiveness as an underlying indicator and expression of biochemical abnormality, which produces, not only the psychopharmacologic epiphenomena, but also the epiphenomena of specific clinical symptoms (Neppe, 1983a, 1983b). Expression of such clinical features is limited by the brain to a few such experiences. The patient may experience hallucinations. He or she may experience symptoms pertaining to delusions and thought disorder or emotional changes, such as depression or euphoria. Alternatively, he or she may experience anxiety, agitation, aggression, alienation and distortion in terms of caring experience. He or she might experience differences at the psychomotor expression level, and at the motivation level. In more extreme cases, he or she may experience alterations of consciousness, insight, judgment, and overt dangerousness to him or herself or others. Finally, he or she may experience specific focal cerebrocortical features, such as apraxia or aphasia. This limitation in expression of symptoms by the brain is also appropriate with regard to subjective paranormal experience. So, for example, it is well demonstrated that out-of-body experience, or autoscopic experience, may be induced by stimulating certain areas of the temporal lobe of the brain (Neppe, 1984c; Penfield, 1958). This may be mechanistically quite different from out-of-body experience as it occurs in the paragnost. The limited expression is a final common pathway (Neppe & Holden, 1989; Reed, 1972). Great dispute exists with regard to a second final common pathway: the commonality of the near-death experience (Neppe & Tucker, 1989). Similar comments can be made with regard to deja vu (Neppe, 1983b) and also with regard to hallucinations (Neppe, 1983a).

Hallucinations are particularly relevant because using a psychiatric model they persistently are interpreted as expressing major psycho-pathology, generally psychosis (Van den Berg, 1982). Yet there are normal hallucinations. Well-known, for example, are so-called hyp-nagogic and hypnopompic phenomena occurring in normal subjects and also in the narcoleptic, and not regarded as pathologic as such (Neppe, 1983a).

Less well-known are the surveys by Sidgwick and associates (Sidgwick, Johnson, Myers, & Sidgwick, 1894) and 50 years later by West (1962) who demonstrated, in a very large survey (Sidgwick, approximately 10,000; West, more than 1,000) of normal people, that the incidence of hallucinations, predominantly visual hallucinations, occurring at least once in a lifetime in the population, is of the order of 10–14%. These visual hallucinations cluster around a death, even when that death is unexpected and unknown. The significance of this finding is relevant, not only to parapsychological research, but to the psychiatric context of a major trauma being linked in terms of reported past memories of a strange experience, such as a visual hallucination. This, therefore, would potentially accentuate inaccurate anecdotal memories (Devereux, 1974; Ehrenwald, 1948; Greyson, 1977).

Given the small ways of expression of the brain, some of which may be subjective paranormal experiences (SPE), (Neppe, 1980a) it is im-portant to analyze which psychiatric diagnostic groups are most likely to exhibit SPE, and whether these have been perceived as pathologic or normal. Table 1 lists the major groups dealt with.

TABLE 1

Psychiatric Conditions Most Likely Associated
with Subjective Paranormal Experiences:

Group 1. Schizophrenics;
Group 2. Hallucinogenic Mobilized Psychoses;
Group 3. Subjective Paranormal Experience Psychosis;
Group 4. Trancelike Dissociative Phenomena;
Group 5. The Psychotic Psychic;
Group 6. Epilepsy and Non-Epileptic Temporal Lobe Dysfuction.

Schizophrenics

Schizophrenics and other psychiatric patients with similar psychoses, like acute exacerbations with schizoaffective illness, and patients with manic episodes, often present, with hallucinatory and delusional experiences that are very much linked to the sub-culture (Neppe & Smith, 1982). If they are religious, they may perceive themselves as Jesus, or as Judas, and may therefore want to act out, in a grandiose or persecutory manner. Those with mystical type experiences may perceive themselves as higher beings, or alternatively, may regard themselves as being extremely psychic, and having clairvoyant and telepathic abilities (Neppe & Smith, 1982; Rogo 1975).

Such symptoms are particularly relevant because they reflect the Schneiderian "first-rank symptoms" of psychosis, namely: passivity phenomena and alienation (Schneider, 1959). Alienation and passivity phenomena relate to a distortion of the patient's ego, whereby influences are received from outside producing an influence on thinking, emotions, drives, impulses or bodily functions. When not only influence occurs, but the outside influences are perceived by the patient as controlling these phenomena, the experiences at times become alien. Such features are hallmarks of psychosis, and the major component is the reference to self, with distortion of ego boundaries (Neppe, 1988a, 1988b).

Logically an extension of this distortion of self is the perception that the patient is receiving information from outside by telepathy or clairvoyance; that others are reading his mind; and that he can read others' minds; that his thoughts can be broadcast; and that there is therefore no need to communicate by speech. Patients may develop a fixed delusional system pertaining to their being psychic, or being able to predict the future. It is interesting that such patients are unable to substantiate any factual evidence, and when they do give examples, the examples are usually inconsequential, and sometimes non-sequiturs. ("I knew I would see my father, and I did, three weeks later." Or: "I knew I would see my father, and, when I did, I was aware that he was the devil.") These features therefore have links with psychosis. Very often the patient talks in vague terms or contradictory terms, and when confronted in this regard, will attempt to explain the phenomena in an even more delusional kind of framework (Neppe, 1984b; Neppe & Holden, 1989).

These patients do not cope at the biopsychofamiliosociocultural level, and they will tolerate high doses of neuroleptic agents—fulfilling the two criteria I have suggested for psychosis. Moreover, this antipsychotic group of drugs will assist in allowing them to attain greater awareness of reality. Thus, the schizophrenia-like psychoses, and, at times, manic illness, may present with a grandiose component, looking like psychic experiences, but manifesting other groups of vegetative and cognitive symptoms, which are clearly inappropriate and associated with decompensation and impaired functioning of the patient.

Hallucinogenic Mobilized Psychoses

The second sub-group relates to patients who have had hallucinogen drugs, either during their episode acutely, or in the past. Two commonly used ones are LSD and PCP. These drugs produce a schizophrenia-like state, either acutely or in more chronic form, but with certain special differences. Very often the mystical element, in terms of mind expansiveness is particularly exaggerated, and this produces distortions in appreciation of time perception. Such distortions are common in schizophrenics, but hallucinogen-mobilized psychosis is the prototype example (Neppe, 1982c).

These patients have difficulty differentiating seconds from hours, days from minutes. Their estimate of time is very wrong. They exhibit a certain apparent mystical expansiveness, whereby they describe feelings of all-knowing, and awareness of realities that they could not even have believed were possible: these experiences may be extremely frightening, or may be associated with euphoric qualities. At times they talk of flashbacks back to such experiences. All these experiences may be reflecting their acute psychotic reality, either under the acute influence of hallucinogens, or through their presenting with a more prolonged schizophrenia like kind of illness, which seems to have initially been mobilized by hallucinogens. This condition does not have the typical negative features of schizophrenia: the withdrawal, the apathy, the autism, the out-of-touchness with reality components, and the substantial lack of insight. Instead, these patients have some insight, are aware that something is strange and that something is different. They have positive hallucination type features, but very often they have visual hallucinations as opposed to the classical, complete auditory hallucinations one sees in schizophrenia (Neppe, 1982c; 1983a).

Such cases are at times more difficult to differentiate in terms of psychic experiences because the pseudo-philosophicality and their mind expansiveness at times makes them look like geniuses or extremely intelligent people, until one listens carefully to the quality of thought, and the distortion of interpretation of reality base.

Subjective Paranormal Experience Psychosis

The third group of conditions, of importance at a clinical level, is Subjective Paranormal Experience Psychosis (SPE Psychosis) (Neppe, 1984b). This condition was originally described by myself in the early 1980s to fill a gap in the literature relating to people who gave a history of ostensibly genuine subjective paranormal experiences, starting in childhood. However, at some point in their early adulthood, they presented with acute psychotic decompensation.

The major feature that had changed—heralding the psychosis—related to self-reference ideation. Suddenly their awareness, their "psychic experiences," were not about others or about the things of little relevance to themselves; instead, they started having experiences about themselves producing enormous distress, because of the dysphoric nature of such experiences such as beliefs that they may die (Neppe & Tucker, 1989).

This condition was characterized by a cluster of features as follows:

1. onset of subjective paranormal experiences (SPEs) during childhood, often before the age of five, certainly before the age of ten;

2. history of numerous subjectively well-validated subjective paranormal experiences (SPEs) which related to others, never to themselves;

3. history of onset of a psychotic episode at any stage of one's life manifesting as self-reference "delusions" pertaining to at least one of these subjective paranormal experiences;

4. such an SPE may relate to the subject's death;

5. a phase of acute turmoil precipitated by self-referential SPEs with the conviction that the SPE is true, but turmoil because it cannot be proven;

6. a phase of very sudden recovery after the SPE has been shown to be false;

7. absence of progression with no phase of deterioration longer than six months;

8. absence of family history of major psychiatric illness;

9. presence, at times, of family history of subjective paranormal experiences;

10. or alternatively, marked antagonism within the primary family group to psi;

11. absence of response to the appropriate management of the conventional differential diagnosis which is most reasonable;

12. no previous psychiatric history;

13. maintenance of congruous and appropriate affective responses;

14. exclusion of physical causes (Neppe, 1984b).

Trancelike Experiences: Paragnosts and Hysterics

The fourth group of subjects have trancelike experiences. Again, there is a subdivision of those that are coping and functional, and apparently claim trancelike experiences as part of their mediumistic communications. These subjects, in general, have subjective paranormal experiences generally of very diverse kinds, such as out-of-body experiences, and various kinds of contemporaneous, retrocognitive and precognitive clairvoyant or telepathic type experience, either in waking reality or during dreams. They may or may not claim psychokinetic experiences. Their trancelike experiences are usually associated with an alteration or defect of consciousness and they have an amnesia in general for any verbalizations that occur during this phase. This amnesia is not, however, invariable, and it is not uncommon for these subjects to exhibit a dual consciousness. The quality of verbalization or vocalization may vary both in kind of voice (i.e., own or other) and in degree of veridical information (Neppe, 1982b; Neppe & Smith, 1982).

As opposed to this "normal" sub-group is a second group of patients who have hysterical dissociative episodes whereby they assume a different form of identity or behavior and exhibit amnesic components. This generally follows on a major stress in their life, and has an acute onset and relatively acute offset. At a later point in time there may be patchy memories, and generally these episodes can be recreated in such altered states of consciousness as hypnosis. The core component of such conditions relates to the appropriateness of the psychodynamics (Neppe & Smith, 1982).

The problem with the two subgroups of these conditions is that it is possible the subject may exhibit trance kinds of experiences, and also hysterically dissociate. In any event, clearly any vocalizations obtained during so-called psychic trance experiences may well be contaminated by underlying psychodynamics and emotional state of the subject (Devereux, 1974).

The Psychotic Psychic

The fifth group is similar to the first, the group of patients with subjective paranormal experience psychosis. But in this instance, it is approached from the other end. Patients who are psychotic or exhibit other forms of what is perceived as special, bizarre pathology, such as seizure disorders, are accepted within the subculture, or within their preliterate culture, as having special mystical abilities. They are trained to become indigenous healers, witch-doctors, sangomas, or shamans (Neppe & Smith, 1982).

This subgroup of patients is biochemically distinct because they exhibit toleration of high doses of antipsychotic agents, and need control of their symptoms with psychotropic medication. Alternatively, their mystical behavior—seizures—responds to anticonvulsants (Neppe & Smith, 1982).

Non-epileptic Temporal Lobe Dysfunction and Temporal Lobe Epilepsy

There is an important, sixth group of patients with non-epileptic temporal lobe dysfunction and with temporal lobe epilepsy who may hypothetically manifest subjective paranormal experiences. This hypothesis is based on the reverse research, whereby I demonstrated, in the early 1980s, that there is a very substantially increased incidence of possible temporal lobe symptoms in subjective paranormal experients (Nelson, 1980; Neppe, 1980b, 1983c, 1984c). These are subjects who claim a large a number of SPEs of at least 4 different kinds, and these SPEs have been subjectively validated on at least 16 occasions. They form the tip of the iceberg of apparent substantial paragnosts. Without exception they manifested temporal lobe symptomatology, both relating to their SPEs (i.e., a state phenomenon), and also, independent of their SPEs (i.e., a trait phenomenon) (Neppe, 1983c). This suggested that an anomalous pattern of temporal lobe functioning may allow them to experience an exogenous or endogenous reality, which most people are unable to experience (Neppe, 1984c).

It is interesting that the "normal" subjective paranormal experients, however, exhibit possible temporal lobe symptoms of qualitatively different or unusual kinds. They experience, for example, pleasant, perfumy, or flowery olfactory hallucinations, (Neppe, 1983) in addition to experiencing, at times, the more common olfactory hallucination of temporal lobe epilepsy, namely, unpleasant, burning, or rotting smells (Neppe, 1981a, 1983). In addition, these patients do not experience temporal lobe epileptic type deja vu, but subjective paranormal experience deja vu (Neppe, 1983b). These point to qualitative differences that may still localize the area of integration of SPE to the temporal lobe, which, in addition, for theoretical reasons, would be a good choice (Neppe, 1981a, 1981b, 1982a, 1984c).

Consequently, I set out to establish whether or not the reverse was true. Do patients with non-epileptic temporal lobe dysfunction, or patients with temporal lobe epilepsy, have more subjective paranormal experiences? Unfortunately, this research is not easy. Firstly, the great majority of the population, generally 70–90%, in numerous surveys in different countries, claim at least one subjective paranormal experience in their lives, with the consequence that the occurrence of SPEs in this population is of no great significance (Neppe, 1981c; Swiel & Neppe, 1986). What may be more relevant is the occurrence of *frequent* SPEs. This is common ground in patients with temporal lobe dysfunction and temporal lobe epilepsy.

It is interesting that, in my experience, when these patients are placed onto anticonvulsant medication, such as carbamazepine (tegretol), they invariably improve, in terms of their temporal lobe symptomatology, and this improvement parallels the diminution or non-occurrence of subjective paranormal experiences, as well as a diminution in creativity, in musical ability, and ability to write poetry. Results at this point relate to my open studies and my pilot experience with these patients involving careful evaluations. The numbers are extremely low, in that the majority of patients with temporal lobe epilepsy do not want to talk about their SPE symptoms lest they are labelled as uncontrolled. There are numerous constrictions and restrictions to such discussions because of the medical and legal implications of operating machinery and driving vehicles for patients who are still seizing. This appears to be an extremely promising direction of research, however. It is interesting that we have described a family with coexistent temporal lobe dysfunction and subjective paranormal experiences (Hurst & Neppe, 1981, 1982). It appears that a family history of epilepsy is a common phenomenon amongst paragnosts. Again, this is fraught with diagnostic difficulties because the patient with epilepsy is seldom available for further investigation. There are anecdotal components to this.

Perspective

This paper has attempted to evaluate psi in the clinical psychiatric context. Clearly the phenomenon occurs. At times the description appears to have psychotic elements. There is always a psychodynamic flavoring to experiences of various kinds, but the essence of pathology appears best based on the biopsychofamiliosociocultural model of the patient not coping, and the patient being able to tolerate, and respond to, appropriate psychotropic medication, particularly neuroleptic medication or anticonvulsants, such that this may implicate underlying biochemical traces.

It appears that the area of the brain most involved is the temporolimbic system. However, clearly psychodynamics are of enormous relevance in any psychotherapeutic relationship, and attempts at explaining phenomena may involve psychodynamic explanations, even in the organic patient.

REFERENCES

American Psychiatric Association Committee. (1987). *Diagnostic and statistical manual: DSM-III-R* (Third revised ed.). Washington, D.C.: American Psychiatric Association.

Bleuler, E. (1911). *Dementia praecox of the group of schizophrenias*. New York: International University.

Devereux, G. (1974). Extrasensory perception and psychoanalytic epistemology. In G. Devereux (Ed.), *Psychoanalysis and the occult* (pp. 16–46). London: Souvenir Press.

Ehrenwald, J. (1948). *Telepathy and medical psychology*. New York: Norton.

Greyson, B. (1977). Telepathy and mental illness: Deluge or delusion? *Journal of Nervous and Mental Disease, 165*(3), 184–199.

Hurst, L. A., & Neppe, V. M. (1981). A familial study of subjective paranormal experience in temporal lobe dysfunction subjects. *Parapsychological Journal of South Africa, 2*(2), 56–64.

Hurst, L. A., & Neppe, V. M. (1982). Psi-genetics: An organic perspective. *Parapsychological Journal of South Africa, 3*(1), 54–57.

Kraepelin, E. (1899). *Psychiatrie: Ein Lehrbuch fur Studerende und aerzte* (6th ed.). Leipzig, East Germany: Barth.

Laing, R. D. (1976). *The facts of life: An essay in feelings, facts and fantasy*. New York: Pantheon.

Nelson, G. K., & Neppe, V. M. (1980). The neurophysiological wave correlates of a controlled sample of subjective paranormal experients. *Parapsychological Journal of South Africa, 1*(2), 99–101.

Neppe, V. M. (1980a). Subjective paranormal experience. *Psi, 2*(3), 2–3.

Neppe, V. M. (1980b). Subjective paranormal experience and temporal lobe symptomatology. *Parapsychological Journal of South Africa, 1*(2), 78–98.

Neppe, V. M. (1981a). Review article: Symptomatology of temporal lobe epilepsy. *South African Medical Journal, 60*(27), 902–907.

Neppe, V. M. (1981b). Review article: Non-epileptic symptoms of temporal lobe dysfunction. *South African Medical Journal, 60*(25), 989–991.

Neppe, V. M. (1981c). A study of the incidence of subjective paranormal experience. *Parapsychological Journal of South Africa, 2*(1), 15–37.

Neppe, V. M. (1982a). Differing perspectives to the concept of temporal lobe epilepsy. *The Leech, 52*(1), 6–10.

Neppe, V. M. (1982b). Psychiatric interpretations of subjective paranormal perception. *Parapsychological Journal of South Africa, 3*(1), 6–17.

Neppe, V. M. (1982c). Schizophrenia: A guide to clinical diagnosis. *South African Journal of Hospital Medicine, 8*(4), 88–92.

Neppe, V. M. (1983a). Anomalies of smell in the subjective paranormal experient. *Psychoenergetics-Journal of Psychophysical Systems, 5*(1), 11–27.

Neppe, V. M. (1983b). The hallucination: A priority system for its evaluation. *Parapsychology Review, 18*(4), 14–15.

Neppe, V. M. (1983c). Non-responsive psychosis: A biochemical difference. *South African Medical Journal, 63*(21), 797–798.

Neppe, V. M. (1983d). *The psychology of deja vu: Have I been here before?* Johannesburg: Witwatersrand University Press.

Neppe, V. M. (1983e). Temporal lobe symptomatology in subjective paranormal experients. *Journal of the American Society for Psychical Research, 77*, 1–30.

Neppe, V. M. (1984a). Delusions, culture and the media. *South African Medical Journal, 65*(23), 915.

Neppe, V. M. (1984b). Subjective paranormal experience psychosis. *Parapsychology Review, 15*(2), 7–9.

Neppe, V. M. (1984c). The temporal lobe and anomalous experience. *Parapsychological Journal of South Africa, 5*(1), 36–47.
Neppe, V. M. (1988a). Psychopathology of psi: A new classification. *Parapsychology Review, 19*(6), 8–11.
Neppe, V. M. (1988b). Psychopathology of psi: A perspective. *Parapsychology Review, 19*(5), 1–3.
Neppe, V. M. (1989a). *Innovative psychopharmacotherapy.* New York: Raven Press.
Neppe, V. M. (1989b). Near-death experiences: A new challenge in temporal lobe phe-nomenology? Comments on "A neurobiological model for near-death experi-ences." *Journal of Near-Death Studies, 7,* 243–248.
Neppe, V. M. (1989c). Psychopharmacological strategies in non-responsive psychotics. In V. M. Neppe (Ed.), *Innovative psychopharmacotherapy* (pp. 94–122). New York: Raven Press.
Neppe, V. M., & Holden, T. (1989). Innovations in schizophrenia management. In V. M. Neppe (Ed.), *Innovative psychoparmacotherapy* (pp. 58–93). New York: Raven Press.
Neppe, V. M., & Smith, M. E. (1982). Culture, psychopathology and psi: A clinical relationship. *Parapsychological Journal of South Africa, 3*(1), 1–5.
Neppe, V. M., & Tucker, G. J. (1989). Atypical, unusual and cultural psychoses. In H. I. Kaplan & B. J. Sadock (Eds.), *Comprehensive textbook of psychiatry* (5th ed.) (pp. 842–852). Baltimore: Williams & Wilkins.
Neppe, V. M., & Wessels, W. H. (1979). Psychotic toleration of neuroleptic medication. *South African Medical Journal, 56*(27), 1149.
Penfield, W. (1958). Functional localization in temporal lobe and deep Sylvian areas. *Research Publications of the Association for Research in Nervous & Mental Disorders, 36,* 210–216.
Reed, G. (1972). *The psychology of anomalous experience.* London: Hutchinson University Library.
Rogo, D. S. (1975). Psi and psychosis: A review of the experimental evidence. *Journal of Parapsychology, 39,* 120–127.
Schneider, K. (1959). *Clinical psychopathology.* Hamilton, NY: Grune & Stratton.
Sidgwick, H., Johnson, A., Myers, F. W. H., & Sidgwick, E. M. (1894). Report on the census of hallucinations. *Proceedings of the Society for Psychical Research, 10,* 25–422.
Swiel, D. J., & Neppe, V. M. (1986). The incidence of subjective anomalous experience in naive subjects. *Parapsychological Journal of South Africa, 7*(1), 34–53.
Szasz, T. (1957). *Pain and pleasure.* New York: Basic Books.
Van den Berg, J. H. (1982). On hallucinating. In A. J. J. De Koning & F. A. Jenner (Eds.), *Phenomenology and psychiatry* (pp. 97–110). New York: Grune & Stratton.
West, D. J. (1962). *Psychical research today.* Middlesex: Penguin.

DISCUSSION

HARARY: Isn't it possible that psi is also sometimes a positive response to other things and is in itself part of coping in a positive manner to other events? Also, the use of the term psychics, I assume you're using that term loosely since we don't really know what those are yet. And, can a person be diagnosed as psychotic and still be experiencing legit-imate psi?

NEPPE: You have already answered the first two. The third one, I don't know. Bruce Greyson tried to address the question of psychosis but overall it hasn't been well addressed at all. It is very difficult because psi is such an elusive phenomenon and objective tests in a lab are probably not best done on people who can't concentrate anyway. I think this is the essence of it all. One does very often see escape phenomena. I will just throw around an interesting one. I remember one of my colleagues at a local mental hospital, a male psychiatrist round about 50, whose patient had an episode of crying and was most distressed, going on for days. She kept insisting that he had died. We kept saying, "But he hasn't died, here he is." We brought him along and this relieved her a little, but she was still distressed. A few months later, he died suddenly after not being ill. The exact time relationships are unclear as it only occurred to me some years later that this kind of event could conceivably happen. I started saying to myself, "Hold on. These kinds of events do seem to happen in a psychotic related context as well. Is there a coincidence component? Is there any subjective or objective validation?" Unless one does rigid scientific research, recording predictions of any kind, irrespective of how bizarre they really seem to be, I don't think one can have the answer.

VON LUCADOU: I think it is very important to realize that real psi phenomena are elusive, and the phenomena which are reported by psychotic persons are not elusive. They always say that they have these feelings. I think this is a good discriminator for detecting real psi events and non-real psi events.

NEPPE: Excellent point.

MCHARG: I think I enjoyed the talk as much as Vernon Neppe did himself. I wanted to make one point about known psychics and a psychotic patient who I've mentioned before, a young schizophrenic who I was interviewing for the very first time. He'd never met me before, and this was the time when I had been preoccupied with Jungian synchronicity, but this didn't come into the interview at all. On pressing him as to how he felt that his illness had begun, he said that it had started when he was aged five, and his father and mother were having an argument about Jung's concept of synchronicity. It so happened that his parents had in fact separated at that time. Many years later I had the opportunity of meeting his father and raising this question with him. The father made it quite clear that he had never heard of Jung. This is just an example of what surely was a paranormal phenomenon in the case of the schizophrenic patient.

BENOR: Unfortunately patients don't come to these conferences and don't tend to conform to the categories that we set up. Often times they like to tease us by sitting between them and demonstrating phenomena that cross the boundaries. In South America they teach healers and mediums to control their epilepsy as a way of entering into mediumship and it may be that we have something to learn from them.

NEPPE: That's a very interesting point. What incidentally is relevant in that context, and also in the context of the potential link between epilepsy and psi experience, is the fact that one so commonly finds family loadings of epileptics in people with subjective paranormal experiences. I was in Oregon a month or so ago speaking to somebody who was in charge of watching out for bush fires from a little cabin at the top of a mountain. He explained to me that it becomes very frightening when the lightening strikes. He has a particular place to stand which has special kinds of conductors to avoid him being killed by the lightning which sometimes strikes his cabin. He said, "It makes one fully aware. I'm fully able to see all the way through into the future." I said to him, "Really." I got very excited and asked, "Does that happen often?" He then told me about a couple of instances of precognition. I said to him, "Tell me about the smells you get." He said, "I get these pleasant perfumey smells." I thought I was on the right track so I said, "Who in your family has epilepsy?" He said, "My mother's epileptic." I said, "All right, thank you." So, there is this link up, and it's not a small link up. It's a major link up.

LANG: I want to ask you a personal question about working with the police and smelling some odors that were documented around the death of an individual. Are you saying to me that a normal person can have these kinds of experiences without temporal lobe dysfunction?

NEPPE: Yes. I have used the expression anomalous temporal lobe functioning because you can base the interpretation on different kinds of temporal lobe functioning. In other words, there is a different way of appreciating reality from the ordinary person. I don't think you ought to use the phrase normal-abnormal in that context because all my subjective paranormal experience population were eminently normal, but they all had these features. The fact is, that if one has these features and one has a seizure disorder, then why not treat the seizure disorder? If one was psychotic one would treat the psychosis. But people have these experiences and they're quite normal, and there has to be an area of the brain that allows them to integrate or appreciate these experiences which do not necessarily come from outside. They may originate within the brain: my area of research at a subjective level does not allow appreciation of origins. I look at subjects as opposed to the experiences, and try to link them up in terms of appropriate patterns of brain functioning.

KRAMER: Last year in Holland, there were two conferences where clients and psychiatrists came together to discuss the topic of hearing voices in their heads. It turned out that it was very, very good, especially since the clients and the psychiatrists were able to give addresses about the topic and talk to each other on the same level. It turned out that both the clients and the psychiatrists learned a lot from each other. It has been a tremendous success. Actually, they did it twice because one conference was not enough to cover all the topics they had to talk about.

NEPPE: Just to corroborate that, most of what I have learned about psychopathology, I've learned from my patients.

WICKRAM: We know that hallucinations can be generated by psychopathological crisis, by drugs and unusual sensory stimulation. But DSM-III seems to pay no attention to the fact that if you walk into a room of people who are non-psychotic, nearly 10% of those people, "normal" people, can hallucinate in some sensory modalities. They can do this but the difference between these people and the psychotics is that they can turn their hallucination on and off. They have voluntary control of the hallucinatory process. DSM-III, as far as I can see, pays no attention to that.

NEPPE: Certainly one doesn't find recognized by the American Psychiatric Association in general, the perception of hallucinations as normal phenomena because one tends to see patients with pathology. I don't think patients with normal spontaneous hallucinatory experiences have ever been reported to be able to turn them on or off. In the great majority of instances, the hallucinations have tended to be of visual kind, and tended to have been very rare as phenomena. I think the point that you are making, which is a good one, is the fact that these kinds of experiences occur in the context of people that are coping, that are functioning, and where the hallucinations do not intrude to any marked degree into psychopathology.

WICKRAM: The dimension of coping is critical. The dimension of control is critical. If you can't control, you feel out of control and then you think you're crazy.

NEPPE: The control context you are using there is the control in terms of response.

WICKRAM: Yes, self-control of the material.

VAN DE CASTLE: I'd like to acknowledge that Dr. Neppe has said he has learned about psychopathology from patients. I would like to ask Dr. Neppe where has he learned about psi?

NEPPE: To a large degree, from psychics, exactly the same kind of source.

HARARY: What are they?

NEPPE: Alright, from subjective paranormal experients.

TIERNEY: DSM-III-R makes the distinction between ideas of reference and it excludes delusions of reference. I have never been clear of what the distinction is. Could somebody tell me?

NEPPE: When one speaks of delusions, one is speaking of fixed false beliefs which are inappropriate within the framework of the socioculture of the subject. When one talks of ideas of reference, these may not be inappropriate fixed false beliefs. They may just be the interpretation of something as having a critical relevance to oneself. One common idea of reference which is not delusional is the idea that "maybe they were whispering, I'm sure they were whispering about me." This certainly would not be interpreted as psychotic in the delusional sense. Delusions, by definition, have a psychotic framework to them.

TIERNEY: Do you think it is clinically significant enough to include a differentiation?

NEPPE: Yes. I think the differentiation is clinically significant from the point of view of schizotypal personality disorder, because if one was talking about delusions per se, one would have to say these people have an underlying psychosis. If they had an underlying psychosis, it would be difficult to say they have an underlying personality disorder. Now, of course, we've got to look historically at the schizotypal personality as previously having been called simple schizophrenia. So, we are very much dealing with an interface area.

WEST: I think the basic thing here is the distinction between the phenomena that one sees in people who appear well and those who are very obviously ill. The phenomena in the sick have, apparently, a physiological basis in the majority of cases. Some of them are due to hallucinogenic drugs, some of them are due to drugs which have a toxic effect, some of them are due to the alteration of the biochemistry of the brain which can be shown by their reaction to psychotropic drugs, and so forth. For those phenomena, we seem to have a kind of physical explanation. For the spontaneous psychic experiences that occur sporadically to people in apparently perfectly normal states who are functioning perfectly well in the community, I think we have no explanation, whatever. I think it is necessary to try to explore, not only the hallucinations which are veridical, in the sense that people can attach the content to some particular stimulus, but also those which are not. There are various theories that go around in psychical research which have not been mentioned here, such as they are ghosts, they are spirits of the dead, they are people from another planet, all sorts of things. But really, we just don't know and we ought to find out more.

MEYER: Following up on what Dr. West just said, there seems to be some room in your taxonomy, I think, specifically in the SPE area for people who are normal functioning and have sudden shifts in paranormal experiences. I'm thinking specifically of Grof's work and wondered if you had taken that into consideration?

NEPPE: Yes, I think it's very important, and I think the context of shifts in terms of altered states of consciousness and in terms of psi sensitivity, has certainly been an area that has been addressed. Shifts in awareness of incidents of subjective paranormal experience seem to occur as spontaneous phenomena within individuals. Certainly, one has seen that a major problem from a laboratory point of view is that people always talk about replicating an experiment. Why cannot parapsychology produce the replicable scientific experiment if their findings are appropriate? Well, if one looks at the subjects, the experimenters, and the researchers, as the major piece of apparatus, and if one looks at the complete context of everything having to be just right, it is difficult to exactly replicate all the apparatus. These shifts, therefore, I think are very interesting phenomena because they might in a way allow just that little bubble to escape through.

PARKER: I'm going to take up in my paper aspects to do with perceptual changes and shifts, and states of consciousness. From this point of view, it's very interesting to look at the prodromal phase, the initial phase in the development of schizophrenia. A couple of studies have found that schizophrenic patients are actually sensitive to when they go into a psychotic episode. They know these certain perceptual changes. Do you know anybody who has actually studied this from the point of view of testing psi, whether psi tests have been carried out before the psychotic experience becomes full-blown?

NEPPE: No. I think that would be a very interesting area to study. I think the major limitation is the psychiatric status of the patient, and the fact that they may not be able to fully cooperate in tests requiring particular modes of attention, which may be foreign to them.

HARARY: I was just thinking about the idea of shifts of attention. If we approach psi as neutral information that is available to be observed, then aren't we talking about what it takes to get to observe it? There may be many different kinds of things that can help an individual observe that information in different ways. Also, people, who are in either various states of consciousness or various states of being in touch or out of touch with what we call reality, might observe, relate to, or be able to access that information in various ways depending upon where they are coming from initially.

NEPPE: I think that's a comment which seems very reasonable.

THE NORMALITY AND ABNORMALITY OF PARANORMAL EXPERIENCES: PREDICTIONS FROM CLINICAL, COGNITIVE, AND PSI MODELS

Adrian Parker

Introduction

My title I believe gives expression to what I think is a common experience among clinicians having an interest in psi-experiences: it is clear that for many individuals reporting paranormal events, these experiences are to be best understood as part of a larger personality breakdown. Yet there are also a number of apparently healthy individuals who report paranormal experiences and while they may find these experiences initially disturbing, these individuals do not appear to show any form of psychopathology. Finally there exists a third group, more difficult to assess, who either as a consequence of, or in some cases concomitant with these experiences, seek a conceptual framework for them by joining various occult and mystical groups.

The central question is then: are paranormal and abnormal experiences intimately or just incidently linked? Certainly parapsychology and clinical psychology share a common heritage in the field that was once called abnormal psychology. Indeed when boundaries were not so carefully drawn up at the turn of the century, psychical research was considered mainstream enough to be represented at the First International Congress of Psychology. Although I know of no standard textbook of clinical psychology or psychiatry that nowadays gives a mention to parapsychology, there have been numerous big names among the psychotherapists who have declared an interest in parapsychology. Here I am thinking of not only Freud and Jung but of even contemporary examples such as Jerome Frank and Carl Rogers. It is also true that much of what the early investigators of the Society for Psychical Research regarded as part of their subject matter—mesmerism, automatisms, mediumship, and dissociated states—now is conveniently placed under the rubric "altered states of consciousness." However even this area is a kind of exotic no-man's land and when the term does appear in psychiatric textbooks, it is usually treated as synonymous with disturbances of attention and ascribed to malfunctions in the brain's reticular activating system.

It is then the aim of this paper to attempt to find or re-discover areas of cross fertilization between clinical psychology and parapsychology. In doing so I will have recourse to refer to input from not only clinical research but also from cognitive psychology, applying the form of attribution theory so enthusiastically recommended by Susan Blackmore and James Alcock. It is my suggestion that we test these models along with the paranormal model for the purpose of making differential predictions. As regards taking the paranormal model seriously, the view taken here is, while it cannot be said that this is "proven" (an impossibility in empirical science) there are good grounds for continuing to work with it (Parker, 1987). Although it would be premature to have any firm ideas about the outcome of predictions from various models, it does seem clear that we can gain from this a greater understanding of how these experiences relate to human functioning and states of mind. What I would like to focus on in particular is where I believe parapsychology has already an important potential contribution to make to clinical psychology. This concerns the two dimensions that seem the most promising as regards relating paranormal experiences to other psychological phenomena: the *need for absorption* and *perceptual defensiveness*. I believe these dimensions can also teach us something of a fundamental nature about psychotic experiences.

Before getting into differential diagnostics, it may be useful to give some illustrative examples of competing explanatory models. The accompanying brief with the invitation to this conference indicated that examples of psi in clinical practice would be of primary concern. Now having worked for the last two years primarily with teaching and research, I had no current examples readily available. Not long after this at a lecture given by Robert Morris, the chairman of this conference, during his visit Gothenburg, I met with a psychotherapist colleague who had more then two years previously been involved in treating on a private basis the mother of the son I had then been seeing in the context of my previous work at a child psychiatry unit. We had not had contact since then and I naturally had wondered how it fared for our former patient. Two days later on returning from Stockholm, I learned that this patient had been seeking me and wished to arrange a consultation. This was arranged and I think it turned out to be meaningful for her and her son. Coincidence or not, it was also meaningful for me since it gave me a needed example to present here.

Now of course to attribute this to more than coincidence may be merely an example of attribution of meaning, by as Blackmore and Troscianko (1985) would put it, setting the chance baseline too low in order to gain illusory control of and make sense of random events. However given that the majority of the populations of Western countries where surveys have been carried out report experiences they interpret as paranormal and which often seem intrinsically improbable, it seems doubtful that this can be a general explanation. Other cognitive theories abound attempting to relate belief in the paranormal to credulity, lack of critical thinking, and irrationalism (Alcock, 1981; Zusne, 1985). On the other hand, turning the argument on its head, I am not the first among those who take the paranormal hypothesis seriously to highlight the role of meaning in promoting apparent paranormal events. No lesser a world authority on quantum physics than David Bohm (1988) has theorized on the role of meaning in linking mental and physical events and in providing a facilitatory framework for paranormal phenomena. Perhaps the nearest that there is to a generally accepted theory in parapsychology—the conformance model of Rex Stanford's—gives a primary role to meaning and teleology as influencing behavior and decision-making processes. Clearly there are competing models here.

The Clinical Model

Let me introduce the second non-parapsychological model of psi experiences by a further clinical example. I am presently replying to a letter (which also happened to arrive at an appropriate point in time) which relates many features typical of cases I encountered when I worked clinically. This concerns a 14-year-old boy who reports hearing inexplicable sounds and footsteps, seeing black shapes even crosses. Occasionally door handles appear to rotate and he is drawn by a power to certain doors. Voices tell him to do certain things under threat of punishment. It is claimed that one of the apparitions seen, was witnessed by a friend. The letter ends asking whether this can be a poltergeist disturbance. For a clinical psychologist such experiences are alarming since they are indicative of a schizophrenic process.

This is a process which usually has its debut in adolescence and is characterized by the breakdown of ego-boundaries giving rise to symptoms such as "thought transference" and "the presence of a force or persons not there." It would seem to ring true in this case and it naturally raises the question of how do we reconcile the fact that many of the phenomena of parapsychology are regarded as symptoms in psychiatry? A look at DSM-III-R, the current psychiatric diagnostic system (see Table 1), shows clinical psychology and parapsychology share some of the same subject matter.

The reporting of apparent paranormal experiences is of even greater diagnostic significance according to so-called Schneiderian first rank symptoms of schizophrenia. These concern the breaking down of ego-boundaries with ideas of thought invasion and thought broadcasting. Schneiderian first rank symptoms form the basis of the much used diagnostic interview procedure called the Present State Examination, developed by Wing and his associates at the Maudsley Hospital.

Now a problem immediately arises when we consider the percentage of the populations of Western countries who report paranormal experiences and believe in extrasensory perception (Palmer, 1979; Haraldsson, 1985). In a classical theory of schizophrenia as a disease entity, it would be absurd to believe that between 55 and 75% of the population show symptoms of it.

Among those who take parapsychology seriously, there have been two attempts to resolve this issue. First, by supposing that the claim of schizophrenics that others are reading their thoughts and influencing them, might actually be right, and alternatively by specifying criteria how one can distinguish a genuine paranormal one from a pseudo one which is symptomatic of disturbance. The classical review by Bruce Greyson (1977) "Telepathy in mental illness: Deluge or delusion?" indicated that the empirical testing of schizophrenics' claims of telepathy, revealed results which clearly favor the delusion verdict. It may well be the case (as Rogo, 1982 pointed out) that the definitive experiment specifically designed to test individual delusions, has yet to be done but there do nevertheless seem to be grounds for supposing that we are dealing with different phenomena in the psychiatric field from the parapsychological one. From this perspective, several writers (Ferguson, 1987; Neppe, 1988) have attempted to identify set criteria for

TABLE 1

DSM-III-R. Numbers 6 and 7 of the Nine Diagnostic Criteria
for Prodromal or Residual Symptoms of Schizophrenia:

6. odd beliefs or magical thinking, influencing behavior and inconsistent with cultural norms, e.g., superstitiousness, belief in clairvoyance, telepathy, "sixth sense," "others can feel my feelings," overvalued ideas, ideas of reference.
7. unusual perceptual experiences, e.g. recurrent illusions, sensing the presence of a force or person not actually present.

how a genuine paranormal experience can be distinguished from a delusory one symptomatic of a psychotic process. A complication lies in the fact that a paranormal type experience is often in itself experienced by individuals as frightening and disturbing. This not withstanding, it does appear to be a distinctive feature of the psychotic state that these experiences become a central preoccupation of the individual, are perceived as part of a larger delusional system of beliefs and most critical of all, as threatening to the integrity of the self.

A further attempt to resolve the problem created by the current proliferation of occult type experiences among the normal population involves the notion of *schizotype personality*. This along with other personality disorders such as schizoid personality and borderline personality was first introduced to DSM-III as a means of reconciling the more all encompassing criteria for diagnosing schizophrenia in the USA with the stricter criteria used in UK. (Arthur Koestler commented that he was 33 times more likely to be diagnosed schizophrenic in the United States than in England.) A schizotype personality is a supposedly schizophrenia prone personality within the normal population. Evidence is however lacking as to whether any of these personality disorders are actually more prone to schizophrenic breakdown. Central to the diagnosis of a schizotype personality are paranormal beliefs, magical thinking, and unusual perceptual experiences. Examples among occult movements of the expression of schizotype personality are not hard to find. Undoubtedly on this basis, the Swedish mystic, Emanuel Swedenborg, would be regarded as a classical example of a schizotype personality. However this case begs the question, since with Swedenborg there are well attested examples of what would seem to be a genuine paranormal ability including the occasion that impressed Immanuel Kant, when Swedenborg told of the exact place of a fire that had broken out in Stockholm before the news could have reached Gothenburg where he was staying. A more contemporary equivalent to Swedenborg, is to be found in the curious work that has gained current popularity known as *A Course in Miracles*. This is an apocalyptic guide to self enlightenment dictated through an inner voice during a period of seven years to Helen Schucman and William Thetford, who by a stroke of irony, were professors of medical psychology at Columbia University!

What is important here is that for clinical psychologists, the introduction of schizotype personality disorder meant the possibility of replacing the illness view of schizophrenia, with a dimensional view of psychosis and psychotic-like experiences; certain individuals being more at risk than others. The work of Loren Chapman and Jean Chapman (1980, 1988) at the University of Wisconsin is outstanding in this respect. They have developed scales for perceptual aberration (especially body image distortions) and magical ideation and then showed that these predict how subjects will be independently rated on the basis of interviews as to the degree of psychotic and psychotic-like experiences reported. What might be viewed as contentious here is that the magical ideation scale is "designed to measure belief in forms of causation that by conventional standards in our culture are invalid, such as thought transmission, psychokinetic effects, precognition, and the transfer of psychical energies between people." Mixed with fairly standard questions about belief in various paranormal phenomena are items of a more morbid nature such, as "I have had the momentary feeling that I might not be human."

Perceptual aberration as a predictor of psychosis is in itself not new—the work of the Humphrey Osmond group in Canada (Hoffer, Kelm, & Osmond, 1975) came to the same conclusion and predates the Chapmans—but it is the thread of relationships they found between perceptual aberration, various occult beliefs, body image distortions and the occurrence of psychotic episodes that is of interest. However, even if we disregard the arbitrary pathological labeling given to some of the experiences, the obvious weakness of this work is the tautology inherent in some of the measures. For instance the interview rating of psychotic episodes is based in part on the degree of belief in thought transmission which itself also features in the magical ideation scale. More important in the present context, the question remains would mere belief in basic paranormal phenomena (i.e. ESP) show any relationship to the more pathological bizarre experiences? The only study to my knowledge to address this, was carried out by Michael Thalbourne (1984) and the findings are particularly interesting and convincing, given that they were precisely the opposite to his own expectations! Thalbourne dealt with the tautology aspect by removing the items relating to belief in basic paranormal phenomena from the magical ideation scale and thereby creating a more purified psychosis scale. He then found this psychosis scale to show a surprisingly significant relationship to the standard (sheep-goat) scale of belief in ESP. Although the relationship between belief in psi and schizotypy was not a strong one, the finding is an important one and one that demands an explanation. It is also important to know whether it is just belief in paranormal phenomena or also apparently veridical experiences that show this relationship. Furthermore, mere psychiatric labeling can hide much heterogeneity. I think I can illustrate this best by my own "twin study."

Recently I have had contact with two Swedish twin sisters, one resides in England and the other in Sweden, who have had frequent out of body experiences and written books about them. The Swedish resident, Agneta Uppman, has reported a least two experiences which have veridical value and on one further occasion both twins appeared to be able to briefly communicate in what seemed to be simultaneously occurring OBE states. What is interesting in the present context are the different reactions of the twins as regards interpreting their experience. Neither of them are dogmatic as regards the interpretation of out-of-body experiences. Agneta is probably the most agnostic and has rejected the solicitations of various occult and New Age groups which abound in Sweden. Her sister on the other hand seems to have had a greater need to seek some interpretive structure for her OBEs and sought contact with the Swedenborg Church in England. Now it is difficult to assert which comes first, the belief structure or the experience, but at least in some cases a paranormal experience may lead to an openness to a wide range of beliefs which might gain one a psychiatric diagnosis. Moreover, as one might expect "out-of-body experiences," while they are not directly specified as "body image distortions" by the Chapman group, they are nevertheless considered as "other schizotypal symptoms" in the general profile of psychosis proneness (Chapman, Edell, & Chapman, 1980). In contradiction of this, it does however seem clear both from a scrutiny of the Chapman's own data and from a study by Blackmore (1986) that when OBEs are carefully defined and distinguished from various body image distortions (such as depersonalization) they are not over-represented in a schizotype or a schizophrenic population.

What of individuals with attested abilities—the high scoring ESP laboratory subjects—what do we know of their beliefs and reactions to having a "proven" ability? There is surprisingly little to go on here but it seems likely once again that there is much individual variation. Two subjects that I tested (Parker, 1974) reported psychic experiences but preferred to interpret them as intuition and both became frightened at the prospect of "being discovered." Last year I was able to contact and interview Miss L. B., a former Swedish high scoring subject. A psychology graduate, she had moved on to have experiences which made ESP trivial and mundane and now works as a counselor with a religious foundation. Evidently the relationship between experience, ability, and belief in this area is a complex one and one where notions of simplistic diagnostics and linear causalities may do more to confound than illuminate the issue. In view of this uncertainty surrounding the meaning of the relationship between apparent paranormal experiences and schizotype personality, it may be as well that we return to basics and ask what is actually known about schizophrenia and schizotypy.

Indeed if there is one issue in mental science that rivals that of the paranormal in terms of controversy, it surely must be the nature of schizophrenia—and this is despite the enormous research effort to resolve the issue. Various theories and findings accumulate—from brain hemispherical asymmetry, suspected virus infection, to excess dopamine. Much of the status of biological psychiatry is staked on a supposed genetic link between these brain abnormalities and psychotic behavior. Appealing as it might be, the supposition does not withstand skeptical scrutiny. Much of the genetic evidence has serious methodological flaws and even the often cited twin studies of Kallman may have been in some measure due to fraud (Rose, Kamin, & Lewontin, 1984). The most recent claim of a breakthrough in this area was published in *Nature* 1988 by a research team from the Middlesex School of Medicine in London. Using genetic markers to study the genetic code of five Icelandic and two English families with a high incidence of schizophrenia, they believed they found a locus on chromosome 5. This was heralded by the press as a breakthrough, yet the linkage was only strong when all "fringe types" of diagnoses (including schizotype personality and various neurotic disorders) were added to the schizophrenia diagnoses. Moreover, *Nature* published in the same issue a joint Swedish-American study which failed to replicate these findings. The most generous interpretation of these findings would be in terms of a genetic vulnerability model of mental disturbance—which is a clear contrast to simple causal genetics.

The same month that *Nature* released these findings, the *British Journal of Clinical Psychology* published what would seem to be the most devastating attack yet on the concept of schizophrenia (Bentall, Jackson, & Pilgrim, 1988) and which, in this writer's opinion, evoked a mere placating response from John Wing who is probably Britain's foremost acknowledged authority on schizophrenia. The lack of agreement in diagnosis, the lack of consistency in findings, and the failure of factor analysis to substantiate a unitary behavioral entity, led the critics to conclude:

> Given that schizophrenia is an entity which seems to have no particular symptoms, which follows no particular course and which responds to no (or perhaps every) particular treatment, it is perhaps not surprising that etiological research has failed to establish that it has any particular cause.

This is not to say that nothing has been learned. The authors of the above review in pointing out the way forward also singled out the work of the Chapman group in suggesting that schizotypy or psychotic like experiences may be normally distributed in the population like other psychological traits. In addition they give credence to the little known work initiated by the Scottish psychologist Graham Foulds, which suggests that mental illness is hierarchical. In clear language, it's necessary to become extremely neurotically crazy before becoming psychotically crazy. Putting this together, it suggests that if there is a genetic factor here, what we may be talking about is a predisposition to unusual perceptual experiences or even dissociation of personality in the face of stress. Let us not forget that splitting or dissociation was fundamental to Bleuler's original conceptualization of schizophrenia.

There is also one study that I think is particularly illuminating in this context. This concerns a follow up study of babies of schizophrenic mothers that is well controlled with both blind assessments and a comparison group (Heston, 1966). All the children were adopted within the first three days after birth and grew up without contact with the mother. (The environmental influence of the schizophrenic parent is thus minimal.) The results of the follow up into adulthood are very instructive: 10% were diagnosed as schizophrenic (none were amongst the control adoptees) and 55% had serious psychosocial impairments. What is however most interesting in the present context is that many of those regarded as "normal" were judged to have creative and colorful life histories. The ability to perceive the world in novel ways may also provide a basis for creativity. Another finding which I think is of interest here comes from the World Health Organization (1979) survey of schizophrenia in different cultures. They found strong support for the view that although psychotic states seem to be universal, their intensity was more benign and their duration shorter in developing countries. Cultural and family support were implicated as important in determining this outcome.

The conclusion I draw from all this work is that schizophrenia and schizotypy are the *disturbed* outcome of a predisposition to perceive the world in unusual ways—that is to say the ability to have unusual perceptual experiences. The predisposition may be genetically inherited and normally distributed. This is, of course, not so far removed from the claim that mystics and schizophrenics share the common ability to experience altered states of consciousness, but react to them differently.

The Cognitive Model

It may be of interest to note that this emphasis on a predisposition towards unusual *perceptual* experiences is actually commensurate with the contribution of the earlier mentioned cognitive approach. In recent years cognitive psychologists have attempted to apply models from the way normal individuals reason to delusional beliefs. A wide range of so-called anomalous phenomena are considered game including paranormal beliefs, hypnosis, and schizophrenia. The individual is considered to be responding to the social demands of the situation and building temporary or permanent belief systems about the universe on the basis of the data he or she is provided with—and like normal individuals he or she stubbornly requires a great deal in the way of disconfirmatory data to change his or her belief system. In schizophrenia it is the anomalous perceptual experience that is primary and the delusions and thought disorders that derive from this (Kihlstrom & Hoyt, 1988; Maher, 1988). Individuals seek out events that are coincidental with or contrary to the anomalous event and form hypotheses around these. There is a suggestion that believers in the paranormal may consistently underestimate the level of what can actually be due to pure coincidence (Blackmore & Troscianko, 1985).

Beyond this, attempts to identify cognitive errors in the thinking of those who believe in and report paranormal events, have however only succeeded in identifying magical ideation as a possible characteristic (Zusne, 1985). This naturally begs the question: what is the nature of the anomalous event? Moreover, why are some individuals more prone to it than others and how do we explain the ways individuals react differently to it? I believe these to be serious shortcomings of the cognitive model.

To answer these questions it is necessary to relate the predispositional concept arrived at above to some of the work done in parapsychology, in particular to what we know about absorption and perceptual defense and explore the ways that paranormal experiences may fit into the models. It is possible that these factors can explain much of the variability in human experience and behavior in this area.

Absorption and Perceptual Defense

The parapsychological model of "subjective paranormal experiences" supposes an extrasensory communication process to exist which is favored by internal attention states. The long tradition of experimental research and spontaneous case studies linking ESP to means of inducing these states such as sensory deprivation, ganzfeld, and hypnosis gives support to this notion. In its simplest formulation the parapsychological model further supposes that ESP functions as a process like ordinary perception which is influenced by the defense mechanisms of personality (Edge, Morris, Palmer, & Rush, 1986). Such defense mechanisms are of course likely to be less active during periods of altered states of consciousness. It is natural then to focus interest on measures of the ability to alter and focus consciousness and the measure known as perceptual defense.

Absorption is defined as "a total attention involving a full commitment of available perceptual, motoric, imaginative, and ideational resources to a unified representation of the attentional object" (Tellegen & Atkinson, 1974). The questionnaire designed to measure this dimension has been used in a variety of psychological research and absorption is reported to be an important variable in dissociation and self awareness, hypnosis, dream vividness and recall, cross modal perception, and out of body experiences (Irwin, 1985b; Råmonth 1985a, 1985b). The few experimental investigations of ESP in relation to the absorption dimension would appear inconclusive but an investigation by Irwin (1985a) found a strong association between reports of spontaneous ESP and absorption. Ironically, many of the questions in the Absorption scale, while not identical with those of the clinical instruments, would appear to relate to the same areas that clinicians use to identify schizotype traits and psychotic-like experiences (see Tables 2 and 3).

TABLE 2

Examples of Possible Related Questions on the Perceptual Aberrations Scale
and the Absorption Scale (in italics)

Sometimes I have had the feeling that I am united with an object near.
Sometimes I feel as if my mind could envelop the whole world.
I have sometimes felt that some part of my body no longer belongs to me.
If I wish, I can imagine that my body is so heavy that I could not move it if I wanted to.
Sometimes I look at things like tables and chairs, they seem strange.
Sometimes I experience things as if they were doubly real.

TABLE 3

Some DSM-III-R Criteria for Schizotype Personality and the Absorption Scale

Ideas of Reference:
Things that might seem meaningless to others often make sense to me.
Odd beliefs or magical thinking:
I often know what someone is going to say before he or she says it.
Unusual Perceptual Experiences e.g. illusions sensing the presence of a force or
    person not actually present.
Often I sense the presence of another person before I actually see or hear him (her).
I sometimes step outside usual self and experience an entirely different state of being.

Although these instruments may be sharing the same dimension (i.e. unusual perceptual experiences and altered states), the truly pathological aspect involves of course threat and lack of control, and in some cases bizarre personal interpretations of the experience. In extreme cases the experience may even take on a dissociated form and be regarded as alien to the self. In this sense it is not surprising that the Absorption scale has been used as a measure of the ability to go into dissociated states (Råmonth, 1985a, 1985b). What is it then that determines the pathological or benign or even pleasurable content of the experience? I suspect this may relate to the defensive nature of the dominant "ego-state" of the individual and the degree of emotional conflict. This naturally involves a view of identity and the self as polymorphous but this appears to be a view that is gaining support in psychology with the return of the concept of dissociation and the current interest in borderline personality and more recently in sub and multiple personality (Rowan, 1989).

Given this view of personality, it is not difficult to suppose that some individuals predisposed to these perceptual alterations, will, with an open, non-defensive self concept, react to them positively while others who are more perceptually defensive may be threatened and perceive them as alien. Much will of course depend on whether such experiences are enforced ones or sought after ones. In other words in this theory *schizophrenia is an enforced state of perceptual absorption in inner conflicts leading to perceptual aberrations which by nature of the individual's defensiveness are interpreted as alien and become delusory.* A third, perhaps predominant group, will naturally seek some conceptual structure for their experiences by interpreting them in the form of some occult belief, and this is of course the group labeled schizotypal.

The instrument that would seem to offer the most sensitive test of defensiveness, is the Defense Mechanism Test (DMT) developed by Ulf Kragh and G. W. Smith in Sweden. Strictly speaking, it is a percept-genesis test rather than a projective test and is designed to evaluate how the individual reacts to a threatening image in terms of the influence of anxiety on perception. The DMT has a good reputation both in and outside Sweden, although some controversy surrounds what it is actually measuring (Sjöberg, 1981; Cooper, 1988; Kline, 1988). Use of the test has been pioneered in parapsychology by Martin Johnson at Utrecht University and Erlandur Haraldsson at the University of Iceland. A remarkable replication rate has been achieved (Johnson & Haraldsson, 1984). However, because of the expertise required, the use of this test has been almost confined to the Johnson-Haraldsson team. Only one attempt has been reported to date to assess its discriminatory value in altered states-ESP work (York & Morris, 1976) and here the lack of a complete DMT series and other methodological problems would seem to prohibit any conclusions being made (Johnson, 1989).

Although the DMT is a test analogue of assessing defensiveness in a threatening situation, it is nevertheless at best a crude measure and the same is certainly true of the Absorption scale. It is also well to remember Michael Persinger's comments on how difficult it is to gain replicable correlations of psi with other variables when the level of the so-called psi-effect is usually somewhere between 1 and 5% above chance. Nevertheless results with the DMT are not only encouraging in their own right but they have a certain construct validity in relating to other lines of research which suggest openness to experience may be an important factor relating to psi (e.g. Honorton & Schechter, 1987).

Some Predictions

No attempt has been made to my knowledge to explore the potential relationship between the need for absorption, defensiveness, and psi. It is conceivable that individuals who have a natural predisposition to or even a need for experiencing alterations in perception and consciousness, and who are open to the content of it, may be receptive to ESP. Rather than relying on purely correlational findings, it may be more effective to actually assess how individuals with a need for absorption and with a known profile on perceptual defense and magical ideation actually react to a testing procedure (such as the ganzfeld) designed to facilitate perceptual changes with the possibility of a psi content. The way such individuals evaluate their experiences afterwards would in addition provide data on which some predictions from the cognitive and clinical models could be tested.

With a cognitive theory, we would expect individuals showing magical ideation to make evaluations that would attribute more significance to chance resemblances between their experiences and free response ESP targets. A clinical theory would make a similar prediction but with the proviso that the effect would depend on the degree to which subjects score highly on magical ideation and perceptual aberration. From a parapsychological viewpoint, it would seem unlikely that magical ideation and cognitive errors would show any clear relationship to actual success on the ESP test. It might be theorized that potential ESP experiences in this group would be often strongly colored by personal needs, although this may not always be so. With the previously mentioned reservation concerning the insensitivity of our instruments, the effect we would be most looking for would be a relationship between absorption, non-defensiveness, and ESP. One could speculate further. It has been reported by the previously mentioned Osmond group and also in a more recent survey (Philipson & Harris, 1985) that the prodromal (initial) signs of a psychotic episode are perceptual changes in form, color, and depth. One of the most promising, but in recent years least tested, hypotheses in parapsychology states that ESP occurs during a sudden change in state or alteration of consciousness. Accordingly, it can be reasoned that any test of the claims of schizophrenics to paranormal ability is best conducted during this prodromal period.

Clearly the field is wide open for research which might help break through some of the impasses which exist in clinical psychology as well as parapsychology. It is probably an opportune period for such a venture since the rise of and popularity of occult groups has demanded both attention and resources from the psychiatric field to explain paranormal experiences. It has been said (Editorial in *Nature* to Lander, 1988) that schizophrenia is arguably the worst disease affecting mankind, even AIDS is not excepted. Paranormal experiences appear universal in every culture and as we have seen are an important part of the diagnostic picture of psychosis. Any greater understanding of these will also further the understanding of psychotic states.

REFERENCES

Alcock, J. (1981). *Parapsychology: Science or magic: A psychological perspective.* Buffalo, New York: Prometheus.

Bentall, R., Jackson, H., & Pilgrim, D. (1988). Abandoning the concept of "schizophrenia": Some implications of validity arguments for psychological research into psychotic phenomena. *British Journal of Clinical Psychology, 27,* 303-324.

Blackmore, S. (1986). Out-of-body experiences in schizophrenia. *Journal of Nervous and Mental Disease, 174,* 615–619.

Blackmore, S., & Troscianko, T. (1985). Belief in the paranormal: Probability judgements, illusory control, and the "chance baseline shift." *British Journal of Psychology, 76,* 459-468.

Bohm, D. (1988). A new theory of the relationship between mind and matter. *Journal of the American Society for Psychical Research, 80,* 113–136.

Chapman, L., & Chapman, J. (1980). Scales for rating psychotic and psychotic-like experiences as continua. *Schizophrenia Bulletin, 6,* 476-489.

Chapman, L., & Chapman, J. (1988). The genesis of delusions. In T. Oltmanns & B.Maher (Eds.), *Delusional beliefs* (pp. 167–183). New York: Wiley.

Chapman, L., Edell, W., & Chapman, J. (1980). Physical anhedonia, perceptual aberration, and psychosis proneness. *Schizophrenia Bulletin, 6,* 639–653.

Cooper, C. (1988). The scientific status of the DMT. A reply to Kline. *British Journal of Medical psychology, 61,* 381–384.

Edge, H., Morris, R., Palmer, J., & Rush, J. (1986). *Foundations of parapsychology.* London: Routledge & Kegan Paul.

Eklund, M., & Chapman, L. (1983). Magical ideation as an indicator of schizotypy. *Journal of Consulting and Clinical Psychology, 51*, 215–225.

Ferguson, M. (1987). Problems in diagnosis concerning psychopathology and psychic phenomena. *ASPR Newsletter, XIII*, 23.

Greyson, B. (1977). Telepathy in mental illness: Deluge or delusion? *Journal of Nervous and Mental Disease, 1665*, 184–200.

Haraldsson, E. (1985). Representative surveys of psychical phenomena: Iceland, Great Britain, Sweden, USA and Gallup's multinational survey. *Journal of the Society for Psychical Research, 53*, 145-158.

Heston, L. (1966). Psychiatric disorders in foster home reared children of schizophrenic mothers. *British Journal of Psychiatry, 112*, 819–825.

Hoffer, A., Kelm, H., & Osmond, H. (1975). *Clinical and other uses of the Hoffer-Osmond Test.* New York: Krieger.

Honorton, C., & Schechter, E. (1987). Ganzfeld target retrieval with an automated testing system: A model for initial ganzfeld success. In D. Weiner & R. Nelson (Eds.) *Research in parapsychology 1986* (pp. 36–39). Metuchen, NJ: Scarecrow.

Irwin, H. (1985a). Parapsychological phenomena and the absorption domain. *Journal of the American Society for Psychical Research, 79*, 1-12.

Irwin, H. (1985b). *Flight of mind.* Metuchen, NJ: Scarecrow.

Johnson, M. (1989). Personal Communication.

Johnson, M., & Haraldsson, E. (1984). The DMT as a predictor of ESP scores: Icelandic studies IV and V. *Journal of Parapsychology, 48*, 185–200.

Kihlstrom, J., & Hoyt, I. (1988). Hypnosis and the psychology of delusions. In T. Oltmanns & B. Maher (Eds.), *Delusional beliefs* (pp. 66–109). New York: Wiley.

Kline, P. (1987). The scientific status of the DMT. *British Journal of Medical Psychology, 60*, 53-59.

Kline, P. (1988). The scientific status of the DMT: A reply to Cooper. *British Journal of Medical Psychology, 61*, 385–386.

Lander, E. (1988). Splitting schizophrenia. *Nature, 336*, 105–106.

Maher, B. (1988). Anomalous experience and delusional thinking: The logic of explanations. In T. Oltmanns & B. Maher (Eds.), *Delusional beliefs* (pp. 15–33). New York: Wiley.

Neppe, V. (1988). Psychopathology of psi. Part II. A new system for classification. *Parapsychology Review, 19*(6), 8–11.

Palmer, J. (1979). A community mail survey of psychic experience. *Journal of the American Society for Psychical Research, 73*, 221–252.

Parker, A. (1974). Some success at screening for high scoring subjects. *Journal of the Society for Psychical Research, 47*, 336–370.

Parker, A. (1987). Psi in search of consensus. *Behavioral and Brain Sciences, 104*, 602–603.

Philipson, O., & Harris, J. (1985). Perceptual changes in schizophrenia: A questionnaire survey. *Psychological Medicine, 15*, 859–866.

Rogo, D. S. (1982). ESP and schizophrenia: An analysis from two perspectives. *Journal of the Society for Psychical Research, 51*, 329–342.

Rowan, J. (1989). *Subpersonalities: The people inside us.* New York: Routledge.

Råmonth, S. (1985a). Absorption in directed daydreaming. *Journal of Mental Imagery, 9*, 67–86.

Råmonth, S. (1985b). Dissociation and self awareness in directed daydreaming. *Scandinavian Journal of Psychology, 26*, 259–276.

Sjöberg, L. (1981). Värdet av DMT vid urval av flygförare. *Nordisk Psykologi, 33*, 241–248.

Tellegen, A. (1982). *Brief manual for the differential personality questionnaire.* University of Minnesota.

Tellegen, A., & Atkinson, G. (1974). Openness to absorbing and self-altering experiences ("absorption"), a trait related to hypnotic susceptibility. *Journal of Abnormal Psychology, 83*, 268–277.

Thalbourne, M. (1983). Are believers in psi more prone to schizophrenia? In R. A. White
    & J. Solfvin (Eds.), *Research in Parapsychology 1984* (pp. 85–88). Metuchen, NJ:
    Scarecrow Press.
World Health Organization. (1979). *Schizophrenia: An international follow up study*. New
    York: Wiley.
York, M., & Morris, R. (1976). Perceptual defensiveness and free response clairvoyance
    in the ganzfeld. Unpublished manuscript.
Zusne, L. (1985). Magical thinking and parapsychology. In P. Kurtz (Ed.), *A skeptic's
    handbook of parapsychology* (pp. 685–700). Buffalo, NY: Prometheus.

DISCUSSION

VAN DE CASTLE: Adrian raised the question of what happens to
successful subjects later on in life. I had shared with you yesterday that
I had been a successful subject in a couple of laboratory experiences
and you are all aware what has happened to me. So I question the
words that you had used with regard to Martin Johnson's high scoring
subject later on. You said she had no interest in ESP because of her
reluctance to take a card guessing test. I think parapsychologists may
be suffering from paradigm paralysis. Equating interest in ESP with
being willing to take an ESP test, is to me a very limited view of what
ESP is. I don't know if she said she's not interested in ESP, but it
seemed quite clear to me that she was not interested in ESP tests.

The other comment concerns Blackmore's hypothesis about being
too ready to interpret events and to attribute significance to insignificant
events. I would say that as a long term dream researcher, when people
have difficulty with recall I tell them to be very appreciative of whatever
little recall they get to start with. If they show their gratitude for that
amount of recall, they'll find their recall will start significantly im-
proving. Could there have been anything involving in this other event
that occurred? I'm going to go back and beat the drum again about
the idea of psi being there for some sort of growth or enhancement
aspect, and put forth a hypothesis. You were coming to this conference
as a clinical psychologist, but had no particular personal examples to
show and feeling not as comfortable as you would if you had one when
lo and behold, some girl with whom you have had no contact for two
years, suddenly, mysteriously contacts you to provide you with some
anecdotes that you could now use. If we were into making interpretations or predictions, I would say you felt better after that happened
because you now felt you had a more solid paper, when before it might
have felt more skeletal. Somehow you came out of that synchronistic
event feeling somewhat enhanced, somewhat better prepared, yet how

quick you were to dismiss it. You want to assure us that it had no significance. You will not attribute any kind of meaning to it. You will not fall into the Blackmore pool and make any unusual interpretation of that at all. I would say, if that gets to be a typical attitude and we don't get appreciative of those little things that come along, we will never get the big ones either. I think you have to take those events, nurture them, accept them, and be open to them, then maybe some bigger ones will come along.

PARKER: I really don't know how to reply to all of that. I'm tempted to say you are right. It is interesting to hear that as a high scoring subject, you have this wider view of paranormal experiences now. I think that the way you interpret them, is perhaps very similar to the way that this girl I followed up interprets them, in the wider context. Certainly you can criticize parapsychologists for not taking into account the fuller implications of the findings, but there are realities here. We work with critics and funds are stretched. I think we also have to have an open mind or we may be deluded; it's possible that other theories have something to contribute, also.

DIERKENS: When I hear all these papers about schizophrenia, schizoid personality, and brain damage, which are paranormal, I appreciate all the work, but, I have been somewhat depressed because I think, it's wrong. I think that all of psychology is based on a "realistic" paradigm and after 30 years of studying psychology, I think that paradigm is not useful. There should be another paradigm. You can call it a spiritual paradigm or a consciousness paradigm, it doesn't matter. But I think it must be something completely and absolutely different. When you listen to what people say about their experience, and you listen to how they speak about the objects, about time, about the space, about the people they see, you find that there is some organization to the information which is completely different. The organization of the unconscious is completely different from the organization in the conscious. I mean unconscious in a Freudian sense. Since his first book, he tried to show the primary process of the unconscious. You can't understand the real meaning of a dream if you just try to use your logical consciousness. So, I think that it is the same for that other paradigm. The way the information is received is very different. Of course, the brain is there and the psychology is there, but the reality is not of the brain. It is analogous to a closed water pipe. A medium is someone who has contact, they can take water out and close it. Goats cannot, of course. Schizophrenics are perhaps broken pipes. I think there is a lot of effort and a lot of work being done, but I think it does not provide much in the way of results. Why don't you get a completely different paradigm and experience that different paradigm? Maybe doing some meditation on the DSM-III-R could be the beginning.

PARKER: I want to make clear that I presented three different explanatory models of psi experiences. I haven't really said much about brain damage. I think it is important to make predictions from these models. Of course, some of the predictions may be wrong, and we may need to reevaluate them. I agree with you that it is difficult in the area of how personality and defense mechanisms relate to psi experiences, to make specific predictions. But I think we have to begin somewhere, and then we can reevaluate things and make new models.

DIERKENS: I don't think that it is good to do it from the reality paradigm, we need something completely different.

PARKER: It sounds as though you want to come up with a fourth explanatory paradigm.

HARARY: I thought that was a great question about what happens to people who have some proven ability in the laboratory. Maybe I could include myself in that list. I could tell you that it is unbelievably difficult to explore any kind of psi potential in the field of psi research as it is presently construed. First of all, many researchers have a very hard time dealing with strong positive results. I have seen positive data destroyed or buried in filing cabinets. I have seen people lose their psychological sense and researchers almost deliberately, unconsciously screwing up experiments and then claiming that the perceiver failed. But years later, when you finally get hold of the data, you find that the perceiver was successful. It is ridiculous. The effect on many people who have done very well, I have to say, is that it is hard to keep a balanced point of view, and many people don't. I personally have a very hard time being around a number of people (I don't include Bob Van de Castle in this) who have gotten reputations for doing well in the laboratory. The idea of being psychic has become an identity to the point where they're into that all the time. They are in collusion with certain researchers, who will say, "This is my psychic. Let me trot him or her out to do my experiment." And they will say, "Here is the person who will tell you I'm special, my researcher." After a while, many healthy people lose interest in being a part of that scene. We don't really attract a lot of healthy people into the field, with regard to experiencing psi. What do you get out of it? You get some kind of ego trip because it is implied that you are special. Personally, I'm not. There is also the idea that some of these people are in competition with each other over who gets to be more psychic. The best thing we can do is to set up the game differently. Don't say to people that they are going to get one hell of a strange reputation for being an unusual person if they go through this experiment. When Darlene and I have done experiments in which we have tried to teach people to respond to psi impressions, people have done well and we haven't set them up as psychics. We have told them right off that it is going to be about learning to use a creative human ability which most people probably can gain access. If you set that up in the beginning, and they then say their life has been enhanced by learning about this aspect, they won't be off on some trip, climbing over each other, killing each other, trying to get in front of the camera to say, "Let me wax philosophical about why the researchers discovered me as a special human being." The fact is that you walked into that laboratory with something in mind. For me it was to find out what was going on. That is not always the case, sometimes it is to get a reputation. To process the information and work with people in the training context, teaching them how to process psi information, you have to have a pretty clear head. Being schizophrenic would not be the best way to go about it. You have to be able to separate out which feelings are psi, or what we call extended abilities and extended perception and communication, from your own other thoughts, imagination, free association, and so forth. You really have to be in a calm state and not feel as though your whole identity or your whole sense of reality are on the line. You have just got to say, "Here's the information. I don't make the news, I just report it." Darlene and I are always kidding with that line. I think you tapped into this whole well spring of very good questions when you asked what happens to people long term. In short, a lot of them don't want anything to do with the research after a while; and the ones that do, I think you sometimes have to be suspicious about what they are still doing hanging around after they found out psi is real. Why don't they get on with their lives?

PARKER: Nevertheless, I think it is clear that they don't become psychotic. I don't think there is any evidence for that. In fact, Dr. West cited in his talk, the follow-up of people over a 30 year period, though it wasn't a formal follow-up, suggested that there is no indication they are more liable to develop schizophrenia. Of course, there may be some people who in society have a need for conceptual systems and join occult groups, and would then be classified by clinicians as schizotype. But that is only labeling.

KRAMER: You said something about textbooks not having chapters on parapsychology. I suddenly realized that most of the psychology textbooks in Dutch which are used in higher education, actually do have a chapter, or at least a few pages.

PARKER: Can I just correct that? I meant psychiatry and clinical psychology course books for the education of clinicians.

KRAMER: That is what I was going to say because in higher education, you learn a little bit about parapsychology, but when you go to a university to become a psychologist, they use American books which never have chapters on parapsychology. That means that everyone learns about parapsychology except psychologists in Holland. You said something about a test in which one of the questions was, "Have you the feeling that your arm or your leg becomes longer or shorter?" It might seem a little bit strange, but it reminds me of a few clients I used to have who actually had the feeling that their heads were moving. It was very strange because sometimes they attributed it to an evil power that moved their heads or to some telepathic contact they had with something. They claimed something was moving their heads because they could not concentrate on work or their studies. The important thing is that sometimes you could see that their head was actually moving, and sometimes very heavily. But in a lot of cases you don't see it. They have the feeling their heads are unwillingly moving, but as an observer, you cannot see it. The problem is, it turns out to be very important in a clinical setting. But if you don't ask for it, the people don't tell you because they think it's of no importance to you as a psychologist or a parapsychologist. So, it might be wise sometimes, in questioning people about their paranormal experiences, to ask explicitly for that kind of phenomena. Sometimes, they simply do.

I would like to say to Dr. Dierkens that I can understand that you feel a little bit disappointed about all the pathological talking about psi effects. I heard that reaction often when I gave a lecture about the clinical aspects of parapsychology. People say, "Oh, I'm sorry because it's a beautiful psi experience." I think the difference here lies in whether you do research in psi, or if you are working as a clinician in daily practice. When you are working in a daily practice, you are confronted with a lot of cases which show you the other side of psi phenomena. People come to you because they have problems. They don't come because they are functioning well. They come because they are not functioning well. Sometimes, you simply need elements from psychopathology to cope with that, otherwise, you cannot help them. So, it's not one way or the other. I mean it's not a matter of being sick or being healthy. It is simply that in some cases people have such tremendous problems which they relate to paranormal experiences, that you need the assistance you can get from psychiatry to help those people.

PARKER: I don't think I really have anything to add to that. I think I agree with the content of those statements.

FENWICK: I liked your three models and think it's one way one has to go. The question for me is the following one. Here we have a set of experiences which we find in several different states. Do these experiences themselves mean anything more than the fact that the person is experiencing them? That immediately throws me back onto the various models that I bring to the interpretation in my data. I have a lot of sympathy with Dr. Dierkens who was saying that if you are going to use a scientific model, then you will come out with scientific results. Scientific results, by definition, cannot be anything but brain function. You will always end up by looking at different aspects of brain function. Because of the science we use, we will never get any further with that. We will have just a whole series of models, because mind is not included in our present day science. That is why CSICOP (Committee for the Scientific Investigation of Claims of the Paranormal) has such fun with us. And so they should. It is absolutely right that there is very little parapsychologists can do to incorporate modern day science. Mind and consciousness are excluded by definition from science. Your models are lovely ones, and I go along the same line as you, but how would you graft your data onto a wider framework to explain the nature of reality?

PARKER: I think your question, in fact, addresses the whole claim of psychology to be a science in it is own right rather than just a science of epiphenomena that can be reduced to physiology or biochemistry.

FENWICK: But, Adrian, you have no evidence for that. Or if you do, I want to hear it. What evidence is there that psychology is a science in its own right and does not make scientific assumptions?

PARKER: The constructs that are used in psychology can hypothetically be reduced to physiological models of the brain at some hypothetical future day. The fact remains that such terms as constructs, consciousness, self-concept, are fundamental to this sort of neo-behaviorist psychology of today. These are parts of the explanatory models of human behavior. You can be quite neutral as to your theory over mind/body relationship, and you don't have to address it. All you have to do is develop hypotheses around human behavior and self-conceptualization. I don't think one has to have a particular theory of mind/body relationship to be a psychologist.

FENWICK: There clearly is not time to go on with it.

IS HYPNOTIC ABILITY A RISK FACTOR
FOR SUBJECTIVE (VERBAL REPORT)
PSI, SOMATIZATION, AND HEALTH CARE COSTS?

IAN WICKRAMASEKERA

Health care costs were $544 billion or 11.4% of the Gross National Product in 1989 (Durenberger, 1989). In 1950 health care costs were 4.6% of the gross national product. Somatization is a major factor contributing through *overutilization* of physician visits, hospitalizations, high tech tests, surgeries and iatrogenic illness to the escalating cost of health care in the U.S. (Quill, 1988; Katon, Kleinman, & Rosen, 1982). Somatizers are people who transduce perceptions of psychosocial conflicts into somatic presentations (Wickramasekera, 1989b). Somatization accounts for approximately 50% of all visits to primary care physicians (Katon et al., 1982).

I have hypothesized that "unassimilated" *subjective* psi reports (anomalous experiences) are a measurable risk factor for the presentation of psychological and somatic symptoms (Wickramasekera, 1979, 1983, 1986, 1988) (see Figure 1). Clinically we have observed numerous instances of chronic resistant psychophysiological disorders which rapidly resolved when we provided the patient with an invitation to verbalize, reframe, and assimilate distressing anomalous perceptions which they had previously been afraid to verbalize lest they be regarded as crazy or "possessed." Our data (1979, 1983, 1984, 1988, 1989a) and clinical experience renders us comfortable in issuing such an invitation routinely to all patients and particularly to those who score over 9 on the Harvard scale. Often, but not always, the patients are relieved to talk about the incidents of subjective psi and report that I am reading their minds because they have previously not revealed the psi incidents to anybody.

The hypothesis that subjective psi is a risk factor for somatization may or may not be true, and is a topic for empirical study. For example, have professional psychics had bigger medical expenses than the average person? If this hypothesis is true, then the investigation of subjective psi reports may have economic consequences in terms of reducing

Figure 1. Hypnotic ability and subjective PSI (verbal reports).

1. Wickramasekera 1979	Highs = 80%	Lows = 25% (patients)
2. Wilson & Barber 1983	Highs = 92%	Lows = 16% (non-patients)
3. Wickramasekera 1984	Highs = 63%	Lows = 20% (patients)
4. Wickramasekera 1986	Highs = 71%	Lows = 19% (patients)
5. Wickramasekera 1989a	Highs = 80%	Lows = 32% (college students)
6. Wagner & Ratzeburg 1987	$r = .26$ (p < .04)	(college students)
7. Nadon & Kihlstrom 1987	$r = .22$ (p < .01)	(college students)
8. Council, Greyson, & Huff 1987	$r = .34$ (p < .05)	$r = .38$ (p < .01)
9. Richards 1989	overall	$r = .175$ (non-significant)
	subset	$r = .53$ (p < .01)

mental and physical health care costs. The empirical study of subjective psi reports as a risk factor for somatization may be an idea that in William James' terms has "cash value" today and whose time has come. The concept of psi as a risk factor for psychological and somatic symptoms may provide incentives to fund basic and applied psi research in the Clinton administration.

I previously (1979, 1983, 1984, 1986, 1988) reported (see Figure 1) several small studies showing that "high" (Stanford or Harvard scores 12–9) hypnotic ability was a risk factor for somatization and subjective verbal reports of psi. These subjective reports of psi in high hypnotizables were found to be *unrelated* to serious psychopathology (psychotic process) in both somatizers and a normal college student sample (Wickramasekera, 1989a). It is noteworthy that one of the most promising empirical sources of evidence for objective psi, the ganzfeld research (Rao & Palmer, 1987), incorporates two procedures (sensory restriction and verbal relaxation instructions for low physiological arousal) that are known to at least temporarily, but reliably, increase hypnotic ability above baseline levels (Pena, 1963; Wickramasekera, 1969, 1970, 1971, 1973, 1977; Barabasz & Barabasz, 1989; Engstrom, 1976).

Hypnosis can be defined as the verbal induction, in select subjects, of reliable and large magnitude changes in perception, memory and mood that can have profound psychological and psychophysiological consequences (Spiegel, Bierre, & Rootenburg, 1985; Spiegel, Cutcomb, Ren, & Pribram, 1988; Laurence & Perry, 1983; Dywan & Bowers, 1983; Wickramasekera, 1979, 1986, 1988). For people of high hypnotic ability these psychological and psychophysiological changes do not necessarily require the ritual of a hypnotic induction (Barber, 1981; Council & Loge, 1988) and can under certain additional high risk conditions (Wickramasekera, 1979, 1986, 1988) be associated with the amplification *or* attenuation of fear and/or pain (Spiegel et al., 1988; Stam, McGrath, Brooke, & Cosier, 1986).

Prior reviews of the hypnosis and psi literature (Van de Castle, 1969; Honorton & Krippner, 1969; Schecter, 1984) have suggested that hypnotic induction amplifies objective psi performance. But these reviews failed to control systematically for hypnotic ability. Hypnotic ability is a normally distributed stable individual difference variable (Barber, 1969; Hilgard, 1965; Kihlstrom, 1985) that appears to be partly genetically based (Morgan, 1973; Morgan, Hilgard, & Davert 1970).

In 1983, Barber and Wilson confirmed my prior report of an association between high hypnotic ability and subjective psi verbal reports. In a sample of very high hypnotic ability (top 4% of the population) non-patient professional females, they found that 92% of the *high* (N=27) and only 16% of the *lows* (N=25, low and medium hypnotic ability control group) reported subjective psi experiences. Subsequently there have been at least 3 independent replications (see Figure 1) of a positive correlation between hypnotic ability (Harvard scale) and verbal-subjective reports of psi with large normal college student samples (Wagner & Ratzenburg, 1987; Nadon & Kihlstrom, 1987; Council, Greyson, & Huff, 1987). Richards (1989) who studied an unusual sample (Association for Research and Enlightenment members N=120) of older adults (x age=47 SD=10.85), which consisted only of "sheep" (no goats), failed to replicate with his "overall sample" the prior finding of an association between hypnotic ability (Harvard) and subjective psi reports. But in a subset of his own sample, on a separate testing session, he replicated the positive correlation between hypnotic ability (Harvard) and subjective psi reports (N=32, Harvard and psi r=.53 P<.01). While hypnotic ability was normally distributed in Richard's (1989) study, the lack of "goats" in the subjective psi domain may have skewed the distribution and attenuated the correlation in his larger sample.

Wilson and Barber (1983) used a procedure that selects for very high hypnotic ability (somnambules) and described a personality construct they term "fantasy prone personalities" or "fantasy addicts" who report intense imaginative involvements in reading, solitary play, and mystical/religious experiences that date back to their early childhood. These "fantasy prone" personalities report (a) multiple psi experiences, (b) and ability to heal others, (c) out-of-body experiences, (d) fantasy of hallucinatory intensity in several sensory modalities, (e) the ability to reach orgasm without physical stimulation, and (f) false pregnancies with abdominal swelling, breast enlargement and termination of menstrual cycle. This sample of "fantasy addicts" (N=27) were all non-patient females and post graduate professionals without notable histories of psychopathology (without psychosis). These women were all selected for very high hypnotic ability with the Stanford Form C and the Creative Imagination Scale (Wilson & Barber, 1978). Wilson and Barber (1983) proposed that the very high hypnotic ability person, the "fantasy prone personality," and the "psychic" are the same person. Lynn and Rhue (1988) wanted to check out this formulation. They started *not* with hypnotic ability but with the ICMI or Inventory of Childhood Memories and Imaginings (designed by Wilson & Barber, 1981) to study fantasy proneness. They screened over 7,000 college students, selecting those with the top 2–4% of scores on the ICMI to be termed "fantasy prone personalities." They were able to generally revise, extend, and partly confirm some of Wilson and Barber's (1983) prior findings. Most importantly, that hypnotic ability (Harvard) and fantasy proneness correlate only .25. Therefore, "fantasy proneness" is not a reliable predictor of hypnotic ability (about 1/3 of non-fantasizers can be classified as high hypnotic ability persons). Hence, excellent hypnotic ability subjects are not identical to "fantasy prone personalities." A minority (20%-35%) of fantasy prone people show signs of psychopathology, but on grade point average and social desirability measures, high "fantasizers" were not different from low "fantasizers" (control group). The high "fantasizers" hallucinations were found to be imperfect and less "real" than Wilson and Barber (1983) implied. Several other studies (Council, Greyson, Huff, & Swett, 1986; Nadon & Kihlstrom, 1987) using the ICMI and a closely related (Rhue & Lynn, 1989) measure of "fantasy proneness," the absorption scale (Tellegen, 1981), have also reported a strong connection between (r=.63-.51) fantasy proneness and subjective psi reporting (see Figures 2 and 3) in large college student samples.

The studies of Wilson and Barber (1983) and Lynn and Rhue (1988) are not strictly comparable because the former started out with very high hypnotic ability people and the latter with high "fantasy prone" people. But one important conclusion to be drawn from the above studies is that *high hypnotic ability people and "fantasy addicts" are not*

Figure 2. Fantasy proneness and subjective PSI.

Inventory of Childhood Memories and Imaginings (ICMI)
Wilson & Barber, 1981
52 item checklist assessing fantasy proneness

Council, Greyson, Huff, & Swett 1986
college students: N = 169

1. ICMI and Psi	r = .63	(p < .001)	N = 169
2. ICMI and Psi	r = .60	(p < .001)	N = 337

Figure 3. Absorption and Subjective PSI.

Absorption: measure of predisposition to become highly involved in sensory and imaginative experiences (like fantasy proneness).

1. Council, Greyson, Huff, & Swett   1986   *APA Washington, DC*

Absorption and Psi   r = .62   (p < .001)   N = 68
Absorption and Psi   r = .62   (p < .001)   N = 336

2. Nadon & Kihlstrom, 1987   *Behavioral and Brain Science*

N = over 1,000 college students
Absorption and Psi r.51 (p < .001)

necessarily the same people (Rhue & Lynn, 1989). This is not an unexpected conclusion because for over 20 years, factor analytic studies (Hammer, Evans, & Bartlett, 1963; Evans, 1965; Monteiro, MacDonald, & Hilgard, 1980) have shown that standardized measures of hypnotizability are a composite of at least two uncorrelated or orthogonal factors. One factor is the capacity to self-generate fantasy of hallucinatory intensity. This factor correlates approximately .50 with standardized tests of hypnotic ability (e.g. Stanford scales). The second factor is a capacity "to make the mind blank" (Hilgard, 1982) and is related to post-hypnotic amnesia. This second factor appears to be a cognitive and/or sensory inhibition factor.

Clearly the capacity to generate rich fantasy is related to subjective psi verbal reports (Wilson & Barber, 1983; Lynn & Rhue, 1988; Council et al., 1986; Nadon & Kihlstrom, 1987). On the other hand, *objective psi* (empirically verifiable) performance may be related more closely to the second factor in hypnotic ability, the capacity to make the mind blank which is related to post-hypnotic amnesia. Investigations of objective psi should use all appropriate experimental controls for psi and focus on superior hypnotic subjects, selected particularly for superior performance on the second factor (mind blank factor) in hypnotic ability (Wickramasekera, 1991).

I have hypothesized that "unassimilated" subjective psi verbal reports are a risk factor for somatization and psychological symptoms. In the last 14 months in association with John Palmer, we have administered both a pilot *overt* and a *covert* test (Stanford, 1974) of objective psi to all patients seen at the Behavioral Medicine Clinic at Eastern Virginia Medical School. The overt test is given together with our standard battery of psychological, hypnotic (Harvard), and psychophysiological tests (Wickramasekera, 1988). The overt objective test of psi is presented (with a straight face), as a test of "subliminal perception" to patients presenting with somatic complaints like muscular or vascular headaches, chronic low back pain, hypertension, etc. The cognitive dissonance reduction, desensitization, and role playing required to present such an objective test of psi to a patient with physical complaints in a medical school context, took the current investigator two years of personal work. No patient to date has refused to take the overt test of objective psi. Based on the work of Rex Stanford (1974), we are also concurrently using a covert test of psi designed by John Palmer. Our empirical results with these primitive and probably insensitive instruments (overt and covert tests) are still unanalyzed and at too preliminary a stage to report today.

In conclusion, it may be important to run single blind studies of objective psi, with subjects selected for high belief in psi (sheep) and who are also high on factor 2 (post-hypnotic amnesia) of hypnotic ability. We should also check on the rate of somatization and other psychological symptoms in these highly select subjects (e.g., professional psychics, etc.). It would be useful from a funding point of view to concurrently study the rate of somatization and other psychological symptoms in "sheep," "goats," and those who report "unassimilated" psi experiences. Is the assimilation of "psi" associated with remission of somatic symptoms and reduction in medical expenses (hospital costs, medical tests, drugs, etc.)?

REFERENCES

Barabasz, A. F., & Barabasz, M. (1989). Effects of restricted environmental stimulation: Enhancement of hypnotizability for experimental and chronic pain control. *International Journal of Clinical and Experimental Hypnosis, XXXVII*(3), 217–231.

Barber, T. X. (1969). *Hypnosis: A scientific approach.* New York: Van Nostrand Reinhold.

Council, J. R., Greyson, B., Huff, K. D., & Swett, S. (August, 1986). Fantasy-proneness, hypnotizability, and reports of paranormal experiences. Paper presented at the meeting of the American Psychological Association, Washington, DC.

Council, J. R., Greyson, B., & Huff, K. D. (1987). Fantasy-proneness, hypnotizability, and reports of paranormal experiences.

Council, J. R., & Loge, D. (1988). Hypnotizability and expectancy-induced hallucinations.

Durenberger, D. (1989). Providing mental health care services to Americans. *American Psychologist, 44*, 1293–1297.

Dywan, J., & Bowers, K. (1983). The use of hypnosis to enhance recall. *Science, 22*, 284–285.

Engstrom, D. R. (1976). Hypnotic susceptibility, EEG-alpha and self-regulation. In G. E. Schwartz & D. Shapiro (Eds.), *Consciousness and self-regulation.* New York: Plenum Press.

Evans, F. J. (1965). *The structure of hypnosis: A factor analytic investigation.* Unpublished doctoral dissertation, University of Sydney, Australia.

Hammer, A. G., Evans, F. J., & Bartlett, M. (1963). Factors in hypnosis and suggestion. *Journal of Abnormal and Social Psychology, 67*, 15–23.

Hilgard, E. R. (1965). *Hypnotic susceptibility.* New York: Harcourt, Brace & World.

Hilgard, E. R. (1982). Hypnotic susceptibility and implications for measurement. *International Journal of Clinical and Experimental and Hypnosis, 30*, 394–403.

Honorton, C., & Krippner, S. (1969). Hypnosis and ESP performance: A review of the experimental literature. *Journal of the American Society for Psychical Research, 63,* 214–252.

John, R., Hollander, B., & Perry, C. (1983). Hypnotizability and phobic behavior: Further supporting data. *Journal of Abnormal Psychology, 92,* 390–392.

Katon, W., Kleinman, A., & Rosen, G. (1982). Depression and somatization: A review. *The American Journal of Medicine, 72,* 127–135.

Kihlstrom, J. F. (1985). Hypnosis. *Annual Review of Psychology, 36,* 385–418.

Laurence, J. R. & Perry, C. (1983). Hypnotically created memory among highly hypnotizable subjects. *Science, 222,* 523–524.

Lynn, S. J., & Rhue, J. W. (1988). Fantasy proneness: Hypnosis, developmental antecedents, and psychopathology. *American Psychologist, 43*(1), 35–44.

Monteiro, K. P., MacDonald, H., & Hilgard, E. R. (1980). Imagery, absorption, and hypnosis: A factorial study. *Journal of Mental Imagery, 4,* 63–81.

Morgan, A. H. (1973). The heritability of hypnotic susceptibility in twins. *Journal of Abnormal Psychology, 72,* 55–66.

Morgan, A. H., Hilgard, E. R., & Davert, E. C. (1970). The heritability of hypnotic susceptibility of twins: A preliminary report. *Behavioral Genetics, 1,* 213–224.

Nadon, R. & Kihlstrom, J. F. (in press). Hypnosis, psi, and the psychology of anomalous experience. *Behavioral and Brain Sciences.*

Pena, F. (1963). *Perceptual isolation and hypnotic susceptibility.* Unpublished doctoral dissertation, Washington State University. Pullman, WA.

Quill, T. E. (1985). Somatization disorder. *Journal of the American Medical Association, 254*(21), 3075–3079.

Rao, K. R., & Palmer, J. (1987). The anomaly called psi: Recent research and criticism. *Behavioral and Brain Sciences, 10*(4), 566–643.

Rhue, J. W., & Lynn, S. J. (1989). Fantasy proneness, hypnotizability and absorption—a re-examination. *International Journal of Clinical and Experimental Hypnosis, XXXVII*(2), 100-106.

Richards, D. G. (1989). Hypnotic susceptibility and subjective psychic experiences. Presented at the Annual Convention of the Parapsychological Association, San Diego, August.

Schecter, E. I. (1984). Hypnotic induction vs. control conditions: Illustrating an approach to the evaluation of replicability in parapsychological data. *Journal of the American Society for Psychical Research, 78,* 1–27.

Spiegel, D., Bierre, P., & Rootenburg, J. (1988). Hypnotic alteration of somatosensory perception. Presented at the Annual Meeting of the American Psychiatric Association, Montreal, Canada, May 7–12.

Spiegel, D., Cutcomb, S., Ren, C., & Pribram, K. (1985). Hypnotic hallucination alters evoked potentials. *Journal of Abnormal Psychology, 94*(3), 249–255.

Stam, J. S., McGrath, P. A., Brooke, R. I., & Cosier, F. (1986). Hypnotizability and the treatment of chronic facial pain. *International Journal of Clinical and Experimental Hypnosis, XXXIV,* 3, 182–191.

Stanford, R. G. (1974). An experimentally testable model for spontaneous psi events 1. extrasensory perception. *Journal of the American Society for Psychical Research, 68,* 34–57.

Tellegen, A. (1981). Practicing the two disciplines for relaxation and enlightenment: Comment on "Role of the feedback signal in electromyographic biofeedback: The role of attention" by Qualls and Sheehan. *Journal of Experimental Psychology: General, 110,* 217–226.

Van de Castle, R. L. (1969). The facilitation of ESP through hypnosis. *American Journal of Clinical Hypnosis, 12*(1), 37–56.

Wagner, M. W., & Ratzeburg, F. H. (1987). Hypnotic suggestibility and paranormal belief. *Psychological Reports, 60,* 1069–1070.

Wickramasekera, I. (1969). The effects of sensory restriction on susceptibility to hypnosis:

A hypothesis, some preliminary data, and theoretical speculation. *International Journal of Clinical and Experimental Hypnosis, 17,* 217–224.

Wickramasekera, I. (1970). Effects of sensory restriction on susceptibility to hypnosis: A hypothesis and more preliminary data. *Journal of Abnormal Psychology, 76,* 69–75.

Wickramasekera, I. (1971). Effects of EMG feedback training on susceptibility to hypnosis: Preliminary observations. Proceedings of the 79th Annual Convention of the American Psychological Association, 6(pt. 2), 783–784.

Wickramasekera, I. (1973). Effects of electromyographic feedback on hypnotic susceptibility: More preliminary data. *Journal of Abnormal Psychology, 83,* 74–77.

Wickramasekera, I. (1977). On attempts to modify hypnotic susceptibility: Some psychophysiological procedures and promising directions. *Annals of the New York Academy of Sciences, 296,* 143–153.

Wickramasekera, I. (March, 1979). A model of the patient at high risk for chronic stress related disorders: Do beliefs have biological consequences? Paper presented at the Annual Convention of the Biofeedback Society of America, San Diego, March.

Wickramasekera, I. (August, 1983). A model of people at high risk. Paper presented at the International Stress and Tension Control Society, Brighton, England, August.

Wickramasekera, I. (1986). A model of people at high risk to develop chronic stress-related symptoms: Some predictions. *Professional Psychology: Research and Practice, 17*(5), 437-447.

Wickramasekera, I. (1988). *Clinical behavioral medicine: Some concepts and procedures.* New York: Plenum.

Wickramasekera, I. (1989a). Risk factors for parapsychological verbal reports, hypnotizability and somatic complaints. In B. Shapin & L. Coly (Eds.), *Parapsychology and human nature* (pp. 19–35). New York: Parapsychology Foundation.

Wickramasekera, I. (1989b). Somatizers, the health care system, and collapsing the psychological distance that the somatizer has to travel for help. *Professional Psychology: Research and Practice, 20*(2), 105–111.

Wickramasekera, I. (1991). Model of the relationship between hypnotic ability, psi, and sexuality. *Journal of Parapsychology, 55,* 159–174.

Wilson, S. C., & Barber, T. X. (1978). The Creative Imagination Scale as measure of hypnotic responsiveness: Applications to experimental and clinical hypnosis. *American Journal of Clinical Hypnosis, 20,* 235–249.

Wilson, S. C., & Barber, T. X. (1981). Vivid fantasy and hallucinatory abilities in the life histories of excellent hypnotic subjects ("somnambules"): Preliminary report with female subjects. In E. Klineer (Ed.), *Imagery: Concepts, results, and application* Vol. 2. (pp.133–149). New York: Plenum.

Wilson, S. C., & Barber, T. X. (1983). The fantasy-prone personality: Implications for understanding imagery, hypnosis, and parapsychological phenomena. In A. A. Sheikh (Ed.), *Imagery: Current theory, research, and application* (pp. 340–390). New York: Wiley.

DISCUSSION

HARARY: I haven't seen any evidence that the ganzfeld, either (a) reduces the signal to noise ratio or (b) makes it more possible to use one's psi ability. What I have seen is that ganzfeld tends to make people internalize and free associate more and also influences the way in which they express possible psi information in relation to other kinds of mental noise processes. There is a problem when we look for some unusual way to bring about psi; a number of experiments are performed and a certain amount of psi is seen, we therefore conclude that this procedure is the thing that brought it about. For example, if you compare the remote viewing results with the ganzfeld results, you'll see excellent results in remote viewing without all the paraphernalia. We could argue about whether people are in an altered state of consciousness while remote viewing; but, they are certainly not hypnotized and they are certainly not in a state of sensory deprivation. They tend to free associate less in their descriptions and be more specific. So rather than seeing one approach causing psi to occur, we tend to see either approach influencing the way in which people respond to psi information, the way in which they express themselves, and how they change that information around in their minds. Also, the idea that people with a certain internal focus also experience subjective psi, is probably true. But then it's a question of investigating the basis for that. That is to say, are you a person who is not familiar with looking at your own internal imagery or paying attention to your feelings? Or are you a person who is prone to thinking about your feelings, paying attention to your ideas, your images, your dreams and so forth? The latter focus might also sensitize you to other creative, perceptual and communicative processes. But it may not be that one part of the process is causing the other. It may be that your general focus brings you in touch with all kinds of things. So, I wonder, don't we have to be careful in how we're defining psi? If we define psi as a certain kind of performance in a certain kind of experiment, we are limiting ourselves to a very narrow definition. Isn't it also possible that we are setting people up to begin with? If we look at the process in a completely different way and don't ask people to be hypnotized, for example, we also find people doing well in psi experiments. Are you saying that you have to be in an altered state of consciousness to function using psi? Are you saying that you have to be a fantasy prone individual? Or, are you saying something else?

WICKRAM: I have no axe to grind. I'm not a parapsychologist and my living and my income are totally unrelated to the rise or fall of psi. I want to make it very clear that I was using only the most prestigious literature. Palmer and Rao replied to the National Science Foundation's critique of psi research. The research that they quote as probably the best objective evidence for psi, is the ganzfeld research. I'm not going to argue about whether that is the best research or not. Palmer and Rao mentioned that research. In the recent review of *Behavioral and Brain Sciences*, Rao and Palmer had an article in which they cite the best evidence, methodologically, of empirical psi as being the ganzfeld research. Now, I do not know what the mechanism of potentiation of a signal there is and I don't know even if it is a signal. The point is that the empirical results are most impressive for that methodology. Now, I haven't the foggiest idea why that is and I don't even care to speculate on it. But I would point out that if you decompose that procedure, take it apart, it can constitute techniques that are known to potentiate hypnotic ability temporarily. Those are empirical things. You can do it yourself. You don't need to use psi. People who spent time in the South Pole experienced an increase in suggestibility. Astronauts have this same problem. That is partly why they feel nausea— the GI tract is extremely responsive to suggestion.

HARARY: I only want to say that just because researchers have done a lot of experiments of a particular kind and they have gone pretty well, it does not mean that the approach taken in that experiment is the only way to do it. Also, we should not then draw premature conclusions about what it takes to get psi going. Sometimes people draw scientific conclusions for political reasons. Clearly, if we look at the remote viewing work, we are looking at the way the process is affected in different circumstances rather than at something external making it happen.

WICKRAM: I am not familiar with the remote viewing material. I just know that when I was preparing this paper I looked at the literature that was supposedly the most scientifically impeccable literature in the field.

NEPPE: I have several comments and questions, if I may, and I think it's probably easiest subdividing these into the various parts. Much of this comes from what has just been discussed. The first is, you have spoken about measuring subjective paranormal experience. What kinds of parameters are you, in fact, using?

WICKRAM: The scales that I have developed have true-false questions. "Have you experienced telepathy, or precognition?" Things like that.

NEPPE: What kinds of terminology?

WICKRAM: I can refer you to those actual scales if you want. The other scales and the other studies have been independent confirmation of my work. Barber and Wilson developed a scale called the Inventory of Childhood Imaginings and Memories which has numerous questions dealing with paranormal events. Kihlstrom developed a scale which also asks multiple questions, exclusively devoted to a wide range of paranormal. I don't have those scales with me but if you ask me about specific items, I can give you the references.

NEPPE: I am asking this because you have used the term subjective psi experience. As the creator of the term subjective paranormal experience, in the 1970s, I feel constrained to comment that I would feel far more comfortable if the measures of subjective paranormal experience you were using, were measures which were being used conventionally in mainstream parapsychology. It may be insufficient that people outside the area of parapsychological research have developed questionnaires which they feel are adequate to measure subjective paranormal experience. Additionally you have used the term subjective psi experience but I have tended to shift away from the term subjective *psi* experience because the term *psi* implies a certain objectivity in the context of phenomena which one can not fully conceive. I would suggest that you use the term paranormal instead of psi. I wonder how adequately one can measure these psi phenomena. Based on my experience many people do not understand terms like "precognitive." They do not understand many terms that we use formally. We need to translate them down to their levels.

WICKRAM: If you look at the items on the scale that Kihlstrom designed, the one that I used, we ask questions like, "How often have you been able to predict a telephone call or the death of someone before it occurred?" We don't talk about precognitive or telepathic.

NEPPE: Obviously not. What I'm trying to get at is the fact that you may find it useful using more conventional kinds of measures which have been used within the literature. For example, Palmer and Dennis developed an excellent measure in that regard.

WICKRAM: Three of these studies that replicated my work used the Palmer scale. Kihlstrom, Wagner, and Ratzeburg used it so there have been independent confirmations with traditional measures.

NEPPE: The second thing is, in my original work, I used a three level scale which I'll just mention to you. The first level consisted of two very broad screens because I was trying to get people who either had no subjective paranormal experiences or had had a large number. So, the first screen was just something sent through the mail asking people about their psychic experiences and how they rank those experiences. One was looking for a rank of no psychic abilities and no psychic experiences, and the other extreme included rankings of moderate or profound "psychic" abilities and large numbers of psychic experiences. Once one had these initial subgroups, they were then exposed to telephone interviews where they were given a broad screen of nine fundamental kinds of subjective paranormal experience. Then, they were given a detailed questionnaire. One therefore had three internal built-in mechanisms trying to, if not validate, at least replicate, ones original findings within that population. One finds that people misinterpret phenomena in a variety of different ways particularly in heterogeneous groups and one has got to be extremely careful interpreting what subjects regard as "psi." It is probably worthwhile, therefore, even couching ones terms, saying that patients with high hypnotic ability *claim* a larger number of subjective paranormal experiences than those without high hypnotic or with low hypnotic ability, as opposed to saying they do or don't have it. That aspect, as we heard yesterday, is just an expression of the extent of significance to which they are attributing their particular kinds of experiences. I think this whole framework is something that is of enormous relevance and enormous importance. The other component which is the emphasis of what Dr. Harary was saying, is the translation from subjectivity to objectivity, where the two may not correlate very well at all.

WICKRAM: I'm not clear what you mean by that.

NEPPE: When one talks about people who claim large numbers of subjective paranormal experiences, this might not mean that in any kind of objective test of psi, be it formally in a lab, or informally in some kind of field or spontaneous framework, these people will necessarily exhibit more psi than those who do not. This is something that has to be proven.

WICKRAM: We can get as meticulous as we need to, but the point is, as long as we remain at the level of verbal report data, the field could be dismissed as a function of psychopathology or a function of hypnotic ability. Until we can actually show objective psi (i.e. things that are empirically verifiable) we cannot begin to get into what might considered paradigm shift. The data that I presented to you simply demonstrates a correlation between verbal report and a personality characteristic. That is very fruitful. For example, if you want to find tigers, it would be nice to have a tiger detector. How do you identify tigers? What part of the woods do they exist in? So, you can identify the organisms that generate these verbal reports at a high frequency or a high density. Whether there is any validity to their verbal reports is a totally separate issue and that remains for future investigation. In my opinion, the objective issue, if psi exists independent of the reports of it, is a separate issue.

WEST: What I want to ask is a follow-up on the last question. As I understand it, what is being said is that one factor in hypnotizability is what is being called fantasy addiction, being able to self-generate hallucinations and also having control over physiological functions, so that when one imagines an illness, this can be accompanied by actual physical and measurable changes. This is a personality attribute of some people and is correlated with reporting a lot of psychic experiences. Now, it seems that the speaker is suggesting that these subjective experiences, because they occur in these fantasy prone personalities, may perhaps have no objective basis at all, may be purely imaginary. I would suggest that that is an assumption. It may be that the people who are capable of producing these fantasies and producing these physical changes are also the same people who are capable of having objective psi experiences. It need not always be imaginary.

Now, my second point is that we are told that there are two factors in hypnotizability, the other factor being ability to make the mind blank. It is suggested that making the mind blank may be associated, not with subjective or imaginary psi, but with an objective psi ability. We have heard that objective tests have been given to these people to see if they have demonstrable psi ability in an experimental situation. We don't know what the results of that are yet. Now the question I would like to ask is, what is the reason for assuming that there is a connection between objective psi and the ability to make the mind blank? This seems to be a hypothesis which came out of the blue. I would like to know the reason behind this hypothesis?

WICKRAM: You understood my first point correctly. Subjective psi, in terms of my research and the independent replication of other people, seems to be related to subjective psi reporting. There is another component in hypnotic ability, which is orthogonal to the hallucinatory component, and that is the ability to make the mind blank—the ability, in terms of actual items on the Stanford or Harvard scales correlated with amnesia. The notion that that may be correlated with objective psi is something we are currently testing. Why it might be correlated with objective psi, or why we think it may have a relationship is totally speculatory. The basis for speculation is that if either external noise or internal noise interferes with a signal that is very weak, then, maybe the ability to put aside all preconceptions or all contrary beliefs may improve the reception of a weak signal. That is purely speculation, I have no empirical evidence to support that. I do know that in the yogi literature, literature on the samadhi state, they talk about a "blank mind" as an important factor in the ability to not just do psychophysiological tricks, but also to do things like levitate and the other kinds of supposed claims of paranormal experiences.

WEST: I believe that in fact, you do have a little more than pure speculation to go on, because you have argued that hypnotic ability and hypnotic states are psi conducive. I know that Keith Harary has challenged that, but it has certainly been suggested in the literature. Now, if hypnotic ability is correlated with objective psi, it is also correlated with fantasy productions, but you don't believe that fantasy productions are correlated with real psi. Then, there must be some other factor in hypnotic ability which makes for real psi. Since you have another factor, then you have a reason for looking at that other factor. So, maybe you have more reason behind your hypothesis than you have explained.

WICKRAM: Thank you. The important point is to see what the data suggests. For example, fantasy proneness has been shown to correlate .25 with measured hypnotic ability. It is not a perfect correlation. There is much variance that is unaccounted for. So, we don't know until we see what the empirical results are. It is possible that the fantasy factor in hypnotic ability is only *modestly* correlated with empirically verifiable psi but that the cognitive-memory inhibition factor in hypnotic ability is strongly correlated with empirically verifiable psi.

THE LIMITATION OF THE NEUROSCIENTIFIC APPROACH TO PARAPSYCHOLOGY

PETER FENWICK

Introduction

A major difficulty for parapsychology is that it is considered a non-scientific discipline. Indeed, it is clear that if there was adequate scientific proof for the action of mind at a distance, together with the necessary mathematical theory to explain this, then physics as we know it would have to be re-written.

A search through the neuroscience journals for 1989 produced no articles on the nature of mind. Indeed, it is evident that the very nature of science as it is NOW understood would seem to exclude parapsychology as an area of study.

The Current Dilemma

Neurophysiologists and psychologists have long faced the problem that there appears to be no place in the brain for consciousness or mind—a fact which has led many scientists to claim that mind as a separate entity does not exist.

For many centuries there has seemed to be no place in the universe for consciousness. In the 18th century, when Newtonian mechanics appeared to give a complete account of the world, the mathematician Laplace said that if he knew the position and momentum of every particle in the universe, he could predict how the world would evolve. Clearly this statement assumed a totally materialistic universe, without consciousness, and evolving according to a set of immutable physical laws. The idea of a mechanical universe, although powerful in predicting the orbits of the planets, has been unsatisfactory from an experiential point of view, as it excludes consciousness. Both psychology and psychiatry suffer from the lack of a satisfactory theoretical framework for the explanation and investigation of consciousness. In order to understand why, it is important to see how consciousness came to be excluded.

Primary and Secondary Qualities

In the 17th century, at the time of Copernicus, Keppler, Descartes, Galileo, Bacon, and Newton, to mention just a few of the outstanding thinkers of that time, the infant science of reductionism came into being. Up to that point, explanations of the external world had depended on the views of Aristotle and other Greek authorities. What the new science did was to propose models of the world which could be checked and were in accordance with observation of physical data. The success of the scientific method gave rise to the modern reductionist science we know today. Galileo in "The Assayer" (1623) said:

> To excite in us tastes, odors, and sounds, I believe that nothing is required in external bodies except shapes, numbers, and slow or rapid movements. I think that if ears, tongues, and noises were removed, shapes and numbers and motions would remain, but not odors or tastes or sounds. The latter, I believe are nothing more than names when separated from living beings, just as tickling and titillation are nothing but names in the absence of such things as noses and armpits.

He stated that science was only concerned with primary qualities, those qualities of the external world which could be weighed and measured. Secondary qualities, heaviness, beauty, love etc. were not within the realm of science.

Descartes expressed the same idea of the difference between primary and secondary qualities. He maintained that there are two radically different kinds of substances, physical, extended substance (res extensa) that is, that which has length, breadth and depth, and can therefore be measured and divided, and thinking substance (res cogitans) which is unextended and indivisible. The external world, of which the human body is a part, belongs to the first category, while the internal world of the mind belongs to the second.

It was these assumptions by the early scientists that led to a division between subjective and objective worlds and to the exclusion of consciousness (subjective experience), by definition, from the external world. If the external world is only to consist of those things which can be weighed, measured, and quantified, then by definition it must be "a valueless exterior," with no place for consciousness. However complex physical theory becomes, consciousness will not appear in the equations. (It can't, because it has already been excluded.)

The Search for Consciousness

With the rise in the 19th century of experimental physiology, and the understanding that the brain was responsible for the appearance of consciousness it was hoped that the examination of brain structure and physiology would give us an understanding of the nature of consciousness. By the end of the 19th century, it became clear that neurophysiology was unlikely to yield any information about the nature of consciousness, although it might well give some information about its mechanism. It would be possible to cite numerous examples from many authors who wrote widely on this subject at that time, but it is sufficient to quote from Charles Sherrington's essays Man and his Nature, which were published at that time, and which sum up then current thinking.

> You may then ask whether it is one cell, a superpontifical cell, which allows the world to come into consciousness, or whether it is many. The brain acts as a democracy, with each cell playing its own place, and through their concerted efforts they allow consciousness to arise.

He described this process poetically as the workings of the enchanted loom. "They weave an ever-changing pattern, never an abiding pattern, the workings of the enchanted loom."

> Sherrington was at as much of a loss to explain consciousness as his predecessors were: The energy scheme describes a star, how the light from a star strikes the retina, and stimulates the cells in the back of the eye. From there, nervous conduction carries the information to the brain where it is distributed amongst the cells of the cortex. But at the point at which the star comes into consciousness, the energy scheme is silent, and puts its finger to its lips.

It was hoped that further neurophysiological investigation would somehow still be able to extract the true nature of consciousness, if only it could be made complex enough. That this was unlikely to occur was shown by the school of thought typified by Gilbert Ryle in his essays on man, when he points out the futility of the search for "the ghost in the machine."

Twentieth Century Physics

Twentieth century physics brought the recognition that the universal mechanical laws of Newton must give way to the laws of relativity for the very large, and to the statistical laws of quantum mechanics for the very small. Once again there was hope that consciousness could be found lurking in the corner of our mechanical universe. Recent work by such physicists as David Bohm heightened these expectations. During the 60s and early 70s, with the big bang theory still in its theoretical infancy, it seemed possible that the conditions in the first few seconds of the universe had to be so precisely chosen if the universe was to evolve in the way that it has done, that these conditions could not have occurred by chance. It was also postulated that as the conditions at the time immediately preceding the expansion of the universe could never be known (technically this is known as a singularity), the possibility of a consciousness and a consciously-directed universe still existed. This led to the idea of the anthropic principle, a principle that states that the evolution of man's consciousness must have been written into the laws of physics from the beginning, simply because he is here to observe it. The logical extension of this was the assumption of an implicate unfolding order which becomes manifest during the evolution of physical laws.

Closing the Gaps

However, in the most modern theories of physics it seems that even these gaps which seemed to allow for consciousness have been closed. There are now perfectly coherent theories which suggest that it is possible to know the physical laws pertaining to the initial singularity of the universe, and that the universe evolved the way it did because it was the most probable of the set of all possible universes. And so once again, consciousness has become excluded. We can no longer appeal to the "God of the Gaps" as modern physical theory does not really leave any gaps to be filled.

This does however, clearly run contrary to everyday experience. We know that we live in a universe where love, beauty, sadness, are part of our experience. And even if the physicists cannot find a place for consciousness it has still to be reckoned with.

So then, why is it that physics is still deficient, in that it gives us a mathematically coherent and highly effective predictor of the outside world, but yet leaves aside some of the most important aspects of that world—color, beauty, love, etc? In order to understand this, it is necessary to look at the very basic assumptions on which our reductionist science is built, as it must be from there that its incompleteness stems. Remember, the primary qualities of Galileo excluded subjectivity, so the data of science is objective. But scientific observation is carried out by scientists and they are subjective, so how can science be totally objective? Our modern understanding of brain function may help to explain this paradox, although the following scheme must be dependent on the assumptions of reductionist science and contaminated by them.

Explaining the Paradox

The external world comes into consciousness through the mind/brain mechanism. Although we experience the outside world as a series of sensory objects, what actually comes to our senses is energy in the form of electromagnetic radiation of different frequencies, very low frequencies for hearing and touch, higher frequencies for warmth, and higher still for vision. These radiations carry no subjective information and have only objective value. As Sherrington said, they are part of the energy scheme. Modern physics would describe them simply as heaps of statistical probabilities.

These radiations trigger neural codes, which are made by the brain into a model of the external world. This model is then given subjective value and by a trick of brain functioning projected outwards to form the subjective world. We call this external world objective, whether we are looking at the meters which monitor the occurrence of resonances in high energy particle accelerators (the data of quantum mechanics), or the ricochetting of two billiard balls (the data of Newtonian mechanics), but it is only a subjective mental model created within our brains. As the nuclear physicist Wigner said, "When we stare at our meters, we merely see reflections of ourselves."

The result of this distorted worldview, is that it appears that reductionist science is capable of explaining our mental models which have value and quality and consciousness, while at the same time covertly saying that value, quality and consciousness are excluded from them. So our scientific models must lead to theories which are devoid of consciousness by definition.

Scientific models of brain function can only explain subjective experience as a mechanical process; anger as an activation of neural impulses in amygdala-hypothalamic structures; love as activity in those neurological systems which underpin mood; transcendent experiences, when the world is experienced as universal love, as the dysfunction of the temporal lobe. Scientists would argue that if we were to understand brain function fully then consciousness could be totally explained by a moving flux of electro/chemical processes within the brain. Even the synthesis of new qualities arising from complexity of brain structure as in the models of artificial intelligence, still makes use of scientific thinking, and so still excludes consciousness. Reductionist science still assumes an external world which is independent of ourselves, but uses a subjectively contaminated mental model to assess it.

A Science of Secondary Qualities

Although psychology has not yet developed to the science of Galileo's secondary qualities, physics has already begun to recognize that the objective and subjective cannot be separated. Some theorists of quantum mechanics include the observer in the observation, for example, where a particle appears is dependent on the collapse of the wave equations which specify it. Until they collapse, the position of the particle cannot be precisely predicted. Thus, observer and observation are intimately related.

Is it possible to evolve a science of secondary qualities and of consciousness so that reductionist psychology need no longer explain phenomena beyond its terms of reference? And if so what consequences would this have for psychiatry and psychology?

Both Galileo and Descartes pointed the way to this science when they split off the objective world from the subjective. The study of secondary qualities must be the science of subjective experience. The aim of such "Secondary Psychology," or "New Dualism" should be the analysis of consciousness and its content. It takes as its data only subjective experiences, is consistent within itself, and sets up theoretical models about subjective experience. It sets out to explain the relationship between different subjective phenomena, as reductionist science does for the objective. This science progresses as does reductionist science, by the setting up of a hypothesis, its testing, possible falsification, and reformulation. In this sense it is a true science, as defined by Popper.

Before the nature of the new dualism can be determined the laws of mind and consciousness must be defined. This can only be done by the detailed observation of subjective experience with the evolution of a coherent schema of the properties of mind and consciousness. This suggests that much work of psychology at the turn of the century could again become valid, though viewed from a different perspective as it is now only concerned with consciousness, not with the structure or function of the brain, which are in the domain of reductionist science. It is to be expected that the study of our everyday consciousness would give one set of rules, just as the study of our everyday world does in physics. These rules would change when the level of consciousness altered just as they do in physics when the scale alters from the very large to the very small. Under this scheme transcendent and mystical experience, both spontaneous and induced by special circumstances, such as near-death experiences, would be seen as valid descriptions of the world. Consciousness is then seen as the ground structure of the universe from which all else arises, study of these experiential states would lead to a more complete understanding of the universe and the rules that govern it. These two views, one through the primary qualities (physics) and the other through the secondary qualities (subjective experience) might then be related to make a unified whole.

Brain Function and Parapsychological Experience

Dr. Vernon Neppe has already written in a previous conference proceeding concerning the relationship between experiences arising from disorders of the temporal lobe, and parapsychological phenomena. This view, which attributes parapsychological phenomena to the functioning of the temporal lobe, runs into the difficulties of mind/body dualism. Providing that as has already been explained above, science by definition is unable to explain consciousness, then the relationship between brain function and experience is a valid field for study. However, the relationships are correlative, and cannot be causative. Fenwick (1983) looks in some detail at the relationship between brain physiology and mystical experience.

In a study of psychic sensitivity and mystical experience, head injury and brain pathology, Fenwick, Galliano, Coate, Rippere, and Brown (1985) were able to show that temporal lobe pathology was possibly involved in patients who had experienced psychic gifts. Their hypothesis came from the parapsychological literature in which it is often mentioned that there is a relationship between head injury and a subsequent development of psychic sensitivity. This observation allows the development of the hypotheses which say that the experiencing of psychic gifts is due to temporal lobe damage, or is due to an alteration of function in the temporal lobes such that brain function is altered and allows a new manifestation of consciousness to arise. These two hypotheses are not seen as alternative by science, as a similar alteration in brain function is postulated in both hypotheses, the difference between them being that in the second case, mind is seen as acting through brain rather than being a distillation of brain function.

The Significance of Temporal Lobe to Psychic Experience

The findings of this study showed that there was a significantly larger number of head injuries in the group who claimed psychic sensitivity experiences. It was interesting that on psychological testing this group showed a significant excess of brain damage compared to the control group, and that this damage was confined to the right hemisphere and was maximal in the right temporal lobe. As a result the mediums experienced some specific cognitive deficits. For example, most of the mediums when in trance had "psychic helpers." These helpers frequently manifested in physical space and tended to stand on either one side or the other of the mediums. Those mediums with right temporal damage and right hemisphere damage could be expected to show poor visio-spatial abilities and thus poor spatial localization of their helpers. This was exactly what we found. Mediums with brain damage described their helpers as being "all around" rather than having a special spatial location. This finding adds support to the hypothesis that mediumistic experiences are specifically conditioned by brain function.

Another finding of this study was that the mediums had more mystical experiences than the controls. This finding would suggest that mystical experiences are to some extent mediated by the right temporal lobe, and indeed, there is evidence in the literature that this is so. A paper by Cirignotta et al. (1980) describes a mystical experience occurring during an epileptic aura (fit). The seizure arose in the right temporal lobe. Additional evidence comes from the author's own experience in which patients with epilepsy who have had mystical experiences have usually had right temporal lesions. That the right temporal lobe should be involved is not surprising, as there is evidence in the literature that the right temporal structures are involved with the mediation of emotion.

There was a relationship between the type of psychic sensitivity and right temporal lobe impairment. Precognition, clairaudience, telepathy, working with a psychic helper, having a psychic guide, and the position in physical space of the psychic helper, were all significantly related to right hemisphere damage. This finding clearly suggests that brain damage can lead to these experiences.

The mediums were more "fragile" than their controls. They had had more serious illnesses, had been knocked out more often, had had more blackouts, and had consulted a psychiatrist more frequently. This suggests not only an increase in physical damage to the brain, but possibly emotional damage as well. A questionnaire study of patients with epilepsy at the Maudsley hospital showed that there was a definite re-

lationship between perinatal brain damage and the experience of telepathy and clairvoyance. This was found in not only those with temporal lobe epilepsy, but also in those with generalized seizures. Again
this finding suggests a relationship between long-standing brain damage
and the occurrence of psychic experiences.

Unhappiness and Illness in Childhood

Kenneth Ring, an American psychologist, in a paper given at an
international conference in Norway described the provisional results
of a recent study he has undertaken into near-death experiences. Not
everybody who has a cardiac arrest and comes close to death, has a
classical near death experience. Many people coming out of the intensive care unit will have experienced only unconsciousness. Comparing
those who did to those who did not have the near death experience,
Ring found that there was a significant difference in their childhood
experiences. Those who described near death experiences had been
more unhappy in childhood or had had more childhood illnesses. This
finding suggests again the possible causative role in these experiences
of brain trauma as well as the significance of emotional deprivation. It
is possible to hypothesize that during the development of the mature
mind, both brain damage and emotional deprivation allow the formation of different psychic structures which mediate and underpin
parapsychological experiences. The question that then arises is whether
or not these experiences reflect an extension of reality or whether they
are simply part of a dysfunctional brain?

Conclusion

Science today, following the postulates of Descartes and Galileo,
studies only the objective external world. Subjective experience is thus
excluded from scientific study, with the result that parapsychological
knowledge cannot be reconciled with the large field of scientific knowledge. With the recognition of the present limitation of scientific theory,
a new science based entirely on subjective experience, will need to be
created. It will be a combination of objective and subjective sciences,
that will finally lead to a resolution of the current separation of psychology and parapsychology.

The study of brain function allows us to gain some understanding
of factors which are important in the genesis of mystical and parapsychological experiences. It is clear that the right temporal lobe is predominantly involved, and that an alteration of function within this area

can give rise to aspects of psychic sensitive experiences as well as mystical experiences. Further work needs to be done on the possible relationship between childhood unhappiness and stress, and the hypothesis that this may facilitate creation of psychic structures which in adulthood can mediate a range of experiences which are not available to those with normal childhoods.

Present orthodox science still has much more to contribute, although a more comprehensive explanation of these phenomena will only be achieved with the fusing of the sciences of objective and subjective experience.

REFERENCES

Cirignotta, et al. (1980). Temporal lobe epilepsy with ecstatic seizures. *Epilepsia, 21,* 705–710.
Fenwick, P. (1983). Some aspects of the physiology of the experience. In J. Nicholson & B. Floss (Eds.) *Psychology surveys* No. 4. Leicester: British Psychological Society.
Fenwick, P., Galliano, S., Coate, M. A., Rippers, V., & Brown, D. (1985). Sensitives, "psychic gifts," psychic sensitivity and brain pathology. *British Journal of Medical Psychology, 58,* 35–44.
Neppe, V. (1986) Window into the mind: A phenomenological perspective. In B. Shapin & L. Coly (Eds.), *Parapsychology and human nature* (pp. 1–12). New York: Parapsychology Foundation.
Ring, K. (1989). Personal communication. Data presented at the Near-Death Experience Conference, Floro, Norway.

DISCUSSION

HARARY: It is just not true that people who have a lot of subjective psi experiences necessarily have something wrong with them, have had bizarre childhoods that led to their having those experiences, are necessarily brain damaged, or have suffered from severe emotional problems. If we are looking for pathology whenever somebody says they have had a psi experience then we have totally alienated ourselves from our own potential. We have said, "Look, all you crazy people experience this stuff—not the rest of us." Well, I have had a lot of psi experiences. I have had electrodes hung all over me and I am fine, thank you. I really think that this expresses part of the problem. I mean, look, we can talk about people who have serious problems and discuss how they may either feel that they are having certain kinds of experiences of psi or that they are not. But the point is there are people who have serious problems who think they are encountering something that they are not. Just as there are people without serious problems in the same situation. There are also people who have serious problems who think they are encountering something that they are! There also are people who do not have serious problems who think they are experiencing something and they really are. They really do what they say they do and no, they do not go into fits; they do not have horrific head injuries; they do not have brain damage. Sometimes people have difficult childhoods because they are experiencing things that the people around them do not feel comfortable with. That does not mean that the difficult childhood created the experience, it may be the other way around. Also often the psi experience is a response that is healthy, that helps you cope, that gives you a sense of something greater, something beyond yourself, something to reach for, some sense that the future is going to be brighter. So what are you suggesting? Should we turn this off? Should we imply that only pathological people, only people with real serious problems, experience psi? I do not think so. No offense but I have never smelled non-existent perfume and there is no epilepsy in my family. I think it is OK to talk about what happens in pathological situations but we must not confuse what happens in pathological situations with what happens in normal situations. There has to be a normal context for psi.

FENWICK: I am talking about three sets of data. These are very specific sets of data. One is a set of mediums who came to me from the College of Psychic Studies in London. Another set are patients who have got epilepsy and therefore brain damage. The third set is a set of people provided by Kenneth Ring, who is a psychologist in the United States who researches into near death experiences. Now, within that population of people there seemed to be a very close correlation between the occurrence of some experience, for example, a birth trauma or a head injury, and the onset of that psychic gift. It would be quite unfair to generalize outside that population and I would not like to do it. If you want an explanation of the phenomena, I think you have to be very careful about what model you are using. If you use a reductionist model, in other words, the perception of the world as we see it is entirely due to brain function, then you will come out with reductionist explanations. The explanations which I put forward at that time, that this was due to a distortion in the temporal lobe structures, would be a perfectly logical model and quite consistent with the data which was presented. However, you may find that that is not a satisfactory model. In other words, if you come to think of the world as it is and how it comes into our consciousness, science is quite unable to explain even the most simple sensory experiences. We know a lot about the actual mechanism. It is all related to the energy scheme. When I say energy scheme I'm also talking about the transfer of information because the two are interchangeable. We come to a point where sensory experience arises. Now, there is not one theory that I know of which talks about how the magnetic fields and the ionic flow within neuronal networks leads to the arising of sensory experience. You can talk, if you like, about parallelism, but that really is just avoiding the issue. We have no scientific theory of the nature of ordinary experience, very simple things. There is quite a good reductionist explanation for the phenomena that I was describing. But, whether that is the entire explanation, and whether you find it satisfactory, really depends on the philosophical point from which you come. But, if you will always imply a scientific frame, then you always will end up with brain function. I'm not sure really that in a conference devoted to parapsychology that we should always be looking at scientific models. I think we actually should be examining other models as well.

NEPPE: Let me just from a continuity point of view carry on where Dr. Harary has left off, I think his points about attribution of causality are obviously very important. If one examines a population of people with psychopathology you may well get one subpopulation who is able to attribute a variety of different phenomena in terms of just answering, "Yes, this has happened to me." That same subgroup may be answering in relation to subjective paranormal experiences or might be talking about them, and might also be prepared to talk about traumatic events in their childhood. Attribution of causality is questionable. Even if one then gets a control group from a psychiatric population, you may find that the (proper) correlation will stand up but it does not imply any kind of causal link. So I think Keith's point is particularly good. I also want to clarify that I have been misquoted by Peter in this paper. To quote him quoting my view: "This view which attributes parapsychological phenomena to the functioning of the temporal lobe runs into the difficulties of mind/body dualism." I have never attributed parapsychological phenomena to the functioning of the temporal lobe. I have said there is a correlation between subjective paranormal experience and anomalous temporal lobe functioning as reflected by the increased incidence of possible temporal lobe symptoms both at a state and a trait level and also incidentally linked up from an electrophysiologic point of view in terms of another study on electroencephalograms. The electroencephalographic study, originally by Nelson, is really the only positive one that has not been replicated. There was a marked degree of interhemispheric asychrony but it was equally distributed on both sides. In our subsequent studies using the same lab, we found several people with subjective paranormal experiences as having normal electroencephalograms. I am interested in the point made in relation to olfactory hallucinations because I have no doubt that you would fit the criterion in terms of our subjective paranormal experience. Although I have not gone through that formally with you, we now have about 18 subjects, all of whom had spontaneously, when asked about olfactory hallucinations, admitted to it. Keith, you are the very first "psychic" I have ever come across who has not spoken about that. We have not been looking for family histories of seizures until very recently. We did find that cluster in one family and it has been an interesting one which crops up with my temporal lobe epileptics all the time. But again one is looking at a pathologic population. There is just one final comment which may allow clarity to all of this. A very interesting finding in relation to temporal lobe pathology has been that the accentuation of stress and emotionality that is linked with all of this may in fact, in some kind of vicious cycle component, seem to be accentuating the temporal lobe pathology in some way. I would like to emphasize the very important point that I talk about anomalous temporal lobe functioning. I do not talk about dysfunction of the temporal lobe in people with subjective paranormal experiences: the temporal lobe is functioning in a way that is different from that of the average member of the population. They have certain perceptual experiences of temporal lobe kind which others do not have. This does not imply temporal lobe dysfunction. In fact they function differently to temporal lobe dysfunctions as well because as indicated, the olfactory hallucinations, and the deja vu experiences are qualitatively different; they are not the same.

FENWICK: Yes, I accept that absolutely. I think that is very nice. Going back to the head injury question, the argument runs something like this—if people show psychic experience after they have had head injuries, you can take either a reductionist view that you so change brain function that the meaning which is attributed to experience, is altered, or a non-reductionist view. This would say that the brain function is changed in such a way that the mediation of experience is different. Those are two quite different statements about the world and I think one has to see this.

PARKER: Rather like incest, perinatal brain damage and perinatal risk factors have been found to be correlated with a wide range of psychiatric disorders. I do not think one can imply much from the thought that they are a risk factor in life.

NEPPE: Birth is correlated with many psychiatric disorders.

VAN DE CASTLE: I am finding myself distressed in some ways because I feel the panelists are going toward trying to make an extremely strong linkage between psi and pathology. As I tried to address yesterday, my own view would be that psi is somehow growth facilitative. If so, it can certainly be an accompaniment of normal behavior or of a psychiatric problem. If we were to link psi with creativity, we could have an equally eloquent panel talking about creativity and referring to some artists and writers who would have been labeled as schizophrenic or manic depressive. Would we come to a conclusion that we should get rid of creativity because somehow it means you are going to wind up psychotic if you are creative? Certainly you can be normal and appreciate creativity. If psi is intended for self-enhancement, self-expansion, self-understanding, we should find more models, more research paradigms that could emphasize that. I was trying to explain yesterday, you can experience psi in this cooperative fashion with all members participating, feeling good about having had a joint psi experience. It seems to me we have too much pathological focus and too many nosological categories. It will distress Vernon Neppe that he has not been able to get Keith Harary into one of those pigeon holes yet and he is going to try until he gets him into one of those diagnostic pigeonholes. Are we going to go on with this labeling and categorizing and seeking out, smelling out? Do you smell perfume? Because then I have got you tagged and this somehow is a negative aspect in connection with psi. So if we could somehow see that psi is here for a reason—it is to facilitate growth and people with mental problems are going to need additional growth. I would also hope that all of us, as normals, would not want to exclude ourselves from seeking the possible experience to grow, and to be creative, and to have some sort of interactive exchange with others or with information that we feel is some sort of an enlargement of our own personal worldview.

WEST: Dr. Neppe has mentioned to us earlier that some surveys have shown, that actually the majority of people report some kind of subjective psychic experience during their lives. Now, unless the temporal lobe anomalies are much commoner than I believe them to be, the correlation between these two things cannot be as high as has been suggested.

NEPPE: This is almost a direct question in relation to this and I think it is very important to make the point, as I have made it, that I subdivided my populations, and one would have to look at the original research methodology in this regard, into people with large, large numbers of subjective paranormal experiences using a variety of validating criteria at that subjective level using three levels of descriptive interview as I indicated. That was an extreme subpopulation compared with the other subpopulation of "non-experients." However, separately, the vast majority of the population reports subjective paranormal experiences but they have small numbers in their lifetime. They do not fit within the framework of anomalous temporal lobe functioning. It is only the extreme subgroups that one is talking about in terms of that. In the criteria that I have used, the people who have never had experiences, who are incidentally at times, depending on the population you look at, as hard to find as those who had large numbers, have had four different kinds of subjective paranormal experience. So your point is an important one and it is a point that I have made repeatedly. The average member of the population has these experiences, but they do not have any evidence for anomalous temporal lobe functioning. If they did, that temporal lobe functioning would not be anomalous.

ELLISON: May I just reinforce what Peter Fenwick has been saying about the importance of models (and what that end of the table has also been saying), how one is limited in the experiments one does, and what one will find in those experiments, by the model used. I mentioned earlier that I have recommended for many years, with no success at all, that fellow psychical researchers experiment on themselves. I experimented on myself and had two out-of-body experiences. Now, the way I did that was to change my conceptual model. I had to imagine that I had an astral body made of subtle material interpenetrating the physical—which is not quite "true." In other words, it doesn't fit realism at all, which is very easy to show in simple experiments. But I had to go along with that model before I could possibly "move my consciousness around in the physical world." I did what the Philip group did. I "believed" in the model and then had as a result of strong imagination an OBE. It couldn't have been 100% belief, of course, because I knew it wasn't true in my ordinary model of reality. I had enough belief in that model to have success. I moved around physical space in an astral body and had very interesting experiences indeed. So, it's enormously important to have the right models and I'm sure Bob Van de Castle has a much wider range of interesting, creative, and stimulating experiences because he has a quite different model. Regarding Peter Fenwick's head injury cases, I asked him a question about that some time ago. I read some of the old Hindu literature and in Patanjali's Yoga's aphorisms the idea is given there that if you practice meditation then you will develop the *siddhis* or psychic powers. So, I wondered, if you practiced meditation—in other words, developed yourself— whether you could "rewire" your right temporal lobe? (I'm an electrical engineer) I asked Peter Fenwick whether this was possible and he told me it was. He might like to comment on that. Finally, another experience with Peter: we set up an EEG machine in a bio-electricity lab in our university. He asked me, as the first guinea pig, to relax while he observed my EEG. I didn't understand and I said, "Do you want me to relax thinking or not thinking?" He told me he had never been asked that question before, so I switched off my thinking. (Having been a long time meditator I was able to do that.) We got rather a lot of theta rhythm, about the four hertz region. I had that interesting experience. Somewhat concerned Peter also examined my whole EEG picture; and I had a statement to say that I am normal.

FENWICK: Only just normal, Arthur. Concerning the comment about changing your model of the world by meditation, one of the things we do know is that you can change brain rhythms by meditation and there is some evidence from the biofeedback literature that if you change your cerebral rhythms in one circumstance, you can change them in another. The correlation between EEG and mental state is a very distant one, but nevertheless, what you are arguing for is a change in cerebral physiology due to a practice of some sort. I think this would absolutely agree with what we think, in other words, the mental state that we bring to a situation determines what we see. I suspect it's got a neurophysiological basis as well.

CASSIRER: Let me be unfair to Dr. Fenwick for a few seconds. You made your experiments with mediums from the College of Psychic Studies in London, and you found a correlation between brain damage and those mediums. I, however, was thinking of the great mediums of the past: D. D. Home, Mrs. Osborne Leonard, Mrs. Piper, and so on. I have never heard of any suggestion that they were dropped on their heads as babies or that they suffered from any of these physical abnormalities. Would you care to comment?

FENWICK: I wouldn't interpret anything outside my data. Within that set of data head injuries or cerebral trauma were important. Within Ring's data of people who had near-death experiences and people who did not, then the people who had near-death experiences had either unhappy childhoods or prenatal brain damage. Those were only three very small studies and to try to explain the whole phenomenon just on three studies, I think would be quite unfair. So, I very much accept what you say. There are bound to be people who have these experiences without any evidence of brain damage at all, and indeed this would fit much better into a model of the world, than one which says that all these phenomena are just due to brain damage. I wouldn't say that.

GENERAL DISCUSSION
DAY TWO

BENOR: In this conference on psi and clinical practice we have been in the model of psychologists and parapsychologists being the ones in charge of managing the phenomena. I'm working with healers; I've worked with mediums and psychics who do counseling in a clinical practice that is, as far as I can tell, every bit as successful as that of psychologists and psychiatrists and other therapists. It is a neglected area for study. These people seem to do as well, and sometimes much more deeply and thoroughly, in their work as conventional therapists.

FENWICK: Could I just make a comment on that? Dan, I absolutely agree with you. You know the famous study which put us all out of work. It compared a group of psychiatrists, a group of social workers, a group of nurses, and a group of people who just came and talked to other patients. The people who attended the groups were people with neurotic illnesses, and all groups did the same, it was really just talking that helped.

KRAMER: I agree with you. I'm also involved in working with psychic healers and what you see is that most of the time they can help their clients very well and very quickly because they are on the same level with them. One of the things I often hear from my clients is that, "It's nice to go to doctors, psychiatrists, and psychologists but they all talk a language which I don't understand. They have the impression that they understand what they are talking about." One of the good things about psychic healers is that they are coming from the same population as the clients. That means they mesh. That provides very quick results in some cases.

VON LUCADOU: I want to come back to the problem of models. It seems to me that we are speaking about psi as subjective psi experiences or real psi experiences and different models. But it seems to me that there is not only the alternative of the random paradigm which says that psi is something like an information transfer or a force. There are rather elaborate theoretical models in parapsychology which describe psi in quite different ways. One is, for instance, the observational theories. If you do not like them, then I would offer others—the chance model of psi, which is quite different from the observational theory, or my own model of pragmatic information. I know that we first have to confirm in experiments that these models can be verified or falsified, but, since I'm also doing counseling at the moment, I tried to develop the model of pragmatic information. I developed this model with my colleague, Klaus Kornwachs. I simply tried to bring this down to earth and apply it in counseling cases. I found it works pretty well. But with this model the usual paradigm is far too simplistic. It's not a simple force, or a simple information transfer, or a simple reductionist model; it is a systems theoretical model. For people who do not have a theoretical background, I simply use their own language. I describe to them what I think they feel and what I expect that they will find. They say, "Well, that's true, exactly." If they speak in terms of ghosts or entities, I can predict how they behave because there are very simple rules which came from that model. For instance, one very simple rule is, whenever you use ESP like a simple information transfer, it will disappear. I find this in my practice and a person immediately understands what I'm saying. So, I think it's not very useful to discuss clinical issues without discussing the theoretical issue of what psi really is.

SUSANNA VAN DE CASTLE: As part of the general public, I think we look to you as parapsychologists, to find some answers or some possibilities for what is happening. I don't think that there is a clear answer and, from what I understand, there may not be a clear model. Maybe we should stop trying to find a specific model of something that is energy and not tangible, and start looking for a model that has flexibility depending upon the areas of perception for each individual.

PRICHETT: One thing that I would like to ask which has not been talked about directly is the relationship between memory and the paranormal. There is a difficulty here, I think, between the scientific and the non-scientific paradigm and parapsychology, in that a lot of things to do with psi, particularly reincarnation, seem to imply that long term memory is not actually located in the brain. Whereas the scientific paradigm tries to maintain that it must be in the physical brain. Has anybody got any comments on this?

FENWICK: It's a very difficult one and I certainly don't have enough data with which to answer it. From a scientific point of view, when the brain dies, all information disappears. But, in non-scientific models, such as that postulated by Ruppert Sheldrake, information is held independently of the brain and is held within the universe itself. I think that one has to be quite clear how one comes at these things. If one comes at it from a scientific point of view, then of course, one has to say that it's not possible. But I think that one has to recognize that science is only one very small part, or one partial description, of the outside world. Other models are equally valid.

NEPPE: There's just one sentence I want to add to that, and that is, memory is the prototype example, as I think you were implying, of not being able to easily localize a phenomenon within the brain. Certain aspects can be localized to the hippocampi, and other aspects to various parts of the temporal lobe, but basically you are dealing with much that is non-localizable. The implication of what you were asking raises all sorts of questions, the same questions relating to mind and consciousness. Then you're shifting to a realm of philosophy. And here philosophy and science do indeed meet and we have heard some attempts at answers. I don't know if we've got all the answers.

MORRIS: Does anyone on the panel of participants have any one last short comment?

NEPPE: I do have one tiny comment, and that is just correcting the factual error that there is nothing on parapsychology in conventional psychiatric textbooks. The *Comprehensive Textbook of Psychiatry* which is regarded as the bible of psychiatry, has traditionally had a chapter on parapsychology and psychiatry. One issue was written by Montague Ullman but for reasons best known to that comprehensive textbook does not appear in the latest edition which came out this year. However, the entry of "subjective paranormal psychosis" is discussed in my chapter (see Neppe & Tucker, 1989).

HARARY: I have been thinking about all the different points of view on psi experiences and noticed I still avoid the word psychic. It is clear that some of us are very familiar with seeing people who are suffering from various kinds of delusions and we ask ourselves, "Under what circumstances do these delusions occur?" Others of us get defensive and say, "Well, you know, psi isn't always a delusion." The original folks say, "Well, I didn't mean that it was always a delusion." Bob Morris said to me during one of the breaks, "Nobody said anything about training." So I'll say something quickly. We are gathering evidence in our research indicating that with the proper guidance you can actually learn how to experience psi. It appears that you can actually learn to develop quite astute capabilities at processing psi information. This will not turn you into a guru. This will not make you special. This may drive you crazy if you try to bring it into a psi research laboratory, but it doesn't have to drive you crazy. Some of us have seen psi in a growth oriented context. I think there's a distinction between what's going on spontaneously in Western culture, given the fact that we're not in a culture that has its act together around these experiences yet, and the whole question of learning to work with psi in a reasonable way. It seems that you can. Darlene and I have taught people how to do things that used to be thought to be the sole domain of special and unusual people. We found out that there apparently are a lot of people out there in the general population who can develop quite fine capabilities, they just hadn't been asked, and didn't think that they could. When we made it OK for them by saying, "This will not turn you into something weird, why don't we work on this together." We got some good results. We have to overcome the word psychic and all of the archaic thinking that goes along with it.

PARKER: I began my paper by asking the question whether or not psi and psychotic-like experiences are intimately or merely incidently related. The theme of several papers, and here I am thinking in particular of the papers of Keith Harary, Donald West, and Wim Kramer, is that having a subjective psi experience does not necessarily imply pathology. The reverse seems also true, having a disturbing experience does not exclude genuine psi irrespective of the implications of this for parapsychology. This presents a challenge for orthodox clinical psychology and psychiatry which persists in regarding all such experiences as delusory and symptomatic.

Yet it would seem that verifiable spontaneous psi experiences are rare and that the picture is confused by personal psychodynamics giving rise to what might be called pseudo-psi. Many of the latter experiences can perhaps be explained by both the cognitive theory of psi type experiences described by Ian Tierney and myself and by the clinical theory of psychotic-like experiences occurring in the normal population (schizotype personality). These experiences, whatever their nature, often demand crisis intervention and supportive psychotherapy but as Wim Kramer cautions us, we would probably be wasting our time searching after finding good evidence of psi amongst this clientele.

Might it however not still be the case, that at least in some instances persons having anomalous states or unusual perceptual experiences are in a potentially psi-conducive state and that the genuine article becomes heavily diluted with a delusory content? Here I think that Robert Van de Castle's paper was not only challenging in the claims he reported, but also made us aware of the role that dissociation and self conflict can play in paranormal experiences. Indeed, I firmly believe we must make the best of the *psychological aspects* of parapsychological theory and come up with predictions in both this field and the general field of abnormal psychology. Now it would seem to be a consensus finding from various lines of research that absorption internal attention states is a variable implicated in psi experiences. If we re-read the Rhine work with the high scoring subjects Lindzmager and Ownbey, it is apparent that they achieved their results during periods of absorption or dissociation. Spontaneous trance states were already in 1941 accredited an important role in a survey of the experimentation by Smith and Gibson. It would seem natural in this respect to look closer not only at altered states of consciousness but at the role that the defense mechanisms of personality play in the interpretation of psi and pseudo-psi. These in relationship to the ability individuals may have to experience altered states may help to elucidate some of the complexity in this area. However, we must not forget that categories such as psi and pseudo-psi are conveniences coined by our scientific mind and in nature it may sometimes be impossible to purify the experience into one or the other.

WEST: Having listened to clinicians discussing pathological cases it seems to me that the link between psi and schizophrenia is liable to be over-emphasized. The prevalence of histories of ostensibly psychic experiences revealed in survey work is far too great for more than a tiny proportion to be related to schizophrenia. On the other hand, surveys also show that there is a minority who claim to have numerous experiences of different kinds. One suspects that these are the "fantasy-prone" personalities, but that does not prove that all their experiences are fantasies; they could be "psi-prone" was well as "fantasy-prone." In any case they are good subjects for research.

CLOSING REMARKS

ROBERT L. MORRIS: I would like to note a reminder that when we talk about psi in clinical practice, we really are talking about circumstances involving the prevention and alleviation of difficulty of some sort. A client is involved, a counselor or clinician is involved. The difficulties can be mental and physical. Clinicians can be therapists, administrators, general medical practitioners, specialists, social workers, and others. They may be interested in parapsychology, not interested, or hostile. I think what we have discussed this weekend has many implications for the nature of our research. We do our work in an extraordinarily powerful and complex social context. If we are to get to the place where we are to really understand the full personal implications of psi, we may have to go through phases that are almost analogous to the classical Aristotelian hero, who first must experience duress and sorrow in order to achieve anything resembling catharsis. Perhaps we must inevitably pass through considerable psychological turmoil in order to integrate the self into our social context in the way that we have in mind.

Even prior to the beginnings of formal psychical research, people have been aware of a linkage between ostensibly psychic experiences and psychopathology. This connection has been problematic for us in the past and threatens to be even more so in the future. At the same time it represents an opportunity for parapsychology to contribute both theoretically and practically to our understanding of mental health and dysfunction.

The intertwining of psi and psychopathology presents many concrete problems. Most members of the mental health professions presume that purported psychic experiences are indicative of distorted thinking or delusional beliefs. Thus parapsychologists are seen either as colluding with such thinking and thus detrimental to the mental well-being of society; or, worse yet, as providing evidence that threatens their own current understanding of the range of influences between mind and environment. If psychic functioning is real, their job becomes much more difficult. They are thus most eager to see any such evidence invalidated. The result can be bias, deliberate ignoring of the evidence, ridicule, and active opposition. This can be readily communicated to potential clients, who then seek better information or, occasionally, formal validation from the parapsychological community, as broadly defined by society. We as members of that community have an obligation to provide the most valid, accurate information we can about a host of anomalous experiences, some of extraordinary personal power and meaning, which may or may not include a genuine psi component. Ideally we should help people identify for themselves which experiences involve true psychic functioning, including their implications for how they lead the rest of their lives, philosophically and pragmatically, and which experiences may have other, conventional interpretations. Yet we all know it is difficult if not impossible to do so for the majority of events that we are asked to reconstruct. Most clinicians have no familiarity with the current state of understanding within parapsychology, and such understanding is marginal at best, especially in the clinically relevant aspects. Most researchers involved in parapsychology conversely have little if any clinical training. We don't want to encourage everybody to ignore whatever psychic talents they may potentially have, yet we don't want to collude with inappropriately exaggerated beliefs either. If people are troubled by their experiences we wish to help them, not just dismiss them or else ask them to participate in a research project which may not be in their best interests.

As we present our research publicly we also have comparable obligations to society as a whole, both at the individual and institutional level. We do not have the opportunity to conduct an extended discussion about the implications or uncertainties of our work with all who come across a direct or secondary account of it. People may alter their beliefs as a result of what they see or hear from "experts." They may accept premature interpretations or speculative philosophies which only appear to be supported by data on hand. They may open themselves up to influences, psychic or otherwise over which they have no real control and which are poorly understood even by "experts."

Conversely, a further understanding of the relationship between psi and psychopathology may give us valuable new insights into the latter. Our current understanding of thought disorders, unintended imagery, the aetiology of delusional systems and related topics is still far from complete. By developing and evaluating better models both for genuine psychic experiences as well as fake or pseudopsychic experiences we will inevitably improve our understanding of the full range of factors that influence our interactions with the world around us and the distortions thereof that characterize so much of psychopathology. Additionally, many have argued that psychic functioning is an intimate part of the interaction between therapist and client, an interaction that would be greatly enriched by any improvements in our understanding of the clinical aspects of psi. Actual application of any such improved understanding within a clinical context would be a gradual process, however, given the bias and inertia that must inevitably be overcome by any radical innovation in clinical thought and procedure.

All of this means that, as we come to have success in our research and communicate those successes, we will inevitably confront more and more criticism, both fair and unfair, because our work is significant in both its positive and negative implications. As society comes to increase its acceptance of psychic functioning, there will be even greater demands on us as responsible researchers to provide individuals and institutions with the knowledge and tools to help them separate wheat from chaff. We can't just say, "psi exists, here are some conditions for enhancing its occurrence, but sorry, we really can't give you any advice on how to integrate it into your daily lives, your worldviews, your sense of self." People need and deserve much more than that. It is most important that we help people understand the clinical context of apparent anomalous experiences. The fact that they overlap with some characteristics of psychopathology indicates that such experiences may have some very problematic properties. Parapsychology in the past has rarely acknowledged these clinically relevant aspects of our work, and their importance for the entire social context of our research and how it is valued by others. The present symposium is an extremely important step in moving us in this direction.

Donald West begins by presenting the results of his recent British survey of apparitional experiences, noting that such experiences are still frequent occurrences, although only a small proportion are regarded as meaningful. Interpretation of such experiences, including assessment of their evidentiality, remains problematic unless the description is sufficiently thorough and one has access to information about potential corroborating events. This is a problem for experients and researchers alike. Such cases do suggest that simple alterative explanations do not suffice, and the question remains open of what triggers hallucinations and determines their contents.

Keith Harary surveys many of the issues confronting those who wish to provide useful counselling for those who have had disturbing experiences. He critiques the existing clinical approaches including psychoanalytic ones which treat psi as largely dysfunctional. The existing parapsychological literature just scratches the surface and has little to do with application or helping people find meaning in their experiences and grow from them. The research literature often seems to imply that only certain types of people tend to have such experiences and only in certain states, which is not useful to the bulk of people whose experiences are not so restricted. He identifies four areas in which counselling can help people cope with their experiences: (1) adjusting to genuine, long-term psi; (2) integrating short-term or isolated psi; (3) dealing with deeper psychological problems reflected in experiences which may or may not have a true psi component; and (4) confronting delusional systems with strong defenses in place, not necessarily involving any psi at all. The first two ordinarily may require only brief counselling whereas the latter two call for longer term professional services. In general, Harary makes a plea for counsellors and researchers to be sensitive to social context and the meaningfulness of experiences for those involved.

Ian Tierney, also writing from a clinical psychology perspective, notes that anomalous experiences and their interpretation can lead individuals to encounter social difficulties and thus be at risk of meeting the criteria for institutionalization. As Maher and others have noted, problems can arise when we attribute excessive meaning to our experiences. We need to understand why some attribute meaning and others don't. There are neurophysiological correlates of the experience of meaningfulness, shifts in states of arousal are linked to attribution of meaning, and a host of prior experiences, interests, and beliefs potentially contribute as well. Clinicians can have difficulty in helping people sort out the extent to which they have overinterpreted their experiences—counsellors must be supportive and understanding, without colluding. Tierney argues it's therefore most important that health care officials as well as clients be given more information about parapsychology, including the ways in which we can be misled by ourselves or by clever others.

Jean Dierkens presents a description of recent research with mediums suggesting that they can respond to the meaning of symbols independently of their form. His work thus further emphasizes the importance of meaning in interpreting anomalous experiences.

Robert Van de Castle focusses on experiences of dissociation, especially multiple personality disorder (MPD), noting the frequent appearance of psychic experiences in those who have MPD. Although its reported incidence varies from culture to culture, it is now resurgent in the U.S. Of special interest is the frequent presence of Inner Self Helpers (ISH), personalities that function almost like guardian angels, seem to be actively involved in helping the personalities reintegrate, and show occasional strong psi themselves. Van de Castle illustrates with examples from his own spouse, who has MPD and an ISH. Parapsychologists need to explore such phenomena more than in the past. They should be prepared to confront unconscious processes and associated experiences with strong personal significance, as advocated by Rhea White's depth parapsychology with its emphasis on psi in situations of change and personal growth.

The paper by Wim Kramer provides a description of the range of counselling techniques he and his colleagues have used in Holland, where popular acceptance of psi and psychics is very high. He identifies four types of problems for which people seek advice: (1) people experiencing mysterious negative forces, often within a belief system such as those of immigrants from Surinam; (2) people seeking advice on personal matters from professional psychics; (3) people with an unsatisfactory history of involvement with psychiatry looking for alternative sources of help; and (4) people with feelings and experiences they can't explain, who either merely want solid information or else want confirmation of their special abilities. Kramer finds that SPEs tend to be linked with emotional events, that many people become persuaded that they have special talents shortly after a major life event, and that as emotional instability increases, SPE incidence goes up as well. Two techniques for counselling arc described. The first involves recording major life events and SPEs associated with them, then working with the client to integrate these events with their other emotions. This technique was abandoned by their group in favor of another which is less demanding psychologically, places more emphasis on the SPEs themselves, and is more free-ranging. It works best for those primarily seeking better information. To be effective with these techniques, counsellors in general need more training in clinical areas and less in parapsychological research, but also need considerable familiarity with the range of occult beliefs and practices of the culture involved, so that these can be taken into account during therapy. Kramer finishes by outlining the main principles evolved by their group over the years of exploring how best to meet the needs of the diverse Dutch public.

Vernon Neppe discusses how anomalous experiences relate to existing and potential psychodiagnostic categories, from a psychiatric perspective. Traditional approaches either incorporate SPEs as part of a well-known diagnostic classification, or else add them in to more general catchall categories of psychopathology. Given that this is not the complete picture, one can either decide there is no true psychosis and that all such symptoms stem from problematic interactions with society, or one can rediagnose. For the latter, Neppe suggests two general diagnostic categories: biological (psychopharmacologic), characterized by tolerance of psychotropic or antipsychotic drugs; or functional (biopsychofamiliosociocultural dysfunction), characterized by experience-induced lack of coping at one or more of the levels from biological through to cultural. He elaborates by describing the origin and characteristics of six sets of psychiatric conditions most associated with SPEs: schizophrenia; hallucinogenic mobilized psychosis; SPE psychosis; trancelike dissociated phenomena; psychotic psychics; and nonepileptic temporal lobe epilepsy and dysfunction. Neppe concludes by emphasizing that explanation of the above categories should be a blend of the psychodynamic and biological, the latter emphasizing temporal lobe involvement.

Adrian Parker considers SPEs from both a clinical and cognitive psychology perspective. He focusses on prepsychotic stages and cognitive models of individual differences in those who deal well with SPEs versus those who do not, including magical thinking and reasoning in the area of attribution of cause and probabilities of occurrence. Of special interest are the ability to become absorbed in one's activities and defensiveness. Parker suggests that high absorption may favor psi, and defensiveness affects how one copes with both genuine psi and non-psi experiences. He adds that it is especially important to understand and explain parapsychological experiences, as psychiatry is now devoting considerable attention and resources to the study of cults and other occult groups.

Ian Wickramasekera focusses on fantasy proneness and hypnotizability as representing important individual differences in the occurrence of subjective paranormal experiences (SPE). Unassimilated SPEs can lead to both psychological and somatic symptoms. High hypnotizability is correlated with SPE incidence, but such SPEs tend not to be related to psychopathology. Some fantasy prone people, most of whom report SPEs, do show signs of psychopathology. In considering future lines of research, Wickramasekera defines two components of hypnosis: the capacity to self-generate vivid fantasies; and the capacity to make the mind blank, involving cognitive and sensory inhibition. He suggests the former is correlated with SPEs, the latter with genuine psychic functioning, and that we should focus more on the latter in our research.

Peter Fenwick, also writing from a psychiatric perspective, notes at the start that physics his always had a problem in dealing with consciousness, and that a science of subjective experience is badly needed. He points specifically to the association among emotional deprivation, brain trauma and SPEs, noting that temporal lobe dysfunction seems to be conducive to states of consciousness related to true psychic experiences, that mediums seem to have had more physical and emotional damage to the brain than others, that NDEs are associated with illness and difficult childhood, and that in general long-standing brain damage seems associated with SPEs.

Overall, these papers come at the core problems from a diversity of perspectives, although each author in his own way emphasizes the importance of understanding the meaning or salience of SPEs for those who have them. This is a message that must be heeded by the active parapsychological community, both the formal researcher struggling to find adequate yet ecologically valid methodologies, as well as the counsellor helping clients to integrate SPEs into their worldviews in positive ways. Parapsychologists can no longer afford to ignore the challenge posed by the clinical problems discussed in this volume, if they wish to fulfill their social responsibilities to (a) the individuals with whom they come in contact and (b) the social institutions that must accommodate all advances in knowledge and that ultimately regulate the value (or lack of same) placed upon parapsychology itself. The Parapsychology Foundation has done us all an invaluable service by convening these ten presenters and giving them the opportunity to reflect their own perspectives and experiences. There are major ethical issues confronting a successful parapsychology and much work to be done if we are to deal with them progressively and productively.

I'd like to thank Eileen and Lisette Coly, as I have done in my heart and sometimes verbally, far too little, for once again providing the context for what I hope and think has been a really exciting intellectual and emotional interaction. They do it year after year. My hat would go off to them, were I wearing one. I think we owe a great round of applause to them and to all of the Parapsychology Foundation people who worked so hard for this conference.

LISETTE COLY: I would like to thank you all who came together to make this such a stimulating conference. Our panelists certainly deserve our gratitude for their excellent papers and comments. Those who observed the proceedings also added greatly to the overall success of these meetings with their cogent queries and comments, and we appreciate the time and effort you have given to joining us this weekend. The entire proceedings will be published in book form—papers and complete discussions—which will make a valuable addition to our conference series.

I am sure we all here recognize the excellent job that Dr. Morris did in keeping us all in line and in time also. Thank you so much, Bob, for your moderating duties and also for your valued cooperation in the early days of conceptualizing this conference.

Ladies and Gentlemen, we wish you a safe return home. The 38th Annual International Conference of the Parapsychology Foundation is adjourned.

INDEX